Computing Our Way to Paradise?

Globalization and the Environment Series

Series Editors

Richard Wilk, Department of Anthropology, 130 Student Building, Indiana University, Bloomington, IN 47405, USA, or wilkr@indiana.edu

Josiah Heyman, Department of Sociology & Anthropology, Old Main Building #109, University of Texas, 500 West University Avenue, El Paso, TX 79968, USA, or jmheyman@utep.edu

This AltaMira series publishes new books about the global spread of environmental problems. Key themes addressed are the effects of cultural and economic globalization on the environment; the global institutions that regulate and change human relations with the environment; and the global nature of environmental governance, movements, and activism. The series will include detailed case studies, innovative multi-sited research, and theoretical questioning of the concepts of globalization and the environment. At the center of the series is an exploration of the multiple linkages that connect people, problems, and solutions at scales beyond the local and regional. The editors welcome works that cross boundaries of disciplines, methods, and locales and span scholarly and practical approaches.

Books in the Series

Computing Our Way to Paradise?

The Role of Internet and Communication Technologies in Sustainable Consumption and Globalization

Robert Rattle

ALTAMIRA
PRESS

A division of
ROWMAN & LITTLEFIELD PUBLISHERS, INC.
Lanham • New York • Toronto • Plymouth, UK

Published by AltaMira Press
A division of Rowman & Littlefield Publishers, Inc.
A wholly owned subsidiary of The Rowman & Littlefield Publishing Group, Inc.
4501 Forbes Boulevard, Suite 200, Lanham, Maryland 20706
http://www.altamirapress.com

Estover Road, Plymouth PL6 7PY, United Kingdom

British Library Cataloguing in Publication Information Available

Library of Congress Cataloging-in-Publication Data

Rattle, Robert.
  Computing our way to paradise? : the role of internet and communication technologies in sustainable consumption and globalization / Robert Rattle.
     p. cm.
  Includes bibliographical references and index.
  ISBN 978-0-7591-0948-3 (cloth : alk. paper) — ISBN 978-0-7591-1933-8 (electronic)
  1. Internet—Social aspects. 2. Sustainable development. 3. Information technology—Social aspects. I. Title.
  HM851.R38 2010
  303.48′33—dc22   2009027114

∞™ The paper used in this publication meets the minimum requirements of American National Standard for Information Sciences—Permanence of Paper for Printed Library Materials, ANSI/NISO Z39.48-1992.

Printed in the United States of America

Contents

Foreword

When I began this project, opinions on the contribution of Internet and communications technologies (ICTs) to sustainable consumption were quite divergent. Ironically, this was due to the very limited information available on the contribution of ICTs to sustainable consumption. Most views, as one might expect, were clustered around anticipations that ICTs would enable the dematerialization of physical products—that is to say, that virtual products and services would generate a smaller materials and energy footprint than their physical counterparts—and the immaterialization—a shift toward virtual options—of consumer preferences. Amazingly, this view still largely prevails today, despite the growing evidence against it.

Why the stubbornness of such a belief, and why its increasing ubiquity? Virtual products and services simply seem to be far less demanding on the environment, and are more appealing, convenient, and easier to access than, say, a similar activity or product delivered the conventional way: physical mobility can be displaced with tele-conferencing, teleworking, or telepresence; printing and publication can be displaced with data storage and electronic documents; the purchase of physical products can be substituted with electronic variants, such as music and many other services; and many services can now be employed to increase the energy and materials efficiency of human activity, from products used in day-to-day life to industrial production processes. The potentials remain limited only by imagination, and by the speed with which these products and services can be developed and brought to market. In large part, these and other similar opportunities have grown immensely popular.

Which is precisely what makes investigating the ecological benefits of ICTs, and questioning the stubbornness and ubiquity of a belief in these benefits, that much more interesting. To ask this question, as this book does, is to take the fork in the road less traveled. It leads us on a journey of discovery and surprise, and reveals insights for the application of this new knowledge.

By all accounts, these technologies and their associated applications continue to be developed at a ferocious pace. The available armies of ICTs continue to march forward in lockstep with the deliciously attractive pronouncements by technology wizards and media moguls alike. ICTs have been endorsed, even celebrated, for their potential to reduce energy demands, cut greenhouse gases, expand democracy and equalities, transform business practices, boost economic growth, create jobs and employment, and reduce global human demands for resources, often, although not always, simultaneously. Only the early adopters themselves appear more enthusiastic about the potential benefits of the almost daily deluge of new ICT variants.

However, there remains a gnawing apprehension, perhaps in part caused by the growing body of evidence that suggests these benefits may not always transpire. Consider the paperless office: despite the ability for electronic data storage to offset paper consumption, demand for paper products continues to soar at an astounding rate worldwide. Although the potential exists to offset physical mobility with telecommuting and teleconferencing, travel, both personal and commercial, continues to rise at alarming rates within virtually every country and globally across international borders. Downloading music and video files has inspired an armada of new devices that compound a growing global glut of e-wastes, led by the over four hundred thousand cellular telephones discarded each day in the United States alone. Smart homes and energy-efficient technologies, although far more efficient than their conventional counterparts (where conventional options even existed), continue to, almost paradoxically, push demand for energy in this sector substantially higher.

Despite this reality, report after report extols the virtues of ICTs and their benefits in this increasingly energy- and environment-constrained world. A quick Internet search reveals dozens—hundreds—of reports, each likely printed by would-be knowledge seekers. Satellites and geographic information systems (GISs) allow the captains, sergeants, and privates of the armies of armchair environmentalists to observe, gobble, generate, and regurgitate virtual and real-time information so long as they have an Internet connection. These technologies have enabled the discovery of new species, which have been categorically celebrated as a success with barely a mention of the rush to exploit those new species by pharmaceutical, bioprospecting, or other value-added industries. ICTs have been applied to monitor traditional lands, allowing indigenous populations to bear witness to the disappearance of their forest canopies, spiritual well-being, and historic lands. We call it "monitoring." There now exist more data-rich indicators, and ICTs and tools to feed those indicators, that measure ecological degradation than we have political will to reverse the harmful trends. Compounding this political paralysis, the same technologies, processes, and events drive cultural transformations that border on cultural genocide. Lies, damn lies, and statistics are now complemented by emerging ICTs that, despite their accuracy, enable the wielders to present their powerful and potent images of future events transmitted by their new digital connections, to be used to accumulate political support and short-circuit democratic processes intended to protect the environment. In every situation, it seems, where these technologies can be used for sustainable purposes, counterintuitive uses or results also exist that can be, and are, used to serve less than ideal objectives or generate unanticipated consequences.

One would be negligent to overlook the global economic tremors that threaten to crush so many businesses and nations that employed ICTs to outsource, globalize, expand and diversify, leverage, and make their practices more efficient. These technology investments seemed to cut operational costs and transform into ever more profitable arrangements the business practices of companies worldwide, pushing ever higher global economic growth. But what about the controversies, risks, and outright conflicts of coveting economic growth in an increasingly physically constrained and socially divided world?

The line defining gainful employment generation often bisects socioeconomic status, with those on one side of the scale overworked and overstressed, while those on the other are left with few income opportunities and even less access to the advancing information economy.

One also needs to question why such an advanced society—potentially the leisure society—would even entertain the continued anachronisms of full employment and job creation and growth, especially considering the consequences from, as Herman Daly suggests, a full economy. What about boosting economic growth? Wouldn't that necessarily imply increased production and consumption of natural wealth? These and other ambiguous social benefits also raise the question: why the stubbornness and ubiquity of a belief in many of the proclaimed social benefits of ICTs?

These ecological and social dilemmas have failed to meaningfully question or alter the roles of ICTs in our increasingly globalized world. In the late 1990s and early into the new millennium, there was indeed considerable debate surrounding the role of the Internet in sustainable development, concentrated, as one might again expect, on energy demand. Late in the first decade of the new millennium, thrust into the limelight of environmental debate, there is a widening discourse on the carbon emissions of the Internet. Clear lines of division are drawn: one segment pronounces the limited—if not beneficial—effects on electricity demand, while the other sounds the alarm that the Internet's energy-demand footprint is about to surge, and in fact may already have done so beyond our peripheral of measurement. Beyond the digital divide, more profound cracks involving such matters as traffic shaping and network neutrality are emerging, revealing the potential for complex social tensions alongside the declared benefits.

Despite these dilemmas, that deliciously attractive utopia continues to fascinate and spellbind us, and more of us today than ever before. The global diffusion of ICTs has been almost as instantaneous as the signals and messages they propagate. Huge segments of populations across all geographic areas already sport cell phones, computers, televisions, and personal data assistants (PDAs), and have become imbued with their messages, both conspicuous and inconspicuous. They're almost always on, plugged in, at work, in contact, or otherwise connected. Who of these, just like those on the other side of the digital divide, doesn't feel lost, naked, guilty, or socially excluded when not connected?

But where is the debate on these matters? ICTs enable the rapid diffusion of ideas, making ICTs both the message and the medium simultaneously. Should this not be as much a concern as it might be a benefit?

It simply no longer matters where on this planet you are: the global commons has become one single, connected social party for t'weens and researchers alike—exchanging, recording, manipulating, analyzing, and repackaging ideas to suit our needs. This truly seems like a historic period in human progress.

Or is it? Sipping tea in bed in London, global consumers can access at a whim any product of the global age and have it delivered later that day to their doorsteps. Likewise, the global consumer can become global adventurer, cheaply and safely traveling with minimum effort to different geographies and climates. At least this is the impression John Maynard Keynes expressed in 1919. Or consider the description of the telegraph, given in an 1852 issue of *Scientific American*, as an invention of modern times that has rapidly expanded its influence globally; this expansion was considered as wonderful as the technology itself. Sound familiar?

History repeats. Yet despite the volumes of information available today, few alive now experienced the transformations of almost a century ago. It is, for all practical purposes, new this time around.

David Rejeski contends that the emerging potential of ICTs is both ambiguous and important, for it demonstrates the state of our understanding as well as our ignorance. Above all else, it is a warning "for those who would posit IT [information technology] as a means of environmental salvation or an easy road to sustainable development" (Rejeski, 2003, 1). Such fissures are beginning to emerge in our understandings of ICTs and their ability to benefit sustainable consumption. In 2008, one study indicated that the impact of a single Google search on the energy demands of the Internet is equivalent to the energy demands of an eleven-watt bulb operating for fifteen minutes to one hour, depending on several input variables. Another study equated the energy consumption of two Google searches[1] to that of boiling a kettle, giving new concern to the sustainability of your morning coffee while you surf the morning paper. Just imagine the number of Internet searches you run each day. Now magnify that by the number of other Internet services and users in millions of households and businesses, all shrouded in a cloud of technological optimism assuming perfect substitutability, complete dematerialization, and virtual immaterialization, yet all equally demanding physical resources—from the servers that must operate 24/7 to host each and every one of the millions of Internet web, blog, and social-networking sites to the computers, cellular telephones, PDAs, and uninterruptible power supplies and standby-mode or recharging devices, all of which provide incredible convenience and mobility, fed by an insatiable lust for electricity.

Globalization, a process ICTs have only recently contributed to, has been around for a long time, and has waxed and waned over the centuries. Certainly some phases have been more euphoric than others, such as the 1920s and 1990s. Just precisely where we now reside along this roller coaster ride is for future historians to determine. Today's historians also warn us to pay attention to the past, for it has important lessons for our future.

One message I have come to understand is how very little we know, how much more there is to learn, and, simultaneously and

---

[1] Where each Google search would consist of the multiple attempts typically necessary to identify the desired information rather than the single-entry, one-click search.

perhaps paradoxically, how much data and information we already have thanks in large part to modern globalization and the spread of ICTs. When I began to address the questions of how ICTs and globalization would affect global ecological states and trends and the human cultures that inhabit them, the lack of knowledge among such abundance of data was perhaps the greatest enigma. That puzzle remains today. Questions were and are being answered and data was and is being generated, but understanding, let alone action, remains critically deficient.

The purpose of this book is to raise some of these questions and to elicit dialogue on the issues that ultimately shape, enable, and constrain our choices, applications, and adaptations of ICTs in a global world. Through this journey, new opportunities, policy options, and research directions should emerge.

There is much to learn from history for globalization and the application of ICTs. This warrants our attention if the forces of ICTs and globalization are to contribute to our basket of tools to achieve more sustainable consumption in the future. Perhaps it is time to sift through this information, listen to the past, and identify the valuable patterns history reveals. For the scholar or perceptive observer, there is much to learn. As George Santayana insightfully noted, doomed to repeat their mistakes or overlook exciting opportunities are the fool and those who fail to learn history's lessons.

Acknowledgments

Many great people helped in the evolution of this book and the shaping of the final product. I simply couldn't begin to list all the individuals who were inspirational and encouraging during formative stages with whom I was fortunate enough to have had discussions. Some of the people who were of great help editing and critiquing earlier versions of the manuscript include Steven B. Kurtz, Sandra Paul, and Colin L. Soskolne. I thank the Canadian federal government for allowing me the opportunity to conduct the original research that became the genesis of this book. I also graciously thank my editors, Joe Heyman and Richard Wilk, for allowing me both the opportunity to express that research and other ideas in a book, and for their patience and insightful comments throughout this project. Similarly, all the great people at Rowman and Littlefield, especially Jack Meinhardt—who probably suspected this project would never conclude—and Marissa Parks and Patricia Stevenson who were nothing short of wonderful with their indulgence and advice as I prepared the final manuscript. There are many points when the stress and time a large project appropriates teaches families how precious time is, and how important our different roles are. For that, I thank my family (Deborah, Benjamin, Christopher, and Chelsea), especially my wife, Deborah, for carrying the torch at those times, and dedicate this book to Benjamin, Christopher, and Chelsea, who will, with a little effort from all of us, inherit a sustainable, bright, and promising future.

1

ICTs and Globalization: Asking Important Questions

They are known by many different names: *Internet and communications technologies (ICTs)*, *agile computing*, *ubiquitous computing*, *information society technologies*, or simply *information technologies.* While subtle differences exist, each of these might be defined simply as any product or system that communicates, stores, or processes information. The influence of ICTs has been dramatic, and their future evolution is anticipated to profoundly alter everyday life from the routine and mundane to the novel and unconventional. They are, in fact, already reshaping our everyday lives—modifying transport patterns, work patterns, and relationships, the structure and organization of our economies, energy consumption and resource usage, leisure, and even our cultures and the way in which people perceive the world, including our relationships to and within it.

Some argue for and promote ICTs as the next economic wave, with the potential to generate jobs, wealth, and prosperity to surpass that of the industrial era while virtually eliminating greenhouse gases and pollution. Due to the abstract or service nature of ICTs, the opportunities appear essentially limitless. Due also to this abstract nature, it is assumed the environmental impacts will be negligible or even beneficial.

Riding the wave of global environmental consciousness that began to rise sharply in the early part of this millennium, a flood of reports made these possibilities evidently clear. The increasing application of ICTs performed an important role in this movement: the landmark film by Al Gore, *An Inconvenient Truth*, found its way into living rooms, theaters, halls, and televisions around the world, and, eventually, onto the Internet. Not to be surpassed, an assault of counter-argument films found their way onto the Internet even more quickly.

Following the global economic downturn, attention abruptly shifted to the new green economy, along with the emerging technologies that might provide green jobs and green growth. ICTs are prominent and pervasive in these visions. Advocates of ICTs increasingly make claims about ICTs' environmental benefits, such as the potential to reduce carbon dioxide emissions by fifty million tons annually starting immediately, and reducing emissions by 7.8 billion tons annually below business-as-usual levels by 2020 (Pamlin & Szomolányi, 2008; Global eSustainability Initiative, 2008).

ICTs are focused on process, yet they also stimulate the continuous innovation of products. Accordingly, their effects are pervasive and cut across all spheres of human activity (Castells, 1996, 16). ICTs have the potential to improve energy and materials intensity through efficient product design and delivery, reduced product needs, urban restructuring, and product reclamation opportunities, for example. Through such processes, ICTs may substitute for or optimize existing products, services, or processes, thereby reducing energy and materials intensity. There is limited evidence that some businesses are willing to accept service solutions, although this interest appears to be driven more by economic, technological, and competitive issues, rather than by environmental issues (Heiskanen & Jalas, 2003). Conversely, "there is not much evidence of the propensity of consumers to adopt 'consumption without ownership' or to 'outsource' their activities" (Heiskanen & Jalas, 2003, 195). Might this reflect, and perhaps reveal, important insights into the various motivations for green claims and preferences?

In other cases, reusing and rebuilding discarded systems provides opportunities for education and access, and leapfrogging technologies now mean that many low- and middle-income countries have growing networks of ICTs, such as cellular and Internet connections. Reusing old ICTs and leapfrogging are helping to raise the standard of living for many people in these populous countries, and achieve this standard of living with apparently less consumption than might otherwise occur. These activities may mitigate the need for investing extensive resources in infrastructure soon to become obsolete. Further, they may offer a wealth of information to new consumers on the impacts of their decisions and opportunities to reduce their impact on the planet. ICTs may also bring democratic opportunities to all corners of the world, empowering the poor and disenfranchised alike. Similarly, the distributive properties of the Internet allows for rapid diffusion of information and marshaling of resources to confront perceived social and ecological threats. ICTs also offer novel opportunities to "package" time and reorganize lifestyles to match socially constructed and evolving visions of the good life. Expanding access to information and services for consumers and professionals alike is enabling the pursuit of both new and old processes and activities in less resource-intensive and less onerous formats in favor of more desirable formats.

In this context, ICTs have been widely advocated as an important strategy for more sustainable consumption. The reasoning is that dematerializing the economy, immaterializing consumer preferences, and facilitating social empowerment can lead to greatly improved energy and resource efficiencies along with more equitable distribution of social wealth. Information provision becomes the key enabling factor for more sustainable democracies.

These premises become a little more ambiguous when other factors are considered. According to Moore's Law, electronics dematerialize by a factor of four every three years. Despite the trend toward reduced energy intensity per appliance, product, or process, there has not been a corresponding reduction of total energy and material flows since the introduction and application of ICTs. Similarly, information has been readily available on the sustainability of options for consumers and business alike. However, consumer and business choice is based on complex decision-making architectures. Information, behavior, and attitudes bear little in common, and causal relationships are weak at best. If we genuinely want to enrich our understanding of how the application of ICTs affects sustainable consumption in a global world, we will need more than nebulous hocus-pocus.

Once beyond a purely reductionistic approach, many seductive conclusions about the role of ICTs in global sustainability simply collapse. Whitehead's "fallacy of misplaced concreteness" identifies the degree of abstraction of our concepts that lead us to draw unwarranted conclusions about reality (Whitehead, 1925). Conventional policies that seek to achieve more sustainable consumption often embody this "fallacy of misplaced concreteness" by overlooking underlying social factors that influence decision making. ICTs possess tremendous opportunities to help achieve more sustainable consumption, both environmentally and socially. Despite this potential, imprudent development and application of ICTs without appreciating their conceptual abstraction and social interactions may simply lead to amorphous growth—and the concomitant untenable ecological and social consequences—consistent with prevailing social structures.

To resolve this fallacy, and the emerging controversies and uncertainties, it may be necessary to consider an approach that situates the role of ICTs within the context of broader social practices, institutions, and values. These factors often shape, albeit through a co-evolving process, how our tools, mechanisms, and activities will be applied. Considered in the context of social processes, and how these shape and are shaped by technologies, the benefits derived from ICTs seem severely tempered; the pillars supporting those deliciously attractive pronouncements, just like last year's harvest, simply begin to decay without appropriate preservation of essential qualities and values.

We are now beginning to understand the interactions of ICTs with social processes, revealing ways in which people are incorporating new technologies into their everyday lives and using them to affect their consumption choices, exposing tremendously complex interactions that can and do occur. This suggests that, at the very least, ICTs and social systems are co-evolutionary. It also offers critical insights into potential techniques we might use to preserve important environmental, social, and cultural qualities and values.

But before we can embark on this exploratory journey, we need to expose just what those values and qualities are that will direct those decisions. What are the current roles of globalization in this process, and what are the drivers of current trajectories of globalization? Despite the co-evolutionary nature of technologies and societies, ICT development may otherwise remain stubbornly and firmly established *within* the wider social environment. If so, the endogenous nature of ICT development, adoption, and adaptations must be recognized as a powerful symbolic metaphor of our current social and cultural trajectory—a redefining of our relationships to nature and between people.

The potential social pathology emerging from ICT use is perhaps best revealed by Google itself. The ten most popular Google global searches for 2007 were: (1) iPhone, (2) badoo, (3) Facebook, (4) Dailymotion, (5) Webkinz, (6) YouTube, (7) eBuddy, (8) Second Life, (9) hi5, and (10) Club Penguin. These reveal the acute attraction to the supreme marketing prowess of global advertisers to dumb down adult consumers, lock in youth and infant consumers, and infantilize the global consumer ethic to establish, as Benjamin Barber calls it, the corruption of the Protestant ethic and capitalism, where consumerism is now literally "consuming itself, and leaving democracy in peril and the fate of citizens in peril" (Barber, 2007, 37).

This advertising approach cuts across all industries. When foods high in saturated fats became socially problematic, though they were always physically problematic in a sedentary world, the food industry quickly responded to produce foods low in saturated fats. At the same time, portion sizes (and prices) increased, leaving food consumers simultaneously overly "stuffed and starved" (Patel, 2007). The tobacco industry, under pressure from national governments and international organizations to reduce advertising to children, promptly prepared marketing aimed at children intended to reduce their adoption of tobacco products. The commercials warned children of the dangers of smoking, reinforcing this with the message that "smoking is an adult behavior." If you have or know children, you know that "grown-up" things are precisely what children innately crave the most, and danger only adds an air of excitement that modern-day living has all but eliminated through our ideological prostheses. Alcohol consumption has for decades been associated with fatal traffic accidents. Once organized efforts to combat such now antisocial behavior emerged, the messages insisted drinking and driving were simply no longer socially acceptable. Drinking *or* driving—implied by such messaging—remains completely safe and healthy. Despite the decrease in fatal alcohol-related accidents, many forms of drinking continue, prompting the World Health Organization to issue warnings, well substantiated by evidence, that any level of alcohol consumption is unhealthy. Despite this knowledge, marketing of alcohol, chocolate, and many other social vices fixate on the limited research that suggests potentially beneficial properties under strict circumstances, while ignoring those strict circumstances in order to market their products to the widest possible audiences and gain universal political and institutional support for their causes. The time may likely be near—if it is not already here, despite the global transformations this industry is in the midst of—when driving itself will come under increasing pressure to be curtailed. ICTs offer a powerful and potent set of marketing tools to convey misinformation and package messages in digestible sound bytes that appeal to mass audiences and conform to prevailing social expectations. ICTs also serve as the target of these messages, emphasizing the greenness of a product, company, or process. Under such circumstances, which messages are people more likely to believe and reinforce: those that smoothly align with their worldview, or those that challenge beliefs and expectations and swim against the social tide? One need look no further than the pattern of Google searches and how the Internet is used, or the collection of anti–climate change videos now available online in response to Al Gore's *An Inconvenient Truth*, or the exponential growth in green products despite the fact that 98 percent of those products contain at least one fraudulent "green" claim (Terrachoice, 2009). Free speech cannot result in unbiased information, and those with the greatest resources are still most likely to present the loudest message.

Within this complex set of often conflicting values and expectations—environmental, social, and cultural—resides important information about the current trajectories of globalization and its consequences for and from ICTs.

ICTs are an essential source of information and communications. As a key factor in the processes of globalization, ICTs have the capacity to enable the dispersion of information and communications to every corner of the globe. This raises critical questions of social and ecological justice, since those who own and control the ICT products, processes, and networks have immense power to influence societal norms and social processes globally, despite the global dispersion of democracy that some might argue is afforded by the Internet. Again, with whom will people most likely relate, believe, and align their values, actions, and expectations?

Simultaneously, those who develop and create ICTs have become increasingly specialized, markedly detached from fully comprehending the workings and machinations of the complex networks, ecosystems, and social structures they intend to serve, employ, and manipulate.

The global convergence of information, communications, and related technologies may also generate a global convergence of cultural values. This process could conceivably contribute to a global convergence of physical environments and spaces, too. Consider suburban yards, hotel rooms, living rooms, or transportation networks, vestiges of lifestyles portrayed and aspired to through media, marketing, entertainment, and socialized and normalized around the globe. Plunk yourself in the middle of a large city's business district and try to distinguish it from any other large city on the planet. Might these values and expectations be dominated by those of the high-consuming nations of the world from whence the networks, systems, and technologies materialized, and from which many global aspirations are drawn? There are serious concerns that the very populous nations are becoming imbued with the values and social forces, institutions, and practices driving first-world levels and patterns of consumption. These growing aspirations and transforming values of a burgeoning global population may become very real and significant ecological, social, and human health dilemmas.

Given the prodigious emphasis increasingly placed on the new information economy, a comprehensive understanding of the potential risks and impacts is certainly warranted. Considerable debate over the life-cycle impacts of ICTs and the potential benefits derived by their application, and concerns raised over e-wastes and direct energy consumption has transpired in recent years. Despite this, there has been much less, indeed very little, consideration of the societal influences on and by ICTs. Clearly, a technology itself does not determine how it will be applied. Indeed, technologies are never neutral, as they reflect cultural values and biases. In the context of its social embeddedness, what might be the ultimate environmental and social implications of ICTs? Do ICTs have the potential to become the channel for increased consumption, much as the preceding industrial era ushered in mass consumption, and lifestyles and behavior based on the consumer as a central actor in economic growth and globalization? Will ICTs dematerialize and immaterialize the human economy, permitting continued growth and prosperity with less environmental damage and with increased freedoms and social equality unseen in previous eras? What are the variables determining one trajectory over another? Can we control those variables to ensure more sustainable consumption? If so, where are the vital points for intervention?

This implies the need for a much wider approach to understanding the effects of ICTs beyond the assessment of the much more mundane life cycle or direct impacts, or simple considerations of efficiency gains afforded by new and emerging technologies. Certainly using less energy and materials to produce the same, or even better, microchip or provide a service rather than a product would, all else being equal, help to reduce absolute consumption and environmental impacts. In general, however, such efficiency gains *always* make sense, regardless of consumption levels (Princen, 1999). However, if these gains motivate increased demand for the consumption of energy and materials, we need to ask what else must be done beyond efficiency improvements to reduce excess demand and still ensure long-term sustainability. We must ask what variables or factors are contributing to these counter-intuitive results. Lest we forget, efficiency as an end goal in itself is neither a sufficient nor necessary condition for sustainability. In reality, society and technologies co-evolve, and "all else" cannot be held equal, nor should it be expected—change is inescapable.

How will the democratic and participatory features of ICTs enhance freedoms and social well-being? How will ICTs affect consumer lock-in, new electronic marketing and advertising platforms, media convergence, and power and wealth concentration? Will these forces shape and apply ICTs as tools to expropriate freedoms, amplify the global consumer ethic, and constrain people into lifestyles marked by high living standards and low self-esteem? Conversely, will ICTs reveal consumer trends and motivate sustainable ones? Will the informational capacities of ICTs allow people to assimilate and digest the growing glut of data and information in productive and sustainable formats? Will they eventually lead to sustainable paths? As ICTs increasingly amplify every corner of our lives, will they enable greater prosperity, freedoms, and environmental sustainability, or enhance global poverty, oppression, and commit us to global environmentally destructive trajectories?

New electronic platforms have driven companies toward ever greater efficiencies, and employees have begun to experience the stress of higher employer expectations. Let's face it: does anybody really want a higher daily information load than they already experience or have access to? Certain advocates, having identified the possibility to tailor e-information to anyone's needs, would counter that consumers may filter out all but the most relevant information. Despite this growing reality, why would anyone in our increasingly complex social and ecological world want to go through life receiving a form of "tunnel vision" information upon which to make choices, understand and perceive different ideas, or cultivate creativity? Some, such as Nicholas Carr, posit that heightening info glut has already transformed us into information storage and retrieval managers more than users of knowledge and developers of wisdom. No problem, the techies assert—step aside Google; here comes Wolfram! Just try to imagine how the next classes of search engines will transform our thought processes. It appears to many others, such as Thomas Homer-Dixon, that the information revolution and knowledge-based economy has reduced our time and ability to think and reflect or to advance our social and cultural wisdom. Social networking and other online applications, through the use of data filtering, analysis, sharing, and other tools, are being tapped to capture information, trends, and experiences. These have become a valuable asset in the borderless globalization and proliferation of consumerism.

What would such a world presuppose about the functioning of reality and about complex, real-world events? What happens to the vast quantities of electronic wastes generated annually? Why does consumption demand continue to rise, and can we afford this socially or environmentally? Certainly the billions of people presently suffering repression deserve better. Will a rising tide, and the potential contribution of ICTs, help enhance their well-being or merely widen the divide? Despite the improved opportunities ICTs enable, these and many other questions remain, yet are seldom asked, let alone investigated. The ultimate role of ICTs in a future sustainable world remains remarkably obscure.

The contributions of ICTs and the role of modern globalization in these processes can be extensive and pervasive. Some would argue that globalization is a recent phenomenon; others might posit that it is now in a formative mid-life crisis; still others might contend that globalization is a mature process that has been occurring for centuries. Regardless of whether globalization has passed a mid-life crisis, ICTs unquestionably both influence and are influenced by the velocity of globalization. The transglobal nature and reinforcing properties of ICTs are critical to understanding their effect on globalization and globalization's effects on ICTs. ICTs and globalization clearly improve market access and efficiencies of production and consumption. What is not so clear is their ability to seek more sustainable consumption. Taken together, ICTs and globalization appear to seek out new trans-global, nonterritorial opportunities to extend and enhance the current trajectories of market-driven capitalism—an expanding scale of the human footprint, an increasingly inequitable distribution of wealth, and an efficient allocation of resources. Could it be that, somewhere and somehow along that historical trajectory, our wish simply for an improved quality of life became corrupted by a tacit desire for less sustainable consumption through the global spread of the consumer ethic and a fundamentally contradictory set of values?

Research and policy have typically focused on the proximate cause of ecological and human health problems. This is precisely the context within which virtually all environmentally focused ICT methods operate. This tactic would serve us well if only consumption activity were easily reducible to the sum of its parts. While the assumptions upon which this approach is predicated may be judicious, they will only remain so within certain limits. The transglobal nature of global-ization, consumption activity, and even ICTs themselves dramatically expand beyond those limits. Hence, more recently, attention has been directed toward the underlying social and economic driving forces upon which evolution of ICTs and globalization occur. By shaping the context in which choices are made, values and institutional structures can establish powerful motivational forces that can indirectly produce tremendously greater environmental and social consequences.

Over the course of decades and centuries, technologies and infra-structures have been developed, political decisions have been taken, and global forces have acted upon and responded to events that have shaped the prevailing social framework. Many features of the prevail-ing social framework and more sustainable consumption are incom-patible. Even as attitudes and perceptions are becoming ever more en-vironmentally sensitive, for instance, powerful social forces militate against the requisite changes. This is not new. Societies throughout time have demonstrated incredible resistance to change, despite being confronted by powerful evidence of the need for change. Individuals are frequently exposed to problems—environmental and social, global and local. Revealed by the diverse options to respond, people obviously feel inspired to be sensitive to these problems, often drawing personal associations of empathy. Regardless, a more subtle message prevails that existing (political, economic, and technological) institutions will solve the problems for them (Kilbourne, Beckmann, Lewis, & Van Dam, 2001). Moreover, individual agency has been as much confined as freed by the prevailing social framework. Global, market-driven forces are promoted while alternative options, frameworks, institutions, responses, and choices are effectively concealed and thwarted, despite or even as a consequence of the access to them afforded by ICTs. Resources, such as wealth and time, can be controlled and manipulated—even defined—by some, and desired by yet inaccessible to others. In this sense, the ethnocentric nature of globalization is inconsistent with ecological and, particularly, cultural diversity. Consequently, the velocity of globalization has determined certain patterns difficult to avoid socially, cloaking others in clouds of technological, economic, or political optimism. While this social bias may manifest a predisposition toward improving the efficiency of resource allocation and informational capacity, it exhibits no intrinsic desire to reduce global aggregate consumption nor the social impacts of our global village. Will the adoption of ICTs break this social deadlock? *Could* it break the deadlock?

Perhaps more disturbing is the rapid globalization of this social trajectory. ICTs can play an important role in these processes, too, and in establishing and strengthening the institutional frameworks that support them. A myriad of cultures, from the Inuit in Canada's Northwest Territories to the !Kung in Africa, are rapidly adopting and adapting ICTs, fashioning them for their unique environments and circumstances. They are exposed to, learn, and incorporate the values and behavior of people in remote lands, adopt the posture of consumers, and embrace modern global market ideologies. ICTs enable them to confront threats to their lands and peoples at the same level, in the same frame of reference, and in the same context in which those threats emerged. What might be the social and environmental implications of this trajectory? The importance of this loss of cultural diversity was observed by Albert Einstein when he mused that the problems that we confront today cannot be solved at the same level of thinking in which they were created.

Yet more daunting is the fact that the development and application of ICTs is, as with all science and technology, inherently value-laden. We can begin to understand the pervasive nature of these forces only after recognizing the many-layered underlying assumptions upon which our standards, values, social systems, conventions, and institutional structures across society are constructed. Given this, one would have to be extraordinarily naïve to expect the amorphous evolution—in terms of conformity with prevailing social constructs—of ICTs to derail the consumerist growth locomotive. Yet this is precisely how most pundits of ICTs present their case. The mere existence of the efficiency- and democracy-improving aspects of ICTs seem sufficient to lead proponents in the belief that this alone will achieve more sustainable consumption. Hidden from this conviction is the ideological basis shaping the course of those ICTs, and, in many cases, those convictions. Progress must (but has yet to) acknowledge this bias, and then seek to cooperatively transform social conditions to be harmonious with human and ecological realities.

These neoclassically derived economic assumptions underpinning the evolution of globalization and ICTs fail to accommodate, as even the remotest possibility, the redistribution of income and power. This is essential to maintain a Pareto optimum. Since redistribution is out of the question, raising the tide, or growth, seems the only viable alternative to improve the lives of the billions who suffer daily injustices. Talk of sustainable growth is laudable, yet wholly misplaced. Despite rising living standards, wealth inequalities continue to expand and ecological thresholds are continuously being exceeded. Could this simply be the trance of consumerism marching on, effectively imbuing billions of new consumers with the necessary aspirations and tools for "the good life," maintaining prevailing income and power relations? Or is there more to this story?

ICTs might enable more efficient growth, creating the politically palatable perception of win-win scenarios, offering hope to billions by raising their standard of living and achieving a more efficient consumption per gross domestic product. The application of ICTs as a specific form of technology and an outgrowth of an expansionist, market-driven, class-structured ideology does not in any way address the sustainability of that trajectory nor the ideology itself. Rather than a virtue, could the efficiency attributes of ICTs—the primary redeeming feature, along with convenience, advocates profess—be a curse? The significance of situating the development of ICTs and globalization within the broader social background has yet to be fully appreciated or perhaps even realized.

The tools and institutions we have fashioned along this trajectory have been tremendously successful. In fact, they have been so successful that we now find ourselves in a position in which they are hyper-charging globalization. They can only provide tremendous material wealth to a select few in a very crude manner. Excluding the broader context of their development makes ICTs an ineffectual instrument at best: a blunt tool insufficient to confront the growing waves of consumerism and its effects.

This book marries several disciplines to explore the potential contribution of ICTs to the sustainable consumption debate in its role as a factor of globalization. It begins with a review of globalization and sustainable consumption to set the stage for later chapters. This review is followed by a brief overview of the role of ICTs in the global demand for energy and materials.

Many of our social assumptions are not obvious in these traditional analyses, as they are already socially assumed and implied in discourse around ICTs, globalization, and even, to a large extent, in sustainable development discourse. As the book progresses, it becomes increasingly difficult to avoid questioning these assumptions if we are to make progress in achieving more sustainable consumption and identifying the role of globalization and ICTs in that progress.

The book explores the broad picture of the potential future impacts, risks, and benefits, and how these benefits might best be harnessed while minimizing the potentially undesirable consequences of ICTs. It combines research specific to the environmental and social risks of ICTs with research in consumption theory that focuses on the social and cultural processes directing consumption decisions. As a core assumption, the book treats the development of ICTs as a process of technological development within class-based capitalism, and thus the analyses consider the objectives of ICTs as an outgrowth of economic growth and globalization with local, regional, and global consequences for both the natural and human environments. Accordingly, the book considers the social, cultural, and political elements of globalization as central forces in global environmental change, explores how ICTs might function within that framework, and considers policies and actions needed to enhance environmental and social conditions.

The book reviews and assesses the various literature and provides a synthesis of their results. It combines these results with a critical assessment of the expected benefits of ICTs in the context of social theory and globalization. Ultimately, it is hoped that the book offers a detailed exploration of current and expected future trends with respect to ICTs, globalization, and consumption activities. In particular, the book probes the role ICTs may perform in search of more sustainable consumption; repair, protection, and conservation of the environment; and improved human health and quality of life.

This book cannot be all things to all people. The concepts discussed are admittedly quite broad in scope, and herein lies a potential flaw. As we all know, broad strokes overlook important details. Yet the bigger picture is also something often lacking in our modern reductionist analyses. Nevertheless, it is hoped that the result provides sufficient detail and important insights to offer some direction for the application of ICTs toward more sustainable consumption, stimulates further dialogue and research, and sufficiently whets the interests of decision and policy makers.

The book chapters are organized as follows. Chapter 2 provides an overview of sustainable consumption and global environmental change. It explores the linkages between human activity and its human and ecological consequences. Chapter 3 integrates ICTs and globalization into this discourse, and considers the co-evolutionary nature of their development. Chapter 4 provides some insights into the known and anticipated consequences from ICTs in various applications. Many questions remain unanswered, and many new questions have arisen. This chapter offers a brief insight into what has been learned, what questions remain, and future research directions likely to prove fruitful. Chapter 5 builds on the expectations of ICTs to contribute to energy and resources consumption, specifically focusing on the ability of ICTs to dramatically improve efficiency in production and consumption activities. This also serves as an initial foray into prevailing global social values and assumptions. Chapter 6 further develops these ideas, focusing on the social processes of consumption. Chapter 7 provides an overview of a sustainable consumption lens and its potential role in identifying more sustainable consumption pathways. Chapter 8 critically examines capitalism, and neoclassical models in particular, as a factor in the development of ICTs and the processes of globalization.

While current trends appear to reflect the global potential for increasing consumption and the concomitant human and environmental impacts, ICTs also hold tremendous potential to achieve more sustainable consumption. It is my sincere hope that, after reading this book, the reader might better grasp how this could be achieved. Exploring the same strengths that make ICTs a powerful yet potentially dangerous global force, chapter 9 suggests an approach to achieve more sustainable consumption. Chapter 10 summarizes the role of ICTs in sustainable consumption and globalization, the profound challenges that will need to be confronted, and the vast opportunities to do so. The consequences from swiftly globalizing social forces may eclipse these opportunities unless there is rapid recognition of the potential risks. The establishment of appropriate policies and actions are urgently needed to counter these forces.

2

The Poverty of Affluence: Sustainable Consumption and Global Environmental Change

BACK TO EARTH WITH AN UNCEREMONIOUS THUMP

By Thursday afternoon a large, stagnant air mass had settled over northeastern North America, bringing with it stifling hot and humid weather. Electrical demand was peaking from New York to Ohio and up to Ontario. Air conditioners, fans, and a veritable profusion of insatiable, electricity-sucking consumer, business, and industrial artifacts were spinning, whirring, humming, and generating heat themselves, fabricating an orchestrated mockery of the weather. Then, shortly after 4 p.m. on August 14, 2003, everything went dark—all lights, air conditioners, fans, appliances, computers, and cellular telephones and other wireless handheld devices stopped working. The connected, wired, electrically charged and energized world abruptly terminated, came unplugged, disconnected.

The Electricity Infrastructure Operations Center (EIOC) explains that shortly after 3 p.m. on August 14, a 345-kilovolt (kv) transmission line in northern Ohio, due to a confluence of events, sagged too close to a tree, faulted, and tripped off-line. This would not have proven a problem under normal situations. However, August 14, 2003, would turn out to be anything except normal.

Simultaneous to the transmission line going off-line, an alarm processor that had failed to reboot following standard operating procedures by technicians at First Energy went undetected. The alarm processor failed to notify First Energy operators of an off-line transmission line, like the one in northern Ohio.

The Midwest Independent System Operator also experienced completely distinct problems that afternoon. Incorrect information was derived from another transmission-line failure elsewhere. The state estimator, not yet restored to its normal operational mode following troubleshooting operations, failed to provide contingency analysis. Contingency analysis relies on a computer model generated by the state estimator to provide a set of tools to analyze potential problems if the current assessment of the state of the grid was inaccurate. This essential process had been suspended.

Shortly following these initial events, alarm bells began a gentle crescendo. At 3:32 p.m. and 3:41 p.m., two more 345-kv lines tripped, accompanied by sixteen 138-kv lines beginning at 3:39 p.m. as a result of coming in contact with trees beneath them. Concealed from First Energy personnel and energy consumers in the northeastern North American grid, a cascading problem was rapidly unfolding. The only hint of a problem originated from other energy suppliers. By the time the crescendo of activity peaked, few people at First Energy were experiencing music to their ears: large industrial customers were assaulting First Energy with complaints about extraordinarily low voltage; voltage spikes and swings were observed at power plants; and, seeking answers to assess the escalating situation, neighboring utilities and reliability coordinators barraged First Energy with questions.

According to the EIOC, a First Energy system operator, in response to calls, replied that he believed problems originated elsewhere. This despite a nearly simultaneous comment elsewhere in the building by a First Energy shift supervisor to his manager that it appeared their system control was deteriorating. As if to presage the immediate future, the EIOC later noted that at that moment, "Information was not being shared effectively."

Shortly after 4 p.m., the cascading power failures began to accelerate. At 4:05:57, the first 345-kv transmission line to trip as a result of the series of events went off-line. This forced more northbound power through transmission lines that ran south of Cleveland. This high current accompanied by declining voltage implied low impedance to a protective relay. Acting as a precursor to many more transmission lines' and power plants' protective circuits, the relay automatically tripped the system off-line to prevent damage.

These multiple independent yet related problems rapidly coalesced to anything but independent as events abruptly unfolded. By 4:13 p.m., a cascade of catastrophic automatic system responses resulted in the largest blackout in North American history, plunging and uniting fifty million electricity users across the eastern part of Canada and the United States, including New York City, Detroit, Cleveland, and Toronto, into total electrical darkness. When the tally was compiled, the economic fallout cost an estimated $4 to $10 billion in U.S. dollars. Gross domestic product (GDP) in Canada fell 0.7 percent in August 2003, 18.9 million work hours were lost, and Ontario manufacturing shipments were down $2.3 billion in Canadian dollars. In Ontario, the acute load loss of the event resulted in a drop of 23,000 MW from an anticipated peak load demand of 24,400 MW for that day, demonstrating the magnitude of the blackout.

As though events conspired to shatter faith in the infrastructures that support modern economies—consumers to consume and producers to produce—and their associated social networks, the gentle violation of a human structure (the 345-kv electricity transmission line) by an ecological system (a tree limb) abruptly interrupted that economy, throwing into temporary disarray the entire global economy. One clear lesson is that when human society pushes nature too far, it's bound to push back unpredictably and suddenly.

On that eventful August afternoon, many people—indeed, entire economies—discovered just how intertwined their lives, work, needs, and experiences with Internet and communications technologies were. The lives of countless millions were disconnected from the normal consumption patterns they had come to expect—communications, transportation and mobility, and space cooling. So ubiquitous are our computing devices—and so dependent upon reliable and secure energy supplies—that people were severed from their modern umbilical cords, cut off from processes and expectations that had defined much of their comfortable existence within the warm womb of modern, technologically insulated society. As computers, lights, and other electronic gadgetry blinked out, offices and stores began to empty. Electronically induced instinctive responses to life's daily grind literally ground to a halt. Original thought had to take over for millions of ex-urbanites seeking to escape the urban core for homes, contact loved ones, and weather the heat. Mundane tasks such as paying for a taxi required money from bank machines that suddenly ceased to function. Debit and credit card payment processing systems and Canadian Interac processing systems shut down, as did gas pumps and virtually all commerce. A phone call home suddenly required patience and anachronistic innovation as cellular telephones stopped operating and hundreds of people coalesced around the dwindling number of public pay phones. As a result of the simultaneous purge of the urban core, traffic chaos materialized. Public transport scheduling and routing became a nightmare, vehicles flooded the roadways, and traffic control evaporated. Airlines, air travel, and air traffic control were crippled. Hotels were swamped with stranded customers. All normal consumption activities taken for granted each and every moment of our lives were disrupted and reconfigured, or vanished altogether.

CONSUMPTION ACTIVITY

Consumption activities, patterns, and levels of material and energy throughput help define who we are and increasingly both affect and are affected by globalization. The transborder characteristics and the increasing velocity of globalization exert profound changes on the environment, wealth distribution, population health, the performance of markets, and the quality of life for peoples around the world. These effects can in turn induce human responses that alter the transborder characteristics and velocity of globalization. Throughout these processes, consumption activities both enable and impede human development and environmental sustainability.

In addition to their substantial benefits, the extraction, production, use, and disposal of many goods and subsequently the use of many services can generate significant environmental problems. These include resource depletion and exploitation; pollution of the air, water, and land; and growth in the levels of solid, toxic, and hazardous wastes. This can have direct and indirect consequences for human and global ecological health. While pollution is a major cause of premature death in the South, many diseases in the North are now considered "lifestyle" diseases, with people dying from the over-indulgence brought on by affluence. Still, over a billion people lack access to supplies of safe water, adequate sanitation, energy, and nutrition. Over-indulgence can also generate indirect effects, disproportionately impacting less affluent populations. Anthropogenic climate change, for instance, is largely caused by the over-consumption activities of the North. Yet the effects are inequitably distributed to poorer and Southern peoples. Excess consumption, barriers to essential consumption needs, and the complex interactions between all consumption activities can have profound and pervasive consequences.

It's only when we are forced to modify our normal behavior, like that fateful day in August, that we notice this behavior. Rare indeed would be those who stop and take time to think about the consequences of our consumption choices. Everything we do, each activity we perform, is associated with, often directly, the consumption of energy and usually some form of materials. We consume energy from the moment we are awakened by an alarm clock through our perhaps daily shower; eating breakfast; listening to music or news likely truncated with screaming commercials reminding us of our inferiority and incompleteness without newer material artifacts; getting to work or our other daily activities; typing on a computer; shopping; reading a book, magazine, or newspaper; talking on the telephone or watching a movie; to brushing our teeth before retiring for the evening. One need look no further than the alarm clock switched off first thing in the morning to remind us of our dependence on cheap subsidized and likely fossil fuel–generated electricity to see where we might reconfigure our activities to help reduce the impacts, such as climate change, of our consumption choices. Still, we don't. An interesting observation by Huber and Mills (2005) is that the form of energy desired has progressively become more refined over the centuries and millennia. This has profound implications for the layers of infrastructures society has developed that support our consumption activities, like that morning alarm clock. As Thomas Princen (1999) explains, this distancing and shading of our consumption decisions has been a vital factor in our increasingly global over-consumption and mis-consumption. Indirectly, the energy and materials consumed in any one of these rather simple and mundane activities can be tremendous. The linkages between our over- and mis-consumption and the impacts of our consumption choices are typically hidden and displaced from the consumer. These linkages and their consequences are relentlessly complex, as are the myriad of processes embedded within the infrastructures that enable the rather seamless and routine completion of these tasks. Layers upon layers of technologies, infrastructures, processes, institutions, social expectations, norms of practice, and systems of organization and regulation all function more or less smoothly to facilitate our daily routines. This is for good reason. Could you imagine how ridiculous it would be to have to reinvent electricity and wire the necessary infrastructure every time you wanted to turn on a light? This possibility was—or could have been, had time permitted—vividly brought home to those millions of people affected by the August 2003 power failure across northeastern North America. Clearly, specific consumption activities change much more rapidly than do the foundations—both social and physical—upon which they are built.

Lengthy and complex commodity chains, informational distancing, and commodity distancing and shading accompany most goods and services today. In this way, our behavior has become habituated to many regular tasks, less the necessary feedbacks, checks, and balances that reflect the social and ecological consequences of our decisions and actions. We simply expect the networks that facilitate these tasks to be available when and where we want them. Society as a whole has become normalized and institutionalized to these particular ways of interacting to provide the necessary means of survival. The proliferation of wireless networks, for instance, merely reflects this desire for greater convenience and flexibility in their accessibility. The consumption of energy and materials embedded within these processes are pervasive and diverse. It's only when these systems catastrophically fail that we really understand how intertwined our lives have become with the technologies, and with the resources and energy that feed them, as we plummet back to the physical realities of life's daily consumption activities with the disconcerting thump of relinquished tranquility.

However, this begs the question: "Has this habituation been unconsciously taken too far, and, if so, why?" Certainly the inertial resistance of layers of infrastructural and societal organization has something to do with it. But as a species with tremendous predictive, planning, and organizational capacity, one would expect a certain level of awareness and a reasonable response appropriate to the circumstances. Yet confronted by dramatic global consequences—climate change, disruptive loss of stratospheric ozone, depletion and loss of both nonrenewable and renewable resources, rapid loss of both cultural and biological diversity—unquestionably insignificant action is taken by individuals, society in general, or our political leaders and global decision makers. This begs the question: Why?

GLOBAL EFFECTS OF OUR CONSUMPTION ACTIVITIES

While we easily observe the effects of our consumption activity at local and regional scales, the global consequences are far more difficult to perceive or confront. Consider climate change: climate mechanisms are tremendously complex. Modeling and predicting to date has been crude at best. As recently as 2007, for instance, models forecast a potential loss of Arctic sea ice by the later part of the twenty-first century. This outcome may occur much earlier, as indicated by the simultaneous opening of both the northwest and northeast Arctic Ocean passages in late August 2008. Scientists are observing more dramatic changes than anticipated, and fear that a tipping-point threshold has already been crossed. Comparisons between reality and computer model predictions indicate that the Arctic melting is two decades ahead of projections. In the Arctic regions, areas already experiencing the greatest impacts from climate changes, warming may thaw permafrost, which may cause increased methane emissions and establish a positive feedback cycle. Such may already be the case. Since methane is a potent greenhouse gas, it may herald the beginning of a runaway global climate change feedback. In 2007, methane levels, which had previously stabilized, began rising again. Originally, climate models and predictions had not anticipated this effect until the end of the century when greenhouse gas levels were expected to be much higher under a business-as-usual scenario. Instead, like the ice-free Northwest Passage, this event appears to have struck far sooner than forecasted. This alarming development is only compounded by the 2008 discovery of methane plumes in an area to the west of the Norwegian island of Svalbard rising from the Arctic seabed. Tundra and boreal ecosystems currently hold about 14 percent of the world's soil carbon (Arctic Monitoring and Assessment Programme [AMAP], 1997). If this is released, atmospheric carbon dioxide emissions could spike by more than the cumulative contribution from the burning of fossil fuels through 1995. While the feedbacks between production and decomposition of plant matter are complex and uncertain, hopes that plants may efficiently capture increasing atmospheric carbon in a warmer planet helped shape key conditions of the Kyoto Protocol. Ominously, it is now believed that increased carbon emissions will tend to *reduce* plant productivity and increase decomposition, further contributing to the release of carbon emissions, enhancing another positive feedback response (Ciais et al., 2005). This concern must be coupled with the damage to primary productivity, including agriculture, as a result of air pollution that tends to accompany carbon emissions. Further, the loss of various ecosystems to certain crops that produce biofuels, in an ironic attempt to reduce the carbon emissions of energy use, particularly transportation, has been a stimulus for crop and forest conversions. These have replaced strong-carbon-absorbing plants with weak-absorbing biofuel crops intended solely for export (Monbiot, 2005; Pearce, 2005). Other implications of these crop conversions hinge on the reduced access to arable land for food crops, destruction of diverse ecosystems leading to loss of biological diversity and species loss, displacement of indigenous cultures, regional smog that has had dramatic global effects in recent years clear across the Pacific, and the increased release of carbon from peat in swamp forests as clearing is undertaken. What is driving this blatantly pathological consumption behavior—a response to climate change that intensifies the processes of anthropogenic climate change and contributes a series of additional impacts harmful to both human and ecological health? Before delving into that question, we need first to explore a few other issues.

Returning to the Arctic and climate change, snow cover has a dramatic effect on solar energy absorption rates. A warmer climate will reduce snow cover and increase warming. As recently as 1997, the Arctic Monitoring and Assessment Programme suggested that the Greenland and Antarctic ice sheets did not seem to be shrinking, and in fact may be growing slightly. The Jakobshavn glacier in Greenland, for instance, remained unchanged until the year 1900, when the front ice surface began lowering by about 2.5 meters on average per year. Between 1991 and 1999, it began to thicken again, and then rapidly thin afterward. By 2003, thinning rates were twelve meters per year (Science Daily, 2003). The British Broadcasting Corporation has quoted Dr. Gordon Hamilton of the Climate Change Institute at the University of Maine as observing the Kangerdlugssuaq glacier on the east coast of Greenland experience a 5-km retreat of its terminus, an astounding 300 percent acceleration in its flow speed, and a 100-meter thinning in roughly 2005 alone (British Broadcasting Corporation [BBC], 2005b). The collapse of the Ayles shelf in Canada's far Arctic occurred on August 13, 2005. This signaled the rapid deterioration of a massive ice shelf resembling a zone "like a cruise missile has come down and hit the ice shelf" (Canadian Broadcasting Corporation [CBC], 2006a). This breakup adds another sixty-six-square-kilometer, 4,500-year-old mass of ice to the mix of melting fresh water destined for the world's oceans.

This amount of fresh water entering the North Atlantic will almost certainly affect the Atlantic Meridional Overturning Circulation, also known as the Atlantic Conveyor, by changing its temperature, salinity, and density.

The Atlantic Conveyor is an important climate mechanism responsible for European weather. Bryden, Longworth, and Cunningham (2005) have observed a 30 percent decrease in its rate over the last twelve years. As the Arctic region warms, the Conveyor is undergoing dramatic changes. This discovery of a rate decrease has led to recent concerns about its possible shut-down, which could plunge Europe into another ice age. Moreover, as the climate changes, the food chain in the North Atlantic, already under substantial stress from over-fishing (Worm et al., 2006), may undergo complex changes that stress fish, seabirds, and marine mammals (Richardson & Schoeman, 2004).

Many distinct cultures around the globe have experienced troubling effects from the often dramatic challenges climate changes are generating. Subsistence food sources have become more difficult to acquire as weather patterns become more variable and unpredictable. The Inuit of northern Canada, for example, have had to cope with a much later freeze in autumn and earlier thaw in spring. This has reduced the size of sea ice, which now drifts much farther from shore, taking with it the seals upon which many communities rely for food. This leads to shortened trapping and hunting seasons. Thinner and broken ice in winter also makes for very perilous travel for even the most experienced hunters. Overall, as subsistence activities falter, the Inuit depend more on processed foods and industrially manufactured staples shipped great distances at great cost, both economical and ecological, which are often beyond the financial reach of many living in northern communities.

Warmer summers also reduce permafrost, which causes coastal slumping, modifies lake ecosystems, and kills fish. Melting permafrost also wreaks havoc on buildings as foundations shift. Flora and fauna have inexorably crept northward, changing the dynamics of the landscape and biota. Of course, given the biomagnification of toxic pollutants from the long-range transport of chemicals and persistent organic pollutants (which are not even used or produced in these northern regions), many Inuit have dropped their critically important traditional diets in favor of the expensive and low-nutritional surrogates of Western processed foods (AMAP, 1997).

These impacts have helped motivate many Aborigines to enter the income economy, both to benefit from the perceived opportunities and simply to survive, the consequences of which will become more apparent as we discuss these issues in chapters 6, 7, and 8.

Many people in Latin America and Southeast Asia experience effects from increasingly intense storms. "Global warming could increase the number and severity of extreme weather events such as storms, floods, and droughts, and related landslides and wildfires" (Intergovernmental Panel on Climate Change [IPCC], 1998, 215). These are likely to be the source of significant, direct climate-change health effects in Latin America. They are only beginning to be understood and are expected to include extreme weather events, air pollution, water- and food-borne contamination, vector-borne infectious diseases, socioeconomic effects, and population effects (Health Canada, 2001).

Europeans and North Americans are watching their glaciers disappear, forest fires intensify, and heat waves become killers. The European heat waves of August 2003 are blamed for literally thousands of deaths in some of the most wealth-insulated countries of the world, and these are predicted to become worse. Floods and the effects of hurricanes and more severe weather also claim many lives each year. Other potential consequences range from crop failures, water stress, increased vector-borne diseases, transport interruptions, more insect and pest infestations, coastal erosion and flooding, and heat stress to increased air pollution, and the list goes on.

Africans are coping with longer and more intense droughts, and, like the Middle East, are fighting wars over declining resources such as water. Declining rainfall since the 1960s linked to climate change, not overgrazing, appears to have precipitated desertification in the Sahel region of Africa. These conditions have subsequently led to conflict throughout the region. Droughts in the Sahel resulting from climate change, already accounting for several million deaths, are expected to intensify during this century (BBC, 2005a). Since the 1970s, rainfall has decreased dramatically. Computer modeling suggests rainfall will continue to decrease, effectively shifting the epicenter for drought southward. Theories currently link this drying spell to warmer waters in the North Atlantic. Some of the poorest areas of the world are impacted most severely by global climate change.

Small-island developing states are scrambling as they lose shore-line to rising sea levels and intensifying storms. With the release of its first assessment report in 1990, the Intergovernmental Panel on Climate Change warned, "The very existence of entire island countries such as the Maldives, Tuvalu and Kiribati could be imperiled by a rise in the mid range of current sea-level rise projections" (IPCC, 1990). In August 2005, a small community in Vanuatu was moved to higher ground under the United Nations Environment Program to escape the effects of "storm surges and aggressive waves linked with climate change" (United Nations Environment Program, 2005). Sea-level changes of this mid-magnitude prediction could also lead to enormous population displacements from densely populated river delta regions, including Egypt, India, Bangladesh, and China.

Similarly, Newtok, a Yupik Inuit community in Alaska, must be relocated due to river erosion and melting permafrost (CBC, 2006d). Newtok is a harbinger of things to come for dozens of additional native villages scattered along Alaska's western coast, each confronting the increasingly vicious effects of climate change. Shore ice and permafrost, each disappearing as a result of climate change, open coastal communities to powerful storm erosion. After losing their nomadic character, these communities now face increasingly challenging hurdles and costs to adapt. The monetary costs alone—too great for state or federal agencies to absorb—tower over the transformed, largely subsistence economies. "Being absorbed into another culture, even one only 160 kilometres away, could amount to cultural death, exposing residents to urban ills including alcoholism, which is banned in Shishmaref and other dry villages" (CBC, 2006d). Residents fear the subsistence lifestyle their traditions and economy so heavily rely upon would fall off, pushing them to welfare. "We would like to keep our traditions and values as long as we can for the future of our children and grandchildren" (CBC, 2006d). Indeed, these may prove valuable assets to all of humanity.

Scenario models predict that the 4.1 million square kilometers of the Amazon Basin could transform into a grassy savanna before 2100. A rise in global temperature, a decrease in rainfall, and rapid deforestation—all of which are linked to excessive consumer practices—are identified as the culprits. Unless aggressive action to halt global warming and reduce pollution and deforestation are undertaken, the Amazon rain forest could transform "into a savanna-like landscape" (CBC, 2006c). Such a loss would irretrievably transform 20 percent of the world's fresh water and an estimated 30 percent of the world's plant and animal species, many of which are as yet undiscovered.

What we are witnessing is the disruption, destruction, and dislocation of diverse cultures that, in many cases, have not yet participated in the consumption activities responsible for climate change and other global environmental changes. The potential impacts from climate change alone, even neglecting the myriad other local, regional, and global consequences of our consumption activities, is a crisis far in excess of observable responses, suggesting a critical distributional link failure between causes and responses.

In poorer communities and nations, the effects of climate change lead to increased mortality and morbidity, wars, and political unrest. In fact, many of the benefits attributed to development simply do not materialize (CBC, 2006b; Rattle, 2005). Wealthy communities and nations, on the other hand, have somewhat greater resiliency, primarily due to their greater technological insulation—as with medical needs, wealthier countries can pay for needed technologies, which helps define, shape, and distribute those technologies. Nevertheless, as we have seen, they are not immune to the consequences of climate change or to other global or local ecological and social phenomena. The adaptive responses of industrial nations are formulated within the prevailing social framework. This evades directly confronting value structures, institutional arrangements, and lifestyle choices. While simpler, the inherent dilemma of such an approach is that it will invariably lead to a diminished ability to adapt to changing global phenomena (for example, climatic conditions) over the long term. As consumption increases and new ecological and health risks are revealed, greater consumption (technological insulation) will be seen as essential to adapt to and mitigate the emerging risks.

Increasing consumption levels produce unanticipated feedback mechanisms "in which socioeconomic changes resulting from climate change lead to further climate impacts" (Health Canada, 2001, 108). When temperatures and pollution levels rise, more people employ air conditioners. As extreme weather events occur, communities repeatedly rebuild their infrastructure in more aggressive formats. "Insurers have been pressing for the establishment of a national disaster mitigation strategy that should include more funds to invest in community protection infrastructure and public education" (Kovacs, 2001, 57). Biofuels and hydrogen economies are touted as solutions to the effects of fossil fuel burning. Yet alternative energy sources have often been tapped only to supplement existing sources. Ironically, society's approach (economic growth) taken to the social and environmental impacts of increasing consumption (climate change) appears contradictory to the needed outcome (a reduced human footprint). In other words, social systems appear to neglect and override fundamental prerequisites for sustainability, including decision-making frameworks; nurture seems to trump nature. Certain social processes and societal values, it appears, irrationally influence our decisions, behaviors, and lifestyles. Fundamental ecological and societal realities and limitations are usually only accommodated once critical thresholds have been surpassed and direct human health risks are perceived. In the case of imminent global phenomena such as climate change, and the loss of biological and cultural diversity, this may be—if it is not already—too late.

GLOBAL CONSUMPTION ON A FINITE PLANET

The limits to growth were well articulated over thirty years ago. Numerous authors from Ehrlich to Commoner to Carson to Daly to Meadows have warned us of the possible threats should we choose to ignore the warning signs. Social upheaval, political unrest, cultural extermination, and inequities are daily occurrences. These are compounded by stratospheric ozone decay, climate changes, and biological diversity loss directly and indirectly attributable to human activity. Local ecosystems, water, and air sheds have become stressed to levels that induce both acute and chronic health consequences, and political and social unrest. National and municipal infrastructures are in decay in industrial countries, and nonindustrial nations are watching their resources being squandered for the manufacture of consumer products, even food, that are beyond their own financial reach. Global economic distress has beset governments with increasing costs at precisely the same time revenues are evaporating, pushing solutions further out of reach for even the most prosperous communities.

The current trajectory of globalization seems irrational. Continued growth and improved living standards for billions of people, as conventional theories would suggest, is simply untenable. *Our Ecological Footprint*, for example, suggests that human activity has achieved ecological overshoot, exceeding the Earth's regenerative capacity by at least 20 percent (Wackernagel & Rees, 1996; World Wildlife Fund, 2004). Similarly, the Millennium Ecosystem Assessment Project has raised alarm about the state of two-thirds of the planet's ecosystems. "In the early 1960s, humans were using about 70 per cent of nature's output; by the early 1980s, we'd reached 100 per cent; and in 1999, we were at 125 per cent" (Wright, 2004, 129). Moreover, Vitousek, Ehrlich, Ehrlich, and Matson (1986) calculated that we humans—a single species—were appropriating 40 percent of the planet's net photosynthetic output, the vast majority of this by a mere 20 percent of the population. These prominent and stark warnings demonstrate that human activity has markedly surpassed ecological capacities. The World Health Organization and the United Nations, along with numerous groups and governments, have also identified the intense human deficit from existing consumption practices. Social, political, and economic disruption continue to plague the five billion people who are marginalized. A mere one billion people, mostly living in the industrialized nations of the world, benefit from 80 percent of the world's GDP, whereas the remaining must divide a meager 20 percent (United Nations, 2005).

This human deficit has tremendous health, justice, developmental, and social consequences. A redistribution of wealth and power seems essential. Would this necessarily achieve more sustainable consumption? The industrialized nations responded with a knee-jerk reaction to a potential economic threat from terrorism with the infusion of approximately $551 billion in 2003 (Labonte, Schrecker, Sanders, & Meuss, 2004). When economic collapse seemed imminent following the folly of credit and debt misallocations and excessive consumerism during the early part of this millennium, governments pumped trillions of dollars of currencies into markets to stimulate, reinflate, grow, and bail out toxic investments and wealthy corporate CEOs, steady the banking and financial industries, and enable the automobile industry—now too big to fail—to continue pumping out SUVs and greenhouse gases alike. Yet G7 member countries contributed only $38 billion for development assistance, including basic health, in 2001. Poor living conditions, arguably a source for inciting terrorism, are derived from unsustainable consumption and industrialized nations' excess affluence. Annual costs to meet the first seven Millennium Development Goals are estimated at $70 billion. This objective is clearly easily achievable—which is perhaps a colossal understatement—if only our values, institutional arrangements, and political will would permit it.

SUSTAINABLE CONSUMPTION

The Oslo Symposium has suggested that sustainable consumption is "the use of goods and services that respond to basic needs and bring a better quality of life while minimising the use of natural resources, toxic materials and emissions of waste and pollutants over the life cycle, so as not to jeopardise the needs of future generations" (Norwegian Ministry of the Environment, 1995, 9). Definitions such as this leave to interpretation basic needs and their differentiation from wants, along with an implicit assumption that the needs of future generations can be determined. They also avoid explicit limits on energy and materials throughput, the generation of toxic materials, and their life-cycle emissions.

Such definitions must be considered with caution. To their credit, they imply a two-way process of social change through which both consumers and producers can influence consumption. Yet they probably afford too much weight to the expectation that individuals and groups freely choose their personal lifestyles. They also emphasize the role of goods and services in achieving a better quality of life, presupposing a technological and market bias. These definitions do not sufficiently emphasize extant social and institutional arrangements—arguably the source of such bias—and the role these play in constructing and reinforcing values and governing social processes, behaviors, and lifestyle choices (Naiman, 1997; Stern, Dietz, Ruttan, Socolow, & Sweeney, 1997). These speak deeply to social justice, democracy, and freedoms. They suggest the substantial role market economies, theories of power and wealth distribution, and technological preconceptions play in the formation of societal values, policy and decision making, and consumption activities. In this sense, the foregoing and similar definitions of sustainable consumption have also been criticized as both idealistic and insufficient.

While a simple definition would be attractive, sustainable consumption is a complex concept. Most definitions of sustainable consumption, however, share several features. These include recognizing the need to minimize resource throughput, waste, and pollution throughout life cycles; establishing social empowerment and enabling greater agency and more shared freedoms; satisfying basic needs and favoring quality of life over material standards of living; and enhancing intra- and intergenerational justice in access to resources and rights to inhabit a healthy environment. Any comprehensive definition of sustainable consumption must be founded upon a diverse range of environmental, social equity, and moral concerns.

A definition for sustainable consumption should integrate social, economic, and political practices by all societal levels and actors to support and encourage a reduced burden of producing, using, and disposing of goods and services; satisfying basic needs for key consumption goods and services, such as food, water, life-long learning, sanitation, and shelter; health and well-being; and a just and equitable distribution of wealth and power. Such a differentiation must also integrate lifestyles that contribute to a high quality of life and place greater value on social cohesion, local traditions, and nonmaterial values, and minimize the material affluence and the corresponding footprint of these choices; and the application of a variety of tools, both new and existing, to achieve these goals.

The foregoing discussion suggests that current consumption practices are both exceedingly complex and largely unsustainable. It also suggests that we need only to understand what more sustainable consumption might be, rather than agree on a complete and potentially restraining definition for sustainable consumption. In these terms, achieving more sustainable consumption might be more productive to consider as a journey rather than a destination. Such a goal would draw attention to the injustices derived from current consumption practices, help distinguish other practices that are more beneficial, and identify opportunities to correct existing shortfalls.

TOO MUCH OF A GOOD THING

Conventional development models have sought to compensate for their own shortcomings by attempting to incorporate more people into the consumer economy, and through economic growth (the proverbial "bigger cake" or a "rising tide raises all ships"). This has often been at the expense of changes in the distribution and pattern of consumption, which can be more *cost*-effective and resource *efficient*. While growth and efficiency might enable a higher standard of living and more efficient allocation, it does not resolve distributional or scale problems. On the contrary, growth and efficiency merely attempt to expand the pie rather than redistribute or reduce it. However, a world in which wealth was initially distributed evenly would look very different from a world that began with an unequal distribution of wealth (Peet, 1992). In a finite world, continued expansion is pathological. The dilemma is that the majority living lives of poverty, despite their (in some cases manufactured) aspirations, cannot be expected to achieve the levels of affluence the few currently experience.

Growth and efficiency are but two goals of the prevailing social structure. Taken together, these goals direct consumption activities through the institutional arrangements, social frameworks, expectations, values, behaviors, and lifestyles they both foster and deter. These issues are further elaborated in chapters 6 and 8.

Fortunately, widespread evidence has demonstrated the often tenuous links between these objectives and those of improved quality of life and population health, environmental and social sustainability, and economic stability. Increasing material affluence, or standard of living, and quality of life tend to diverge beyond certain "threshold" levels (Elgin, 1993; Max-Neef, 1995; Schor, 1991, 1998). As new consumers transcend those barriers, the "good life" is always just within reach like a tomorrow that never comes (Michaelis & Lorek, 2004; Tisdell, 2003; Wilson & Tisdell, 2001). We must instead transcend ever increasing standards of living, characterized by efficient growth, aspiring instead to a high quality of life nurtured by sufficiency (Reisch, 2001), and turn the page on this ideologically, socially, and ecologically anachronistic calendar.

3

Virtual Morality: Globalization, ICTs, and Sustainable Consumption

Globalization has been described as the integration of trade, finance, and economic practices, the interactive co-evolution of technological, cultural, social, economic, and environmental trends. Held, Mcgrew, Goldblatt, and Perraton suggest, "the concept of globalization implies, first and foremost, a stretching of social, political and economic activities across frontiers such that events, decisions and activities in one region of the world can come to have significance for individuals and communities in distant regions of the globe" (2003, 67).

Scholte (2000) suggests globalization is a more complex process than any one of several conceptualizations that can be readily described by existing words and phrases. Among these he includes *internationalization, liberalization, universalization* and *westernization*—all of which can be suitably accommodated by existing expressions. Globalization, Scholte argues, is the phenomenon where social conceptualizations of space and time *transgress* political and physical borders—deterritorialization. Thus globalization generates transworld or transborder connections that move beyond simple territories or relationships between territories. The importance of this becomes more apparent in future chapters as we consider the social, cultural, and ecological trajectories of globalization, and as we consider the role of ecological economics—a field of study and practice that has advanced the term *transdisciplinary*. Ecological economists use this term to describe the way we must now think in order to conceptualize and organize human activity, and in order to better understand and confront our emergent social and ecological challenges.

Scholte (2000) argues that geography has historically been an essential determinant of the differences between peoples. That is, the "differences between the lives of desert nomads, mountain villagers and island seafarers are largely attributable to contrasts in the places that they inhabit" (Scholte, 2000, 46). Historically, people have had to adapt to their immediate environment in order to survive. Cultures have therefore developed unique features, from food gathering to spirituality, that helped ensure their survival in their unique environments.

Today, that has changed dramatically. "Mountain farmers in yak caravans in Laos and Myanmar now use cell phones to find the best route to market during the rainy season" (O'Meara, 2000, 126). Recent changes, in particular through the application of ICTs, have transformed our sense of place from a purely physical location demarcated by political boundaries, local ecologies, altitude, latitude, and longitude. Our sense of place now transgresses both space and time. The Internet may connect someone to his or her physical neighbors as easily as to someone on another continent. Money can be physical legal tender as much as digital bits in cyberspace shifted effortlessly around the globe. Market processes, climate change, and air pollution are global in nature—they do not respect political or geographic borders. The tiniest or largest electrical blackout has the potential to affect and influence almost anyone anywhere on the planet. Among the lessons of the August 2003 massive power failure was the awareness of just how intertwined we have all become with our electronic gadgetry and ICTs. The lineups at telephone booths reminded thousands of the convenience and simplicity of wireless communications devices. Without electricity, there was no radio, television, or Internet to communicate the cause of the power loss, or what actions people should take. Even where power was not lost around the world, millions of Internet surfers struggled with delayed and limited access to websites whose servers went black in the affected areas. People didn't phone or e-mail their usual electronic contacts to understand the situation; they visited neighbors. The same tasks were completed without the need for electricity, and often with other benefits, albeit often in a less "convenient" manner. Instead of looking at amazing images of the universe on the Internet, millions of people gazed skyward at the real thing in utter disbelief. These phenomena and their effects, whether social or environmental, can be anywhere and everywhere; simultaneously interactive and differentiated. Thus the space and time of place has both expanded and compressed. Territorial space is transcended. Global phenomena escape national control and regulation, a problem and challenge we shall return to.

Globalization includes the processes that enable actors and nations around the globe to be interconnected. These processes include economic integration; the exchange of communications, information, and data; the diffusion of cultural ideals, dominated by those of the West; and increasing mobility. Clearly, globalization is not a recent phenomenon.

At the same time, globalization is not inherently "bad" or "good." It is a process that is shaped by our values and institutions, which in turn are shaped by the processes of globalization. Globalization is influenced by the interactions of global actors with the infrastructures, tools, managerial practices, organizational structures, value systems, and political realities we have created.

On the one hand, as many goods and services become global—from information to food to water to energy—the resilience of human systems seems to increase. Should there be a drought, flood, storm, crop failure, social deterioration, or other form of disaster, local populations may simply reach out through their transnational networks to supply their needs and resolve their problems. Should *local* ecosystems collapse due to human activity, transborder global connections offer the capacity to compensate. Similarly with the sociopolitical environment, wars, unrest, and threats against democracy and freedoms may be managed and corrected through transglobal networks. Given sufficient capital and resources, should either the local environment be consumed or society deteriorate, one can simply move on. Yet does this worldview detach—sever—people, individuals, or societies from their respective environmental and social bodies, histories, and cultures? More importantly, what happens when our challenges become global, and there is no longer any place or anyone to reach out to—challenges such as health, environmental, or economic? The benefits of globalization necessarily imply the globalization of risks, challenges, and impacts too.

This particular path of globalization presents some unique health challenges. Health concerns have been expressed about the rapid spread of infectious diseases, such as severe acute respiratory syndrome (SARS), the West Nile virus, AIDS, and the H1N1 flu pandemic. Health challenges are possibly overshadowed only by the introduction of exotic species that continue to transform ecosystems. Mammals, insects, fish, weeds, alien diseases, plant species, and even biological control agents have invaded all land and marine ecosystems around the world. Often, these have been introduced unintentionally through the activities of globalization. Almost one thousand invasive and exotic species have been identified in forest ecosystems in the United States alone (Douce, Moorhead, & Bargeron, 2006). Many of these have become common household names: the Asian longhorn beetle, Dutch elm disease, mountain pine beetles, zebra mussels, purple loosestrife, emerald ash borer. These species have caused major controversies over pesticide spraying, clear-cutting, allowing infestations to run their course, and other strategies to try and control their damage. The mountain pine beetle, introduced in western Canada, for instance, has caused extensive damage to the Provinces' forest ecosystems. "By 2002, millions of trees in an area the size of Vancouver Island had been infested. By some accounts, the area of infestation triples every year" (Canadian Broadcasting Corporation [CBC], 2000). Aided and abetted by warmer weather, probably a result of climate change, the boreal forests of Canada are proving delicious to these beetles' insatiable appetite for pine trees. Similarly, the emerald ash borer, native to China and eastern Asia and believed to have arrived on imported wooden packing material, was introduced into North America in 2002. Since then, it has infested as many as one hundred thousand ash trees near Windsor, Ontario, and killed an estimated six million ash trees in southeastern Michigan. This is only a tiny sampling on one continent. Ironically, collecting live, exotic beetles has become fashionable in places like Japan. What is the likelihood these could be introduced to other ecosystems, with disastrous consequences? (CBC, 2003).

As with the greater than one hundred thousand novel chemicals produced today, the processes of globalization responsible for these exotic introductions have never been tested for their effects on the environment, human health, or economies.

The regulatory abilities of national governments have historically offered protection from aggressive market forces. They have ensured equitable wealth redistribution through diverse social programs. They have also ensured market regulation and environmental protections (Antipolis, 2001; Global Social Policy Forum, 2001; Gough, 2001; Kirkpatrick & Lee, 1999; Labonte, 2004; McMichael, Butler, & Douglas, 2002). Sadly, these are the precise abilities global trade agreements are now eroding (Labonte, 2002). Under these conditions, the influence of national governments has receded. Between national governance and global institutions lies a vast chasm where social and environmental needs are languishing without firm leadership direction. Particularly problematic can be the attraction of foreign investment. Predicated on the provision of jobs, both industrialized and industrializing countries alike aggressively compete to attract foreign investments. The attraction of foreign investment can influence domestic legislation. Local laws can be created through undemocratic and secretive deals, and too often prioritize profits and rarely give recognition to sustainable development (Ayine et al., 2005). The consequences of capital and labor mobility and of capital concentration have increasingly differential effects on the power and influence ascribed to different local, national, and global actors (Fuchs & Lorek, 2001).

Along with the global transborder connections and movements of foreign investment, aggressive competition, profit-seeking trade actors, and the increasingly integrated financial practices of global markets, we have witnessed the rapid global dispersion of economic and financial distress when these structures, institutions, and practices have collapsed. While certain actors are able to ride out or even benefit from the whirlpool of events—socially, technologically, or economically insulated from the effects—many others simply drown in the ensuing currents.

Globalization also presents other challenges. Some experts have expressed concerns about the rise of "Western" lifestyles. Through various channels, such as entertainment and advertising, "Western" lifestyle choices are being depicted and accordingly adopted. These can fuel epidemics of our modern diseases of affluence: cancer, cardiovascular diseases, diabetes, and obesity. They can also fan the global nature of greenhouse gas emissions and climate change, ozone depletion, loss of biological and cultural diversity, and smog. The spread of "Western" lifestyles can accordingly fuel and be fuelled by globalization. The roles of ICTs in these trends are discussed in the following chapters.

ENVIRONMENTAL, SOCIAL, AND ECONOMIC DIMENSIONS

ICTs enable dramatic efficiencies in products and processes, inducing a restructuring effect that creates jobs and improves earnings, capital, and profits growth. Castells (2000) notes how Alan Greenspan traced the high rate of productivity increases during the mid to late 1990s back to 1993 capital investments in information technologies. The ultimate effect was an increase in productivity during this period of 2 percent on average, including the addition of well-paying jobs in the ICT sector at twice the rate of the balance of the economy.

ICTs are blessed with Moore's Law and its variations: that the logic density of silicon-integrated circuits double every eighteen months. Similarly, bandwidth, storage capacity, and graphical image processing are advancing at an astounding rate.

The computing power of a single computer chip has increased by a factor of 64,000, tremendously expanding computational capabilities while dramatically reducing component size. From the bulky vacuum tube ENIAC, which filled a building floor, computer chips are now microscopic, soon expected to reach the physical limits of miniaturization. The marriage of this computing power with communications has spawned the ICTs revolution. Copper wire—a highly sought after commodity that even attracts criminals—is being replaced by thin glass strands and bundles of optical fibers. These fibers are able to "conduct" light pulses that carry, in digital form, information that represents data, voice, and video signals.

Wireless technologies have extended the reach of land-based telecommunications applications. Communications satellites are bringing a wealth of information to every corner of the globe. Low-orbiting satellites have become cheaper to launch. Unimpeded by geography, satellites more effectively service voice and video needs in existing market areas and are able to create and reach new markets. Private investments have capitalized on these markets: between 1967 and 1997, commercial communications satellite launches soared from 14 percent of all satellite launches to 69 percent, spawning a world of modern variants of the Dick Tracy two-way wrist radio communication device.

ICTs can allow the environment to be monitored and modeled. Satellites enable tropical deforestation to be tracked; the ozone layer to be monitored; forest fires to be overseen; air, water, and land pollutants to be traced; shifts in water bodies to be observed and modeled; and severe weather to be modeled and monitored.

Telecommunications, satellites, computers, geographic information systems (GISs), and software enable the collection, storage, transfer, monitoring, analysis, and manipulation of tremendous amounts of data. This can facilitate the tracking, study, and understanding of pollution, social changes, and human activities and their interactions along with the development of models for forecasting and predictions. This in turn can be invaluable for policy development and program determination to manage environmental and social challenges, particularly in the complex global environment in which decision makers regularly find themselves.

These applications have enabled the study of local environmental pollution and damage, social conditions, and global environmental phenomena. By combining satellite data with other data sets, the generation of computer maps enable the swift and relatively simple identification of patterns not readily obvious through written text or tables. GIS allows the overlay of different and complex data sets to build up a picture of a complex system that simply could not be previously generated. Video and real-time images can now advance these opportunities by overlaying current realities with future expectations to generate realistic video images of proposed changes. Changes over time can also be distinguished, opening up the obvious prospect to investigate different possibilities for, and impacts of future actions. The Internet permits the widespread dispersal of this information for purposes unimagined by its creators. Existing challenges, such as the age of some data, the lack of essential ground-based data required to complement satellite data for reliable and accurate information analysis, training in the use of and distribution of the technologies, privacy and security, and data conversion and formatting may be overcome by appropriate management.

ICTs also facilitate the rapid communication of data, information, and ideas. For scientists and others, this can be a powerful tool. Emergency responses and campaigns can be quickly geared up to take action. Education and job training can be more easily facilitated. O'Meara (2000) notes that the provision of maps of toxic substances by the Silicon Valley Toxics Coalition (SVTC) allows anyone with a computer and Internet connectivity to access data containing information on the releases of pollution from computer production and semiconductor manufacturing in northern California. The application of GISs and computer-based mapping software enabled SVTC to provide this data on the Internet. The argument here is that new communications systems, such as the Internet and cellular telephone technologies, allow faster exchange of information. "By linking far-flung people, the network helps researchers and activists work together to solve environmental problems" (O'Meara, 2000, 122).

A key role of ICTs is the provision of information. However, where they can be used to inform consumers and benefit people and the environment, they may also be used for irresponsible and harmful purposes. Privacy, for instance, has become a significant concern in the digital age. Access to private and sensitive information, the use of that information for unscrupulous intentions, and the capture of images in public spaces, among others, are all rising concerns.

In addition, the generation of certain information and its intended and unintended uses may create significant challenges. Ubiquitous or pervasive computing has the potential to overcome many of the barriers of current information systems—everything from data entry to data transfer to analysis and monitoring. Of course, as these systems become more widespread in everyday life, in addition to simplifying our activities, they also hold the ominous potential to observe, record, analyze, evaluate, and respond to our habits and behavior, lifestyles, preferences and aversions, and choices. One effect might be to generate behavior norms against which aberrations could be identified by certain social actors—from private corporations seeking to sell products to government agencies searching for potential terrorists or political dissidents. Less anticipated might be the (lack of) social transformations. By definition, these, and perhaps more sustainable consumption, will require precisely those deviations that may be perceived as a threat to the prevailing social order—if the motivations for these aberrations are repressed, so too might be sustainable social changes. "Societies not willing or not able to re-adjust to external and internal changes and to adopt innovative ways to cope with new challenges are, in the long term, doomed to ruin" (Cas, 2005, 33). Radio frequency identification devices are already embedded in many consumer products from cellular telephones to clothes. Advertising and direct marketing, timed messages and spatially triggered communications—text or cell phone messages sent to consumers as they enter a mall for instance—and product life-cycle tracking applications are already common.

The resulting social conformity may generate vigilante justice, ecological determinism, and social dictatorship. This phenomenon is already far more ubiquitous than we might believe. For instance, crimes have been solved using social forums, and police now regularly turn to the Internet and ICTs to broadcast and elicit certain features of crimes where the general public might have information. However, this process may as easily be turned on its head. In numerous cases, social forums have served as platforms for vigilante justice, solving crimes despite the safety, legal, and security risks posed. In one such example, an automobile dealer, once noticing that his car had been stolen, posted a short plea for information on a social networking forum. This generated a wave of cyber activity accompanied by a physical vigilante search for the vehicle and the crime's perpetrators. Eventually a small group of cyber-conformists sought out and physically identified, apprehended, and detained the individual until authorities arrived at the scene. Besides the irony of this situation (from a sustainability perspective, car enthusiasts taking vigilante action and prompting a fleet of thrill-seeking drivers to converge on city streets to ensure a future theft-free motoring paradise), it does pose some extraordinarily serious implications, beyond the obvious risk of personal injury and vigilante justice. Ultimately, to what extent might social networking forums serve to create physical social conformity? The implications of this phenomenon remain largely unexplored, and range across government, industry, and institutional behavior-shaping activities, to cyber-bullying. Consider the teenagers who use a cell phone (whether it functions or not) to convey the illusion that they have a strong network of social friends to avoid bullying or to secure group identity. This example demonstrates both the participation in use of ICTs (whether willing or not) in addition to the outside connection to physical reality (social networks). ICTs are proving to be powerful physical and social motivators when applied under just the right circumstances. Should we believe this will only be used for virtuous and moral activities? Who defines *virtuous* and *moral*? Could ICTs or globalization themselves influence our perceptions of virtue and morality?

Leapfrogging—a development path that theoretically proposes accelerated development by "leaping" over the less efficient, more inferior, costly, and polluting intermediate stages (especially technologies and economies) of development—may be the pinnacle of social conformity (if not outright colonization) cloaked in an ideology of neoliberal development and growth dogma.

Leapfrogging by developing countries is seen as a specific opportunity to enhance their position and roles in the global economy: to improve their global competitive advantage, enhance economic growth, raise their standard of living to a level consistent with consumer practices in other nations, and create jobs. "Indeed, telecommunication leapfrogging is seen by Antonelli as a way of diffusing IT, acting as a key that can boost growth rates and improve competitiveness" (Davison, Vogel, Harris, & Jones, 2000, 3). Leapfrogging is an approach to "bypassing some of the processes of accumulation of human capabilities and fixed investment in order to narrow the gaps in productivity and output that separate industrialized and developing countries" (Steinmueller, 2001, 2). ICTs offer the opportunity to advance national markets in developing countries, enabling participation in global markets. Integrating with global markets will, it is believed, "make the developing countries less vulnerable to fluctuations in the global economy in their fragile state of development" (Ensley, 2005).

Cellular telephone technologies are a shining example of leapfrogging in action. The growth of cellular telephones has been nothing short of astronomical. In the United States alone, the number of subscribers grew from 340,000 in 1985 to over 128 million in 2001 (Fishbein, 2002), representing an annual average growth rate of 25.5 percent. In Africa, the cellular telephone market has grown from 7.5 million users in 1999 to 76.8 million users in 2004 (LaFranier, 2005), representing an annual average growth rate of 59 percent, more than twice that of the United States.

As noted by O'Meara (2000), the worldwide growth in cellular telephones surpassed that of fixed telephone lines in 1996. The growth of both cellular and fixed telephone lines continues—a point that we will return to. Indeed, Nokia observed on September 21, 2005, that earlier that summer, Nokia had sold their one billionth cellular telephone—to a customer in Nigeria. Nokia anticipates that "it will be new growth markets like Nigeria that will fuel the growth towards three billion subscribers by 2010" (Nokia, 2005). Indeed, this growth "has exceeded even the mobile industry's own expectations."

While fixed telephone lines also grew, they did not grow as quickly as cellular telephones. In 1996, although there were fifty-five million new cellular network subscribers, forty-nine million land-based connections were established. Clearly, while it is difficult to say whether *individuals* utilized both formats simultaneously, the infrastructure for both were deployed to service customers. It is also unknown whether one format complements another or some element of substitution is taking place. Also, as we will see, there are complex issues that may include substitution and complementarity accompanied by induction, optimization, and other effects, thereby further confusing the ultimate effect of ICTs. This is further discussed in chapter 6. We also consider some fascinating evidence from Canada revealing the consumption, time, expense, and other social changes observed in relation to cellular and land-based telephone communications.

Leapfrogging is possibly beneficial, but one needs to approach it with caution. Can a technology be divorced from the society in which it was created?

That marriage of social needs and values is revealing in this quotation from Kai Öistämö, senior vice president of mobile phones for Nokia:

> The *continued rapid growth* in mobile subscriptions has *exceeded even the mobile industry's own estimates*. Since the early 1990s we have seen voice go truly wireless and mobile phones evolve from voice centric to feature driven devices. Earlier this summer, Nokia sold our one billionth mobile phone—a Nokia 1100 sold in Nigeria. . . . It will be *new growth markets* like Nigeria that will fuel the growth towards three billion subscribers by 2010. (Nokia, 2005; emphasis added)

In fact, Nokia (2005) observes that wireless and mobile phones have evolved from voice-centered communication devices to feature-driven devices. Nokia also states that they have "manufactured mobile phones in high volumes since the beginning of the 1990s." In 1998, Nokia, the world's largest mobile phone manufacturer, had produced over 100 million mobile telephones, which increased to over 207 million units in 2004. That is equivalent to producing one phone every 6.5 seconds. Each phone includes up to four hundred different components. These are important points to which we will return to in chapters 6 and 8.

What happens to those phones and components when they reach the end of their useful lives? In Canada alone, almost 34,000 *tons* of ICTs, excluding mainframes and other large equipment, were discarded in 1999 (EnvirosRIS, 2000). In addition to this waste, almost 16,000 tons were recycled, 24,500 tons reused, and 6,000 tons stored. Globally, e-waste is approaching fifty million tons annually. The waste stream from ICTs, although smaller than the general waste stream, is growing at a much faster rate than the general waste stream—while all wastes are growing, ICTs are becoming a greater, and significantly more toxic, proportion of wastes. Africa, China, and India have much larger populations from which to create a demand for ICTs than do Canada, the United Staes, or Europe. Does this portend a looming waste crisis? Once these countries leapfrog and adopt ICTs, is there any place else that can reuse their obsolete technologies? Will extended producer responsibilities extend to these vast numbers of products, assuming remanufacturing these products is even possible? We must not forget the incredible waste generated during the earlier phases of extraction and manufacturing for these devices that dwarf even their global waste streams.

Some would argue that cellular telephones are only one form of leapfrog-enabling technology, and rightly so. There are many others, and these all implore to be better understood in terms of their consequences for sustainable consumption. Leapfrogging offers both environmental and social benefits and risks. As Jared Diamond has suggested, technological optimism is a popular misconception. Jared Diamond notes that technologies merely produce changes, and all of our current environmental problems simply reflect the unanticipated harmful consequences of our existing technologies. "There is no basis for believing that technology will miraculously stop causing new and unanticipated problems while it is solving the problems that it previously produced" (Diamond, 2003, 44). Despite the prospect of highly populous, rapidly developing, consumer growth–oriented societies to exceed the material profligacy of industrial nations, it represents only a shadow—a symptom—of the ills wrought by this particular global trajectory. We return to these issues in future chapters.

Leapfrogging also requires a number of factors to be present, in addition to the installation and application of certain infrastructure, in order to succeed. Most important is the proper knowledge organization and management, and an understanding of its application in the correct context. Davison et al. (2000) suggest that this knowledge and understanding is (only) gained through the application of previous technologies and its shaping of the newer technology. Certain social norms, behaviors, and institutional structures are needed to support leapfrogging. The potential implications of this issue are further discussed in chapter 7.

Davison et al. note that "while leapfrogging may appear as an attractive option for the late adopters, it may not provide the intended results in all circumstances" (2000, 3). Their conclusion is that a "blind belief" in the immediate benefits from applying ICTs must be subjected to a "reality check" to distinguish appropriate applications to protect scarce resources.

As with any approach, leapfrogging requires resources, and low- and middle-income countries often have limited access to resources, which must be distributed wisely. Donor agencies and donor countries similarly are limited in how they can distribute their available resources—although when the need or political will arises, as we have seen, incredible resources can be procured on very short notice. Redirecting resources toward leapfrogging technologies, for example, means either a redistribution or increase of resources, the relevance of which will become more apparent in chapter 8. The private sector may fill this gap, yet it also requires political stability and an openness to foreign investment, and raises ethical and controversial issues around privatization and commodification. These are issues we return to in chapters 7 and 8.

Leapfrogging has a strong propensity to induce and equip billions of consumers with the tools and aspirations for "the good life." Should these absolute numbers alone not compel caution within development circles? (In fact, the efficiency gains from leapfrogging themselves, excluding any absolute gains from more consumers, may induce increased consumption. This issue is considered in chapter 5.) Lifestyles can shift much quicker (in days) than the structures needed to realize efficiency gains (which can take years). The changes in culture and shift of societal values will ensure much stronger ideals consistent with those of the countries that bred the technologies—countries characterized by market-driven capitalism. These new consumers will sympathize with the institutions of market-driven globalization as they continuously expand their aspirations and material affluence. Could it be that leapfrogging is merely a euphemism for colonialism, debt-based consumer growth, or global growth ideologies?

Imagine the prospect of Internet and other marketing propelled into the twenty-first century by ICTs in very populous countries. Benjamin Barber (2007) considers the example of China, where one-child policies have established families with six adults (two parents and four grandparents) who are increasingly connected to the modern global world and are fixated solely on the needs of one child. What expectations and aspirations might each of those millions of children grow up with?

The tremendous investment required to ensure anything near the benefits anticipated, and the processes required to acquire them also raises some provoking prospects. More and more frequently, a profit incentive is being advocated. This will have the effect of limiting access in certain circumstances. Given that they will include consumption, limited access may not necessarily be unfavorable for achieving more sustainable consumption. However, this may establish a digital divide between the "haves" versus the "have nots," in particular with reference to information access. More precisely, it is likely to establish a digital divide between product and service providers and users of "leading edge" technologies with late adopters, reusers, and recyclers. In such cases, often the late adopters are unable to access the full potential of certain technologies. As advances are made in the technologies and services, there is an incentive to ride the crest of the wave in order to take advantage of the full potential of services offered, and, in some cases, to ensure mere access. In this way, certain providers of ICT services require customers to continuously update their own systems and supporting technologies. For example, security measures for Internet-based platforms, operating systems, wireless formats, and cellular technologies can change frequently. Consider the switch to digital television or cellular technologies, for instance. In addition to this push, there is also a pull whereby newer ICT variants and certain applications offer an increased incentive for their adoption. Those who are able to adopt these (i.e., the wealthy) will simply have (improved) access that the late adopters will not experience. Yet even the late adopters can become trapped in this consumer lock-in contest. They may ultimately come to depend on the systems, and help propel the institutional and infrastructural development in a particular direction. Simultaneously, they may be perpetually limited in the services they may acquire from outdated technologies compared with the early adopters and modern technologies that are available for the right price. In this sense, leapfrogging includes the physical resources where permitted, but necessarily excludes the services these are intended, or able, to provide. Leapfroggers experience all the costs, resource expenditures, misallocations, and hopes, with ultimately few benefits.

Combined with difficulties associated with privacy and information tracking, equality and democracy may actually suffer further erosion, despite what many advocates of ICTs envisage. In addition, control over the research, development, infrastructures, and networks already serves the interests of profit as much, or more than, their functionality. Marketing and advertising, fashion- and trendsetting will eliminate shortfalls. In this context, the development and propagation of ICTs globally is likely to serve the interests of global capital and profit growth, and the more powerful the capital, the greater the ability to influence the velocity of that progress. As Smyth (1990) observes, the irony is that children in Peru watch American cartoon programs, and the Inuit in Canada's north watch American soap operas. This is a point we further explore in chapter 8.

Furthermore, the content of information flow and its access will also be highly influenced by global capital, again with the more powerful capital having greater influence on that content and its distributional features. When considered with media ownership and current convergence patterns, the strengthening digital divide pattern becomes more pronounced and evident. ICTs may also become a new set of tools and resources for social control and reduced agency in favor of a set of rules, regulations, and expectations as established by powerful capital influences. Increased public distribution will attract additional legislative and regulatory mechanisms to control and distribute content, thereby further encroaching upon perceived democratic freedom. As with more conventional media, these mechanisms are likely to be employed to absolve powerful agents from providing content harmful to their own and other capital interests. Both the medium and the messages can be shaped according to social goals. These we consider further in chapter 8.

The converse is that, despite some minor successes in the control of information—notably music and videos over the Internet—the floodgates have been opened. Global capital may no longer be able to protect its historic turf. Yet one should be under no illusion that the turf will not continue to be defined by global capital. As the platforms and foundations transform, the sets of rules, regulations, and aspirations are constantly being reshaped and redefined in favor of global capital strongholds. Given the trajectory of globalization, although the rules of the game might change, the winners and losers, for the most part, will not.

The greater challenge will remain the message of the content: as users of digital media become more comfortable with their access, the use of conventional forms of print and information may decline. The sheer volume of information available electronically is already sufficiently persuasive to preclude much fundamentally important conventional media content, limiting comprehension of complex issues to headlines. The "McReal world" of thirty-second sound bytes may indeed substitute for and transform scholarly debate and important social dialogue. Of particular note has been the debate over Wikipedia, and the profusion of video and audio media with their growing ease of accessibility, portability, and convenience.

Information plays an important role in globalization—from the social and environmental characteristics of particular consumer activities and choices to financial decision-making at personal and national levels to national and global news reporting. Information and data provisioning is a key ingredient of ICTs and an assumed element of shifting toward dematerialization and immaterialization. In addition to the individual "privacy" level, information can be used in different ways at a societal level—potentially compelling, pervasively persuasive, ominously foreboding, depending on who controls and most effectively wields it. The image beginning to emerge is one of social, although not necessarily conscious, manipulation and management at a deeply ubiquitous and fundamentally disturbing—almost globally homogenous—level.

A key feature of ICTs is their ability to simultaneously influence diverse groupings of peoples spatially and demographically through complex information sources, processes, and networks. In this sense, both seniors and youth, Africans and Europeans can be motivated to support or oppose specific ideals, values, behaviors, and lifestyle choices. Convergence enables power to be absolutely controlled by class, creating expectations and manipulating worldviews to shape particular social values, behaviors, and even institutional frameworks, social structures, and conceptual perceptions consistent with global market–based philosophies. This facilitates a form of positive feedback, further concentrating power and the velocity, extensity, intensity, and interconnectedness of globalization (Held et al., 2003). We explore the extent of this phenomenon in later chapters.

There is little doubt that mass media profoundly influences consumer practices. Media can create or ignite dreams and aspirations, inform people of certain options, hide other choices, conceal or at least withhold entire ideas from mass public dialogue, and provide the products and services that have been fortified with symbols and identity. Reisch observes that ICT marketing practices include "loading products and services with symbols and identity using emotional conditioning techniques" (Reisch, 2001, 260). She observes that materialism professes to vanquish failures, "build identity[,] and achieve symbolic self-completion."

Expanding global media networks, satellite communications, the Internet, and other ICTs has positioned the ICT sector as an intensely powerful global medium for affecting expectations and norms. The

Human Development Report 1999 reveals that the expansion of television sets per one thousand people nearly doubled between 1980 and 1995, from 121 to 235. Simultaneously, the spread of global trends, branding, and social norms from Delhi to Warsaw to Rio de Janeiro continues to reconfigure cultures (United Nations Development Programme [UNDP], 1999).

This cultural reconfiguration is firmly unidirectional, placing at risk the very nature of cultural diversity. In 1997 alone, Hollywood films grossed over $30 billion globally, reaching every market and acquiring over 50 percent of revenues from overseas (UNDP, 1999). Latin America, for instance, suffered a deluge of American films, claiming 83 percent of the market. Similarly, less than one-third of television programming originated in Latin America, while two-thirds originated in the United States. Conversely, less than 3 percent of foreign films succeed in the vast American market. The result has been an expanding vacuum of local content, industry, and cultural significance as "the fear of a McDonaldization-type of 'cultural globalization' is substantiated by the undoubted concentration of the global market for cultural products" (Reisch, 2001, 262). Similarly, the Internet reflects a largely English-dominated cyberculture, with some 70 percent of content provided in English only (80 to 90 percent of health- and food-related sites), despite the fact that a majority of Internet users—two-thirds—today report speaking non-English native languages (Singh, Wright, Wilson, Boytsov, & Raizada, 2007). Of over one billion Internet users, 41 percent reside in Asia, 28 percent in North America, and 18 percent in Europe (Hachman, 2009). This has profoundly important implications for the democratization of information.

Such unidirectional informational and cultural flows have profoundly sweeping consequences. It is far from limited to the entertainment industry and Internet use, affecting food and diets, mobility and transportation, housing and shelter, energy and materials use, and all manner of consumption activity. The global metamorphoses ICTs fabricate have embedded deep into our collective psyche new ways of knowing, being, and living at a vast scale, serving specific global interests, trajectories, and trends.

Phillips cites Cohen and Zysman, who note, "Even the *Columbia Journalism Review*, a leading publication tasked with monitoring journalism, has, under the leadership of former *Fortune* editor Marshall Loeb, been steering itself towards 'gossip and celebrity' in order to increase sales" (1998, 144).

One need look no further then Google's own statistics on the most common searches to observe this trend. The top ten Google searches for 2008, which were very consistent with those of previous years, including 2007 as previously noted, were: (1) Sarah Palin, (2) Beijing 2008, (3) Facebook login, (4) Tuenti, (5) Heath Ledger, (6) Obama, (7) nasza klasa, (8) wer kennt wen, (9) Euro 2008, and (10) Jonas Brothers. These do not represent any level of complex social dialogue on all things sustainable—consumption, development, health, democracy, or equality. Quite the contrary; they appear to obstruct intelligent debate. Even the notion of a top ten search—which also includes the categories "top of mind," "politics," "trendsetters," "showbiz," "sports," and "around the world"—itself is indicative of this level of social dialogue. The category of "politics," for instance, lists the top ten sources for political news as: (1) Fox, (2) CNN, (3) ABC, (4) CBS, (5) MSNBC, (6) Drudge Report, (7) *New York Times*, (8) *Saturday Night Live*, (9) *Huffington Post*, and (10) *Wall Street Journal.* This is not exactly a resounding compilation of sources that, for the most part, engage in scholarly debate of relevant and important political issues. In itself, this is not necessarily a disconcerting development, but combined with the shift toward digital media, it is.

Indeed, a survey released in the province of Ontario, Canada, in April 2009 demonstrates the ubiquity of the problem. Noting that students are ill-prepared for university, researchers observed a dramatic drop in first-year students' aptitudes over a three-year period, with poorer writing and numeric skills, less maturity, and a belief that good grades are an entitlement. Of particular note was the increased reliance on Internet tools as research sources (CBC, 2009; CTV globemedia Inc., 2009).[1]

As important, however, is the system of expectations, values, and ideologies imparted to consumers. Aside from the ethical challenges previously outlined, there are also the human and ecological challenges of imbuing literally billions of new people with the consumer ethic, providing access to more goods and services, indoctrinating a class-structured ideology, and "creating" work from production with the sole intent and compulsory urge to generate consumption. Education, for example, becomes a value, an expectation, an entitlement— and a competitive process—to direct students into a competitive labor force (Kohn, 1992), itself an implicit entitlement and expectation to serve the sole purpose of consumption.

Despite the ability of ICTs to facilitate a multidirectional flow of information, the ultimate form of that information will be determined

---

[1] The CBC website referenced includes a video discussing the results. The full two-page report is available at www.quality-matters.ca/QualityMatters/docs/Students_less_ prepared_April_6_2009.pdf.

by our values and the social structures that suport them. Clearly, the fact that "[t]he average American adult sees about 21,000 commercial messages a year" (Mayer, 1998, 73) suggests informational flow is predominantly unidirectional. "[T]he largest 100 corporations in the U.S. pay for about 75 percent of commercial television time and about half the public television time. With advertising for a 30 second segment in prime time costing over $200,000 on network television, only the largest corporations can afford it" (Mayer, 1998, 73). It would be difficult to fathom that those same transnational corporations also receive an equivalently powerful message from people seeking more sustainable options. Mayer states that "we are not just giving consumers information about price, quality, maker, and warranties. We are systematically stimulating the addictive, irrational impulse to feed a spiritual emptiness" (1998, 73). Advertising and marketing, trends and fashion are rarely, if ever, directed at the objective exchange of free market information. "Coupled with big corporations' ability to influence the legal environment of business, corporate 'freedom of speech' encourages a consumer-driven economy, with consumers perennially in pursuit of this year's 'hottest toy'" (Mayer, 1998, 73). Two facts are revealed by the amount of capital expended on generating consumption. First, it must be working for corporations to invest so heavily in it. Second, corporations with deep pockets are about the only participants in this unidirectional flow of information. So the obvious question should be, "Who controls the trajectory of those corporations?"

Early attempts by consumers to bypass this indoctrination—new technologies able to record programs, skip commercial breaks, or web browsers capable of blocking pop-up windows for instance—have been entirely obliterated by the eruption of modern ICTs. Advertisers and marketers have become much more creative using new digital technologies—marrying the interests of capital—to implant their messages directly into programming and websites, and employing the financial force of marketing. The sponsoring of specific scenes and segments of programs allows the blatant exhibition of specific products and brands, preferences and lifestyles, embedding consumerism and commercials directly into programming and sites. Entire programs are now dedicated to promoting specific—luxurious and opulent—lifestyles, or enticing consumers to distill a sense of self-worth through materialism by actively interacting to determine program outcomes. Chris Hedges argues that consumerism has led to an entire global culture that embraces—in deeply pervasive ways—celebrity worship, which has established widespread intellectual poverty (Hedges, 2009). Reality programming constructed on illusion, personal trainers and lifestyle coaches, media in all its formats that present only the biggest, brightest, most successful consumption, all feed us images of what self-worth should be. We must become the manufactured landscapes of the illusion. In turn, the intellectual deficiency this consumerism generates serves consumerism very well. Given the evidence from popular Google searches, it appears to be working.

More provocatively, what is the role of other forms of ICTs in information flows? In a direct sense, ICTs offer a very powerful advertising mechanism and branding technique—consider the iPod, for example, or the power of direct marketing, website loyalty, or text messaging. "The fact that millions of users are potential customers, or at least recipients of marketing and product information, makes the Internet extremely attractive" (Traxler & Luger, 2000, 287). Moreover, consider the primary (but not only) audience being targeted here—youth—and the enormous financial clout they wield today and, more importantly, as future consumers infused with intense global market convictions. The mere potential is adequate to make the most rational, calculating, unemotional marketing executive grin. O'Meara argues, "advertising over the Internet threatens to unleash more consumption of resource-intensive products. . . . Yet an environmentally conscious consumer could perhaps . . . find products that were produced in an environmentally friendly manner and designed for recycling" (2000, 140). Of course, this assumes environmental information would be a determinant of consumers' decisions, and that they thoroughly understand the concepts of design for the environment and disassembly. This is an unlikely prospect if ICTs prevail in asphyxiating essential dialogue on sustainable development and restrict the role of ICT users to managers of data, and the role of citizens to consumers of stuff.

While significant information about products can be found on the Internet, details about specific products are very rare indeed. It requires significant research by a generally already informed consumer to uncover the details about a specific product if it exists at all outside the confines of corporate property. Occasionally, research exists on a category of goods or services, but again, revealing this information, let alone understanding and acting on it, usually requires an already thoroughly informed consumer, who is unlikely to be interested in specific product information for typical consumption purposes in any event. The democratization of information flows is still predominantly undemocratic and fails to equip the average citizen with the tools needed to discern the environmental and social properties of specific goods and services, let alone consumer values. There remains much more than technological optimism required to fill this void.

What about new platforms of ICTs—user-generated content, list-servers, passive websites, and text messaging, for instance? Do these offer a two-way or multidirectional capacity for information flow? Here many possibilities exist. These platforms enable the simple and rapid dispersion of information. They can instantly assemble consumers or activists willing to engage in online protests, virtual boycotts, and digital riots. However, certain social mechanisms and institutional arrangements may dissuade this sort of activity. Individual websites have been targeted by corporate lawyers for slander and similar crossings of legal boundaries. Virtual exchange of files, such as music sharing, have been transformed and commodified. Strategic lawsuits against public participation (SLAPP) suits are becoming ever more common. While often legally unsuccessful, most SLAPPs succeed in the public domain since the costs of defense can be astronomical and corporations generally have deeper pockets to support an extended legal battle than do most consumers. This can incite considerable angst in individual citizens and motivate social conformity. As we shall see, powerful interests seek to continuously reinvent ICTs, media, and public messages for their purposes. Temporary negligence is usually swiftly and decisively corrected. Past successes have been sufficient to send a shudder down the spine of most activists or independently thinking citizen. Furthermore, simple questioning of the status quo can land a name on suspect terrorist lists in numerous countries, rendering individuals immobile and often impotent. We further explore these issues in later chapters.

4

Lulled to Complacency: ICTs and Energy and Materials Consumption

Although typically perceived as a service, ICTs fundamentally consume energy and materials in their research, development, use, and disposal. Research has begun to quantify these resource flows, and to compare the various tradeoffs between ICTs and more conventional choices. Many unknowns remain, and many unexpected questions have arisen. In fact, often ICTs create their own new niche markets or roles. Anticipated "tradeoffs" do not always exist, and new applications contribute new and expanded forms of additional consumption. Yet in other areas, tradeoffs between more conventional choices and ICTs do exist. In such cases, the particular role of ICTs needs to be understood, as do their interactions with the "old" format of goods and services provisioning—do the newer options substitute for, complement, induce, or otherwise stimulate additional consumption or directly displace old consumption? Often old ways of behaving exist simultaneously with the new opportunities that tend to extend the barriers of incumbent technologies and practices. The new technologies and their interactions with society and existing infrastructures and technologies often add increased flexibility and convenience, thus extending the reach of existing activities. This chapter explores what has been learned, what questions are emerging, and future research directions likely to prove fruitful.

By exploring what has been learned, this chapter begins to introduce some of the dynamics between energy and resources consumption and the application, adoption, and adaptations of ICTs. Clearly, not all ICT applications could be explored, nor could all categories. The few considered here serve as characteristic representations of what is likely to be found elsewhere.

The various levels of analysis considered are as follows: first are the direct effects, both beneficial and harmful, created by the introduction of ICTs. These direct effects include the life-cycle effects from the new adoptions. This relatively straightforward step involves analysis of the various stages and processes involved in the research, development, adoption, use, and disposal of particular ICTs.

A more challenging level of analysis involves the determination and assessment of the structural and infrastructural changes likely to be established from the introduction of ICTs—the indirect effects. This analysis becomes much more difficult when it is realized that new technology variants often "create" niche applications by users, typically unanticipated by developers and manufacturers, and thus create new demands on and for supporting goods and services.

However, this level of analysis is often eclipsed by a meta-level analysis that involves consideration of how the social frameworks, institutional organizations, norms of behavior, expectations, and values shift to accommodate and respond to new ICTs and their combinations both with other technologies and with society. This latter discussion is largely left to subsequent chapters.

The following, however, introduces at least five different ways, discussed in greater detail in chapter 6, in which the introduction of ICTs might be expected to influence consumption activities.

THE MICROCHIP: THE FOUNDATION OF ICTS

The value of ICTs spending has climbed from over $2 trillion in 1999 to an estimated $3.2 trillion in 2007 (World Information Technology and Services Alliance, 2004). Silicon microchips are the basis of all ICTs. As a fundamental input, the world production of semiconductors was valued at $150 billion in 1999, marked by a 13 percent annual increase in the previous two decades (Williams, 2004a). Clearly, with this tremendous growth and anticipation for further growth, the impacts of semiconductor manufacturing form a key ingredient of the sustainability of ICTs. Therefore, it might be wise to engage in a brief exploration of semiconductor manufacturing effects before considering the contribution of ICT applications to the sustainable consumption debate.

The large volume and number of chemicals used in silicon chip manufacturing, the high standards and precision demanded, the increasing complexity of design, and the rapid obsolescence (but not a short useful life), some would argue, is pollution incarnate. This in turn suggests the likelihood of human health concerns and social inequalities. Upstream life-cycle effects enormously extend the range of possible environmental and human risks.

Williams calculates that the "total weight of secondary fossil fuel and chemical inputs to produce and use a single 2-g 32MB DRAM chip are 1600 g and 72 g, respectively" (2004b, 2). The secondary fossil fuel inputs for chip manufacture total 600 times its weight, compared with automobiles or refrigerators in the 1 to 2 times order of magnitude. Perhaps more startling is the analysis Williams provides suggesting one of these single small components draws 32,000 liters of water during its production, and there are millions produced daily to supply the global demand for ICTs.

At this fundamental level, increasing consumption derived from the semiconductor industry to feed the growing numbers of ICTs and their variants may prove a very real possibility, despite the expectations of dematerialization. Williams, Ayres, and Heller note that, while the environmental performance of the semiconductor industry has recently improved, this improvement has been insufficient to counterbalance the "growth in demand so as to realize net decreases in material and energy used by the industry" (2004, 1916). Their data illustrates a 6 to 10 percent increase in annual energy, water, and chemical use accompanied by an average 15 percent industry-wide economic growth rate. While the energy and materials throughput of the industry has not been increasing as fast as the growth of the industry, it is still quite substantial, and is increasing. They also observe the potential for unanticipated responses. "While the smaller feature size of newer generation chips could imply less materials use *per transistor*, the increased complexity of processes, the requirement for ever-declining defect densities, and the need for purer starting materials have the opposite effect: the ratio of indirect to direct materials consumption may actually be increasing" (Williams, Ayres, & Heller, 2004, 1916; emphasis added; we will return to this point in chapter 5)

While these results seem alarming, they are not without their critics. Shadman and McManus (2004) disagree with the conclusions of Williams, Ayers, and Heller (2002), citing weight (mass) as an inappropriate measure, and the lack of weighting from the social benefits derived from high-technology products versus those benefits derived from "low-technology products." While such an approach might prove rather vague, if not methodologically challenging, an economic analysis of inputs and outputs or an energy analysis would shed further light on the debate. The critical assessment also takes issue with Williams's lack of consideration of the life-cycle analysis when comparing the automobile and electronics industry.

When their results are scaled up to the level of a desktop computer with a seventeen-inch cathode ray tube monitor, Williams (2004a) concludes the need for 6400 megajoules of energy and 260 kilograms of materials. This represents an energy intensity, or fossil fuel–use-to-product-weight ratio of eleven. Due to the rapid turnover rate of these devices, their calculations suggest an annual life-cycle energy of 2600 megajoules per year. This is 1.3 times that of a refrigerator, implying that the life-cycle energy use of a computer is dominated by production (81 percent) as opposed to operation (19 percent) seen in other home appliances.

Interestingly, Williams (2000) notes that, perhaps contrary to common belief, to date there has not been a lot of evidence to support the assumption that the environmentally damaging stages of silicon manufacturing are located in developing countries, although there is some evidence that such manufacturing is now beginning to shift to East Asia. The caveat is that this is but one production chain (silicon) and it could easily be the exception to the rule.

Ironically, a principle concern of this research is the lack of access to available data. Given that this is an industry that contends and represents the importance of an information economy for the purposes of determining sustainability and conducting academic research, and for developing the essential institutions needed to facilitate sustainability, this is nothing short of perplexing.

While these studies have begun to quantify some of the environmental consequences of our apparently insatiable appetite for electronic devices, they potentially represent merely the tip of the ICT iceberg: static snapshots of a rapidly evolving set of technologies.

In a similar study, Williams provides a systems analysis for the global production chain for the "industrial sectors producing high-purity silicon from raw materials for the related microchip, solar cell, and optical fiber industries" (2000, 9). Williams concludes from this analysis that "[p]rojections indicate that high-tech sectors will represent a significant share of the demand of primary materials" (9). Williams also concludes that "change is needed to address this issue. Such reform involves rethinking the role of governments, sector level industry organizations, and other institutions in organizing and disseminating environmental information" (Williams, 2000, 9)

While these results represent initial indications of the material aspects of ICT components, they unquestionably demonstrate the potential energy and resource demands of a service sector once thought to be weightless. While reduced material and energy inputs are certainly possible with careful analyses, planning, and management, these results indicate the unlikely possibility of dematerializing the economy, of immaterializing consumer preferences, or of absolutely de-linking economic growth from physical growth.

TRANSPORTATION AND URBAN DEVELOPMENT

Audioconferencing and Videoconferencing

Virtual mobility, such as audioconferencing, teleconferencing, and web-based meetings, have the potential to reduce the travel expenses and environmental impacts of organizations. By accessing information and services and by communicating with people who are spatially remote, ICTs may enable business meetings without the same physical mobility currently associated with these activities.

A study conducted in Sweden examined this issue (Arnfalk & Kogg, 2002). More than half of surveyed respondents reported that videoconferencing substituted for either their own travel or that of someone else. Just under half of the respondents reported no change in travel patterns, and a small number of organizations (3 percent) reported that the use of videoconferencing had generated more business travel.

Since these findings represent travel reductions at the organizational, or micro, level, savings for the organization appear to be derived from these activities. They also suggest the potential for significant reductions in energy and materials consumption at the organizational level, particularly if video- or audioconferencing substitute for business travel by air. Thus, firm-level expenses could be dramatically reduced.

While the initial investments may seem considerable, travel expense savings, particularly for air travel, including time expenses, suggest a very short period for return on investment. Similarly, for the employee, less time away from the office, family, and friends suggests an incentive to adopt these technologies.

However, from the organizational perspective, barriers such as access by business partners to the appropriate technology may discourage its adoption. Similarly, compensated travel confers employees special benefits, offering vacation opportunities, learning experiences, and prestige. The advantage of combining business with leisure travel may be reduced energy and materials consumption, unless the leisure travel is opportunistically generated, suggesting that employees may be less willing to avoid business travel. Moreover, business travel is associated with prestige and success, frequent-flyer programs, and other benefits. This implies that business travel might be a more difficult social norm to change. Since it is the most influential people within the organization who travel most, business travel has become embedded within the corporate culture. Employees may simply be less likely to embrace the technology[1] given the benefits of business travel. Clearly, organizational and individual behavior change will be essential to achieve the anticipated benefits of audio- and videoconferencing. This may prove rather challenging, and appears to relate more to sociotechnological relationships than to ICTs' functional properties.

Besides the ability to engage in more meetings, video- and audioconferencing has already generated employee complaints about the lack of time for reflection between meetings. In addition, casual talk during meetings, social interaction, and nonverbal cues are lost, generating a degree of social isolation, a very common concern for participants of webinars and other similar online dialogue and presentation forums. Thus a spontaneous shift is both unlikely and very limited, "even in a company that is characterized by a very high level of 'IT competence' and a general curiosity for new ICT solutions" (Arnfalk & Kogg, 2002, 867).

Other studies have found that more often face-to-face communications appear to supplement mobility with telecommunications rather than substitute for them (Gaspar & Glaeser, 1996; Gillespie, Richardson, & Comford, 1995; Thrift, 1996; Traxler & Luger, 2000). For example, Moss and Townsend (1998b) observe that businesses are more likely to shift within existing urban areas than to move into low-density regions unless the latter are equipped with advanced telecommunications infrastructure, skilled labor, and good airport access due to the inherent need for face-to-face meetings. The picture emerging is one where teleconferencing and virtual meetings facilitate more long-distance business connections that eventually lead to increased face-to-face meetings with associates at significantly greater distances (Gaspar & Glaeser, 1996). While Arnfalk (2002) identifies that the greatest benefits are achieved through the substitution of videoconferencing for air travel—the most resource-intensive mode of travel—other studies suggest that the exact opposite is more likely to occur: videoconferencing will function to increase air travel. In addition, the growth of professional meetings and conventions illustrates

---

[1] Similarly, it is worthwhile to observe that a transport policy simply relying on full-cost pricing to move business toward more sustainable development may therefore be insufficient, since the individual employee is compensated for travel and the business passes along travel costs or claims travel expenses.

the enduring importance of face-to-face contacts. The Swiss National Research Programme project results state that:

> Increased employment of modern telecommunication methods such as e-mail, data transfer or video conferencing will not reduce the number of business trips. The reason: telecommunications enable companies to co-operate with business partners over longer distances and this will eventually cause more business and goods traffic than can be saved through "electronic contacts." (National Research Programme, 2000, 9)

While many new contacts may be facilitated electronically, the eventual desire or need for meeting in person will persist. The sheer growth in contacts facilitated by ICTs and subsequent generated travel (particularly by air over long distances) may exceed the displaced travel derived from the application of ICTs. Ironically, as ICTs contribute to an increased number of personal and professional contacts (facilitated by electronic means), they may raise the amount of physical travel by virtue of their absolute growth and physical distance. "Face-to-face contacts and telecommunications are more likely to be complements, and there is some evidence that with the increasing use of ICTs, the number of face-to-face interactions is actually rising" (Traxler & Luger, 2000, 289).

Indeed, long-distance, regional, and local business connections do appear to be placing increasing demand on transportation infrastructure. For instance,

> In recent years, Ottawa-Hull's 1.2-million population has witnessed record growth in air passenger traffic, fuelled in particular by growth in the region's high technology and tourism sectors. The Ottawa Airport currently serves 3.4 million passengers per year, some 600,000 above built capacity. (Ottawa Macdonald-Cartier International Airport [OMCIA], 1998b)

In addition, the environmental assessment for the Ottawa Macdonald-Cartier International Airport notes similarly that the master plan for the local airport expansion "found that socio-economic conditions support the further growth and development of the airport by virtue of the anticipated growth and vitality of the local and regional economy, especially the high technology market" (OMCIA, 1998a, i).

This document continues, indicating that this sector is expected to generate "significant growth in passenger movements" (OMCIA, 1998a, i). The projected growth also includes "the need for a four lane airport parkway" (iii). The implications for materials and energy consumption extends to the building stock and maintenance for "extensive terminal expansion and renovation" (ii), increasing to "61,120 square meters by 2005 and 71,880 square meters by 2020 (versus the current size of 32,110 square meters)" (ii).

Furthermore, the capacity for computers and communications to confer greater information has been a significant catalyst in the physical mobility of people, in particular over continental and transcontinental distances. Substantial travel has been generated through increased information, awareness, promotions, acquaintances, flexibility, conveniences, and opportunities enabled by these technologies (O'Meara, 2000). Schauer (2000) concludes that the simple fact that people will be in contact with an increasing number of others living at greater distances will increase individual travel. He notes that virtual meetings do not displace the continued need to meet in person for many activities. Also noted is the elevated desire for leisure travel for teleworkers and office personnel, often during peak travel times such as weekends. These observations are supported by evidence demonstrating, for instance, that personal vehicle passenger kilometers traveled in the European Union increased more than 2 percent annually through the 1990s.

Other factors influence the ability to adopt ICTs as a substitute to physical mobility. Current institutional structures, alignments, and arrangements have established competing interests that specifically function to induce physical mobility. In part, these have given rise to the increased air travel over the last fifty years. Reduced costs; greater access; and improved comfort, convenience, and flexibility have generated tremendous growth in entire industries (such as tourism, travel, and airlines) that seek to capture market share and increase physical mobility. The adoption of these structures, such as dedicated travel firms for business and governments, have little interest, at the moment, in reducing physical mobility.[2] In the same way, while it is generally recognized that reduced mobility and improved access could make communities better places to live, local vested actors consistently seek to enhance mobility (Fodor, 1999). Finally, ICTs themselves have become extraordinarily flexible, convenient, and mobile, focusing on the "always on, always accessible, always connected"

---

[2] It is fascinating to note how, faced by climate changes and growing environmental sentiments, the tourism industry as a whole chooses to confront the challenge by establishing carbon-offset programs. While this offers the green image (arguably to expand market share) to an industry or consumer as a means to assuage guilt, it does little to convince travelers to forfeit their travel. Rather, it serves as financial self-flagellation and perhaps functions to relieve some psychological travel tensions. In this context, it may actually function to increase travel, demonstrating the intransigence of reducing such forms of consumption.

attributes of the products and their features—cellular technologies, laptop computers, personal data assistants, and so on. These paradoxes establish conflicting goals that need to be resolved.

Urban Development

Traxler and Luger (2000) demonstrate how ICTs generate new physical collections of economic activity not necessarily based on physical proximity. ICTs help connect economic activities located in urban and rural areas, and enable increased transnational and global cooperation and interaction between businesses. Businesses now increasingly interact on a global basis, even in rather isolated locations worldwide.

However, traditional forces defining urban areas will continue to drive many businesses toward urban regions. Available skilled labor, educational facilities and institutions, social and health networks, and the availability of specialized training programs are only a few examples motivating these business decisions. Furthermore, quality of life, culture, public infrastructure, and private opportunities remain important and desirable factors in decisions to locate business operations and facilities. These factors help explain why empirical evidence continues to demonstrate that established urban areas are not becoming obsolete as a consequence of ICTs (Beyers, 1998; Gaspar & Glaeser, 1996; Moss & Townsend, 1997, 1998a, 1998b; Salomon, 1996). Depending on the ICT application, business activity, and business function, ICTs may reinforce and strengthen compact urban development patterns or contribute to decentralized sprawl patterns.

However, urban sprawl fueled by the ICT sector also appears to be stimulating growth in demand for urban transportation and additional urban infrastructures. Local governments are discovering the enormous burdens on municipal infrastructure from the anticipated immaterial ICT sector. "[U]nprecedented growth in the high-tech sector . . . and the impact of these observed trends on the infrastructure array provided for in the ROP [Regional Official Plan] needs to be reviewed" (Ottawa, 2000, 8), and substantial budget increases will be required merely to furnish new capital requirements of this growth. Rehabilitation and reconstruction of existing infrastructure will also be necessary as will its continuous maintenance.

Despite the potential for ICTs to expand the economic climate of remote and spatially separated regions, it would probably be wise for ex-urbanites and remote regions to maintain healthy economic diversification. ICTs are more inclined to serve niche needs in these areas where resources permit their application to already established business and economic opportunities.

Telecommuting and Telework

ICTs offer the potential to dramatically change the way work is conducted. More and more people are able to work away from the office at least some of the time. This allows reductions in needed office space as well as reductions in the resource intensiveness associated with commuting. This effect may reinforce the role of urban areas as meeting places and strengthen sustainable urban planning and healthy lifestyles (Frank, 2007; Frank, Sallis, et al., 2006; Frank, Kavage, & Litman, 2006; Lowe, 1990; Roseland, 1992).

However, telework arrangements may encourage additional suburban sprawl, increasing both infrastructure and new housing demands, as well as increasing commute distances when people need to attend meetings or be in the office. This latter effect may in itself be sufficient to mitigate or exceed the benefits from reduced commuting trips on other days of the week. Finally, while a home office saves office energy, additional energy (likely disproportionately more due to the loss of economies of scale) is required for the home office. Aebischer and Huser (2000) report a 30-percent household energy increase if one household member is working at home.

While many businesses have identified a significant improvement in energy costs associated with their telework arrangements (British Telecom, 2001; Hopkinson & James, 2002; Simmons, 2000), these studies do not consider the wider social implications of their arrangements. For example, British Telecom (BT) (2001) suggests that business and commercial interests are driving e-business. While they assert this trend is accompanied by a number of environmental benefits, they also admit higher order effects may offset these benefits in the longer term.

Tulbure (2002) models various scenarios for e-working in addition to online informing and paper consumption. In each case, it is concluded that the application of ICTs do not necessarily lead to a reduction in energy consumption or greater environmental sustainability. (This study also assessed the nitrogen dioxide, sulfur dioxide, and carbon dioxide emissions, and concluded similarly that the application of ICTs in these instances do not automatically lead to a reduction in emissions.) He stresses, "Social factors are very important and do influence in a decisive way" (2002, 132) whether the application of ICTs will lead to more sustainable consumption.

Romm (2002) observes that many companies reduce office space in exchange for giving their employees mobile communications so they can spend more time with customers, on the road, and in home offices. In other words, the application of ICTs has permitted a shift from a point office to a mobile, on-road office. Since the incremental addition of one vehicle is far less resource-efficient than the incremental reduction of one office space in a building, this trend is likely to significantly increase resource consumption and environmental impacts. Paradoxically, it perhaps simultaneously increases business efficiency.

Arnfalk (2002) found that less than half of teleworkers surveyed reported a reduction in travel, while 10 percent reported an increase in travel. This suggests that telework does not ensure a substitution for work-related travel. He concludes that telework has the potential to reduce commute travel associated with the organization. However, this potential is dependent on the specific telework arrangement. He emphasizes that

> it has to be recognised that the overall environmental impact depends on the way the technology is used, set up and applied. Consequently, pollution prevention efforts cannot be limited to promoting the applications, but must also influence the way they are set up. (Arnfalk, 2002, 177)

The study did not consider the influence of such arrangements beyond the organization, or micro, level, such as leisure- or domestic-related travel. While firm-level savings may be attributed to such arrangements if appropriately structured, the societal impacts are far from understood. These latter have significant potential to complement or offset firm-level benefits.

Zumkeller (1996) found the relationship between travel and communications to be stronger for complementarity than it was for substitutability. These results have been supported by others, for instance Mokhtarian and Meenakshisundaram (1998). Other insights into the relationships between communications and travel are revealed by KPMG (1997), which identified a considerably greater work-related travel incidence by heavy information technology (IT) users than was found in the comparison group. Indeed, based on the strong and predominantly complementary relationships between telecommunications and travel, Mokhtarian and Meenakshisundaram (1998) note that ICT is unlikely to reduce travel at the macro level. Their analyses demonstrated that the fastest growing communication mode was e-mail, while the second fastest was travel. They conclude that "trips are not giving way to telecommunications" (Mokhtarian & Meenakshisundaram, 1998, 30).

While much still needs to be learned, ICTs contribute to the role of transportation in facilitating information exchange and enabling accessibility (Taylor, Button, & Stough, 2000). ICTs seem to stimulate transportation, although in new spatio-temporal relations than historically experienced. Transportation increases physical mobility, and, given modern urban structures, in many cases this means greater accessibility. ICTs complement this with increased convenience and flexibility.

The complementary effects between ICTs and transportation "may be generated by efficient supply of each infrastructure, where demand is increased in one sector by the availability of efficient infrastructure in the other sector" (Haynes, Lall, Stough, & Yilmaz, 2000, 14). Similarly, an inefficient supply of one infrastructure may limit interaction and thus contribute to a substitution effect. Haynes et al. suggest that a ratcheting effect may explain these findings. This is an important observation since it demonstrates how the two sectors (transportation and ICTs) could function together to serve a wider societal goal, perhaps characterized by market-based capitalism and globalization. Indeed, their analysis seeks to identify policies that might stimulate the "interaction between different types of infrastructure" to identify sectors that "have the highest effects on earnings and output" (Haynes et al., 2000, 14). These issues are further discussed in later chapters.

Firm- or lower level assessments—although simpler to justify on environmental grounds—may overstate the benefits by neglecting the macro or societal transformations. As we progress, this will become more apparent.

Intelligent Vehicle Highway Systems

Along with economic growth has come an ever increasing demand on transport infrastructure. As local road networks become congested with goods and people, the typical response has been to increase road network capacity to meet these growing demands for increased mobility. Historically, this has been achieved by building new roads and widening existing roadway corridors. However, in many cases these approaches are meeting barriers: tough resistance from adversely affected communities and limited physical space to expand further. Planners and engineers have begun to find other ways to increase system efficiencies. Signalization and timing, intelligent traffic control, on-board navigation systems, global positioning systems, and other efficiency-boosting options are achieving improved network efficiencies, and therefore supply, without the need to expand the existing physical road infrastructure.

Intelligent vehicle highway systems (IVHSs) are the variety of electronic communications technologies designed to regulate the flow of traffic; give drivers up-to-the-moment information on road and traffic conditions; provide assistance to certain driving tasks, such as steering or braking to avoid collisions; assess road tolls without hindering traffic; help track and guide commercial fleets (including freight trucks) and emergency vehicles; and make buses and car pools more efficient and more convenient to use. Through a variety of methods to improve system efficiency, IVHSs are expected to free additional space on the highway. Expectations range from an effective doubling of infrastructure capacity to a sevenfold expansion. Fundamental to these applications are ICTs.

Planners and engineers have long known traffic demand management theories reveal that the provision of additional highway infrastructure—regardless of how it is achieved—ultimately results in more traffic generated through the process of latent demand. This results when the perceived benefits of reduced congestion, travel times, and costs entice additional drivers onto the roads, driving longer distances and more frequently. Often the supply created or efficiencies achieved permit greater speeds, allowing longer trips in the same time. This creates a strong incentive for urban sprawl and rising mobility, as the opportunity costs of time fall (that is, commute times remain the same for a greater distance traveled). These approaches adversely affect sustainable consumption as infrastructure (sewers, housing, roads, and so on) must be continually reproduced and maintained at greater and greater resource expenditure. Perceived suburban price advantages such as lower property values and taxes, larger properties, and feelings of solitude and freedom contribute to urban sprawl. Road network efficiencies enhance these perceived benefits. Ultimately, however, latent demand occupies the derived supply, resulting in no net gain despite the tremendous resource expenditures and new lifestyles and expectations people become accustomed to.

Therefore, by reducing the privately borne costs associated with driving (such as reducing congestion, travel times, and costs), an IVHS functions to promote increased automobile use, thus increasing both vehicle miles traveled and number of trips to derive the same state that persisted prior to the network supply expansions generating the initial perceived need to increase supply. Despite the potential economic gain as more people make more convenient trips, this raises serious questions about sustainability, which will be revisited later.

Kanninen (1996) characterized some of the dilemmas of IVHSs by evaluating the contributions to travel demand from advanced traveler information systems (ATISs), advanced highway systems (AHSs), and intelligent transit. ATISs are intended to reduce congestion by offering drivers real-time information and advice about road and traffic conditions and trip planning. By learning of unfavorable road conditions, drivers can choose to travel using alternate routes, modes, or times of day, or even forego trips altogether. The intended result is to reduce overall travel times. However, Arnott, de Palma, and Lindsey (1991) illustrate that this may not be the inevitable result, and that the actual benefits are the greatest when information is only provided to a few individuals. They find an inverse relationship between the number of people receiving information and the benefits achieved; as the number of individuals receiving information increases, the individual benefits decrease.

What the findings by Arnott, de Palma, and Lindsey seem to suggest is a positional nature to ATIS. Lintott (1998) and Hirsch (1976) offer explanations for the inability of positional goods to achieve more sustainable consumption. The contribution of a positional good to each person's welfare diminishes as others acquire them. Positional goods are subject to social congestion. This ensures that increased individual and total benefits derived from such positional goods is impossible. Hirsch captures this concept well. Standing on tiptoes in a room full of people will offer a better view for that individual. However, as more and more people stand on tiptoe, the benefits accruing to each individual diminishes—everyone expends additional resources to merely end up with the same position in which they began. Lintott concludes that the "benefits from consumption cannot be increased in the aggregate" (1998, 239). In other words, as more people acquire ATIS, the benefits of reduced congestion and pollution, the economic gains, and reduced consumption cannot be maintained. Indeed, by increasing economic growth (not gains) for the life-cycle development of ATIS, and the latent demand resulting from the application of ATIS, ATIS might reasonably be expected to lead to significantly increased aggregate consumption. There is little need to calculate the actual life-cycle energy and materials demands for ATIS, as it will certainly be positive, yet perhaps eclipsed by the physical mobility their use induces. ATIS seems to offer the expenditure of additional resources by individuals simply to maintain the same relative social position. Those unable to afford or choosing not to adopt the technology merely fall behind.

Therefore, ATIS would provide the greatest benefits when applied by a limited number of users, and these benefits would decrease as ATIS becomes more widely available. Where ATIS can be made exclusive and remain so, individuals who place a high value on travel times and reduced uncertainty should be responsible for covering the cost of using ATIS. This must require no public subsidization and must ensure ATIS use remains exclusive—not likely possible in reality or without punitive and politically challenging regulations. Moreover, exclusivity raises considerable questions of equity, and the potential benefits may widen the gap between potential private and public benefits. Public subsidization also raises significant concerns about equity, in that those benefiting from ATIS would not have paid their full cost. (The important issues of social equity and sustainable development are elaborated upon later.)

Conversely, the private, for-profit motive for introducing a technology necessitates the widespread dispersion of the product in order to maximize sales and profit. Clearly, the application of ATIS by public transportation is infeasible—routes and schedules are predetermined and fixed. Consequently, the use of ATIS by emergency vehicles may offer the only imaginable example where the greatest benefits may be achieved. Unfortunately, ATIS applied for emergency vehicles offers very little opportunity to reduce aggregate consumption, since emergency vehicles represent an insignificant proportion of resource consumption. Nor would it serve to functionally reduce congestion. Therefore, it would be difficult to conclude that there might be any net benefits of ATIS to reduce congestion, consumption, or even achieve its desired objective of redirecting travelers to less congested routes, and under these conditions, it would be very unlikely such a technology could be profitably developed.

AHSs include advanced vehicle control systems and advanced traffic management/information systems. Barth (1994) has found that if AHSs operate at full capacity, permitting 8000 vehicles per hour rather than the current 2000 vehicles per hour, emissions will increase by a factor of two over current levels. Clearly, in this situation there are potential gains in energy intensity, as well as economic gains by reducing travel times. However, a fourfold increase in vehicles per hour would greatly increase aggregate consumption, and create serious challenges for feeder networks unequipped with AHS. If indeed the objective of this technology *is* sustainability, this increase in vehicles would require a corresponding increase in fuel efficiency by a factor of four—not readily attainable, particularly given the historically dismal performance of the automobile industry. Furthermore, this assumes consumers would purchase no additional vehicles as a consequence of the perceived travel benefits. Again, this would be unlikely as demonstrated by latent demand. Additional vehicle purchases would greatly increase resource consumption, eroding any potential intensity gains. The potential for AHS to reduce energy and materials intensity is inconclusive, yet not promising.

Finally, intelligent transit intends to improve the attractiveness of public transportation by providing real-time information on schedules and vehicles. A key factor with intelligent transit, as with many other public transportation initiatives, hinges on its ability to increase its use and decrease private automobile use simply by enhancing the attractiveness of public transportation. If, however, intelligent transit were combined with other policy incentives and disincentives to private automobile use, it may offer a potential to reduce energy and materials intensity, and possibly consumption, primarily in its capacity to change commuting behavior and entice people out of their cars.

The stated objective of IVHSs is to effectively expand roadway capacity. It does so by increasing the operational efficiency of transport networks. ICTs are integral to IVHS's development and application. The potential for latent demand is unavoidable as travelers perceive a greater utility of travel as supply increases in response to demand. IVHSs will have the net effect of increasing transportation. Kanninen concludes that IVHSs "will not solve all of our transportation problems and might exacerbate some, especially environmental costs" (1996, 9). Considering the goal of expanded system capacity and, correspondingly, vehicle miles traveled, the potential for IVHS to increase consumption suggests that careful selection of each ICT application is important, and must be combined with other policies and actions intended to achieve more sustainable consumption.

Despite the dubious benefits from IVHS applications, one must ask why there even exists such fervent efforts to save, indeed, induce more of what can only be considered already excessive motorized mobility—especially given evidence suggesting that it functions to expand resource consumption and decrease our health, well-being, and quality of life—for which more sustainable alternatives exist. At a time when many communities are being designed and constructed that simply avoid the private use of automobiles, why should ICTs be adopted to serve this costly and dying mode of transport?

Just-in-Time Delivery

By predicting consumer demand, just-in-time (JIT) delivery of products has the ability to reduce excess inventories. This could potentially reduce warehousing costs and the subsequent environmental impacts resulting from large inventories of products awaiting sale at retail outlets. Conversely, manufacturers may then require larger warehouse space, countering the benefits gained by reductions in retail space.

However, JIT delivery in the United Kingdom, for example, has proven successful with the complement of efficient road distribution and logistics sector (United Kingdom Department for Transport, 1999). Amusingly, in this sense, ICTs were also applied to mitigate the potential impacts of ICTs! However, this is an important point: ICTs may solve one problem only to create other potential problems—the unintended revenge of technology—unless it is preceded with a thorough assessment of its consequences. Therefore, in order to complement JIT delivery practices, mitigation, possibly through cascading applications of ICTs, may be required at various stages. This offers significant advantages to those businesses that can predict such needs and develop appropriate applications.

For example, a "freight village" is an area within which activities related to freight transport, logistics, and goods distribution are coordinated, including shippers, warehouses, storage areas, public agencies and planners, and businesses. To encourage intermodal transport, a freight village should be served by multiple modes (road, rail, waterways, air transport). This integrates the functions of freight handling and transfer to maximize efficiency (Victoria Transport Policy Institute, 2002). Similarly, other efforts include freight coordination that promotes transport efficiency by providing a way both shippers and carriers can match freighting needs with available services.

However, freight transport is increasing, and the nature of this increase is toward smaller, less efficient shipments and modes to meet mobile inventory demands—JIT delivery. For example, Statistics Canada notes that in Canada "[f]rom 1990 to 2003, the amount of freight carried by the for-hire trucking industry grew nearly three times faster (75%) than all other modes combined (up a collective 27% over the same period)" (Statistics Canada [StatsCan], 2006a, 11). Moreover, these figures exclude goods shipped by private trucking fleets outside the large trucking companies, such as those owned or operated by companies that manage their own shipping requirements or small, local for-hire carriers. "From 1992 to 2005, manufacturers were able to reduce inventories as a share of shipments by 15%, thanks in part to more frequent deliveries by truck" (StatsCan, 2006a, 12). The report observes that "fuel consumption by the transportation industry continues to rise" (StatsCan, 2006a, 13), despite the fact that shipping companies are moving freight more efficiently—using less energy per dollar of gross domestic product.

Perhaps most disturbing is the continuous trend toward greater mobility in a world ever more punctuated by increasing numbers of ICTs. With the exception of rail travel, all modes have seen a steady increase in the consumption of fuel, even given increased efficiencies in logistics and technologies. So much for dematerialization and immaterialization.

CONSUMPTION

E-Commerce

E-commerce has the potential to significantly modify the way goods and services are purchased. More information may make comparing and buying products simpler. Exposure to more options may enhance competition, reduce prices, and increase demand. There is significant potential from e-commerce to optimize transport logistics and reduce overproduction, manufacturing waste, and warehouse space.

Conversely, online orders function to accelerate the delivery of goods. This leads to an increase in courier, express, and parcel services. It also changes the structure of shipped freight toward smaller units, thereby increasing packaging (Fichter, 2001). As is discussed in the following text, e-purchases can be highly customized, resulting in mass customization. This increases nonstandard-size packaging and therefore reduces the efficiency of vehicle load volumes. Results from the high-level international conference on Sustainability Research and Sectoral Integration noted that "e-commerce has been shown to generate increased demand for electricity and transport" (Fellenius & Andersson, 2001, 6).

Online shopping enables consumers to have products delivered right to their door, fueling the preference of many consumers for convenience and immediate gratification. This has a number of implications. First, consumers have added free time to engage in additional activities that may or may not be resource-intensive. Cost savings (as is explored in the following text) also invariably lead to additional consumption. In addition, through e-commerce, consumers shop at individual e-stores to have products delivered to their door. Consequently, where someone may have driven to one or two malls (perhaps during the same trip or route) for numerous items, e-commerce may generate an individual (perhaps more efficient) delivery for each item.

Research quantifying these resource consumption effects is scant. Part of the reason for this shortage results from the sheer number and complexity of possibilities derived from e-commerce. One household shopping study calculated that environmental savings are reached if one e-commerce delivery replaces 3.5 traditional shopping trips, if more than twenty-five orders are delivered at a time, and if travel distance is longer than fifty kilometers (Plepys, 2002). Ultimately, the absolute number of delivery trips may outweigh efficiency gains. The sheer growth in commerce energized by e-commerce led the National Research Programme (2000) to conclude that it will be unable to contribute to traffic reductions.

Studies such as those completed by Matthews and Hendrickson (2001) and Matthews, Williams, Tagamic, and Hendrickson (2002) demonstrate that key factors, such as shipping distances, return rates, population density, consumer choices, and shopping allocations, are critical determinants affecting e-commerce's physical consumption. Assessing the effects from e-commerce has proven extremely complex.

This is precisely because e-commerce is partly dependent on consumer decisions. Making reasonably accurate predictions on ephemeral social preferences—compounded by constantly evolving formats and interpretations of convenience, flexibility, and accessibility affected by manifestations of consumer culture—is akin to herding cats.

Locally produced products may decline as e-commerce leads to a global marketplace. "Local and regional markets become global markets—everybody who has access to the global network can compete in other previously local and regional markets, but at the same time faces potential competition from businesses located anywhere on the globe" (Traxler & Luger, 2000, 285).

Due to the marketing prowess and "convenience" of pointing and clicking over the Internet, the availability of food staples at local markets may fall victim to imported varieties circumventing the globe. Apples, artwork, or answering services from halfway around the world have now become at least as accessible as those at neighborhood markets.

Yet it is doubtful that consumers will entirely abandon conventional forms of shopping. Sindhav and Balazs (1999) argue that people are unlikely to restrict their consumerism to a single format since many formats continue to be available, consumers prefer the choices these afford, and e-commerce simply expands previously available options. What e-commerce does provide is additional information, augmenting consumer decision making. Since many consumers learn about products online and then pursue additional information at retail locations, this may simply send consumers to more retail locations to compare product features, or, conversely, simplify the decision making process.

The changing "mix" of online and conventional shopping must be factored together to assess changes in consumption. Conventional retail outlets will still need to be maintained to satisfy important societal and individual roles of shopping, even though many (more) consumer decisions may be made through informational provisioning. Consumption might be expected to increase as a duplication of services and service and product delivery emerges. As is discussed in the following text, e-commerce may tend to function as a complement, rather than a pure substitute, to conventional shopping patterns.

Hesse (2002) analyzes the implications of e-commerce in the broader context of structural change. This approach provides a much more comprehensive analysis than the more narrow assessments that tend to overstate the benefits of e-commerce.

Hesse concludes that e-commerce is likely to increase transport distances and delivery frequencies. This would result in an increasing demand for land for the establishment of new distribution centers, as well as a shift toward truck and air freight transport modes. He also finds that e-commerce functions to reduce the time and increase the geographic area of transport operations, thereby increasing vehicle miles traveled and influencing shipping mode. Therefore, he concludes that consumer behavior, delivery modes, and population density are greater determinants of the impacts of e-commerce than are the ICTs that are applied.

Matthews et al. (2002) investigated e-commerce for book retailing and found no definitive evidence to suggest that it is more sustainable than traditional methods. However, they do conclude that e-commerce is considered more favorable when air transport does not contribute an increased share of shipping modes. However, as Hesse (2002), cited previously, concludes, increased air freight transport is likely to result from e-commerce transactions. In fact, this is precisely what is occurring as developers build new dedicated airport hubs and massive warehouse facilities (or "pass-through facilities") near airports specifically to accommodate cargo generated exclusively by e-commerce transactions and carried by multiple 747s (Murphy, 2000).

Fichter concludes that "it is obvious that the Internet economy is not and will not be a 'weightless economy'" (Fichter, 2003, 32). He observes further that "[t]he technology (ICT, Internet) does not determine sustainability, but rather its design, use, and regulation does" (Fichter, 2003, 32). The obvious conclusions are that environmentally sustainable design, use, and regulation of e-commerce technology is an important factor for consideration at all stages.

E-commerce has the potential for manufacturers to sell their products directly to consumers. While this may permit some reduction at the retail level, thereby eliminating some impacts, the ultimate benefits may be more elusive. As Sarkar, Butler, and Steinfield (1995) observe, online retailing generates its own intermediaries, such as those who ensure a safe payment system and those who provide intelligent search agents and maintain the networking capabilities needed for online shopping. While service-oriented, these changing business opportunities will nonetheless require physical infrastructure, such as buildings, computer and communication networks, employees, and transportation networks. Consequently, the direct benefits of reduced intermediaries, such as warehouses, have the potential to be more than offset, and much more so when the analysis of Sindhav and Balazs (1999), previously discussed, is taken into consideration, in that conventional shopping and intermediaries are likely to complement rather than strictly substitute for e-commerce. More striking, and even counterintuitive, is Jespersen's finding that the private service sector is not significantly "less energy intensive than the manufacturing sectors" (Jespersen, 1999, 17). This result is echoed by others, such as Heinonen, Jokinen, and Kaivo-oja (2001) and Marvin (1997).

In fact, analysis of e-commerce should not be confined to retail–consumer interactions: many online transactions now include "freecycles," peer-to-peer trading, and a wide variety of online classified websites. In all of these examples, single-product transactions are conducted. While this may include direct reuse, it does create some rather distorted travel and freight transport behavior, such as the 100-kilometer round-trip to pick up a freecycled item (e.g., packing bubbles or cardboard boxes). While that excursion might displace some demand for the product's manufacture, it must be weighed against the transportation consequences of collecting that item for "free." In many cases, freecycled items are also opportunistic, creating demand for an item, or specifically transport of that item, where no demand would otherwise exist. Despite the great advantages of extending the useful life of many products, such formats are more likely to fill economic and opportunistic voids rather than environmental ones.

Music File Sharing, Digital Photography, and Digital Media

Cohen (1999) argues that the music industry is demonstrative of how ICTs might be applied to help achieve dematerialization. By using the Internet to download (at no cost) music files and the necessary programs to play them, consumers may choose precisely the music desired, in the electronic format of their choice.

Other than music CD inserts and packaging (which can be ridiculously excessive), this format may not necessarily displace resource consumption. The energy and materials required for manufacturing, transportation, and retail space attributed to music sales is transposed to other storage and playback media such as writable CDs, DVDs, and MP3 players. While these typically drive the acquisition of alternative playback equipment, the latter substantially enhances the convenience, transferability, and versatility of converting music from one media to another and between different playback equipment. However, with the ability to rewrite CDs and overwrite MP3s, they can be reused when the listener tires of the music, possibly reducing resource consumption. On the other hand, as the price of CDs is reduced, the incentive to rewrite them is lost. Moreover, MP3 players have become important fashion statements, incorporating cases, colors, styles, and features, leading to ever more rapid obsolescence. Their manufacture and warranty also leaves significant desirability—such as the trend toward hardwired batteries that leads to obsolescence within a few years despite their complete functionality. It is also probably a safe assumption that the production of MP3 devices requires greater resources than CDs. Finally, devices for such media playback appear to be contributing to a rapidly growing glut of e-waste.

Despite these challenges, legal rulings over free file downloading websites seem only to have further confused the final resource consumption analyses. It remains to be seen how, and even if, these legal decisions will affect the use of this technology and its resource outcomes. Clearly, the entertainment industries "do not intend to stand idly by while others build business illegally off of our music" (King, 2002).

Similarly, digital photography offers consumers the potential to select, record, store, manipulate, share, and print photographic images electronically. The obvious advantage is the avoidance of toxic chemicals during the developing procedure. However, with the proliferation of high-quality color printers, there is an incentive to print many of these pictures. Furthermore, as they may be transmitted electronically in various formats, digital photographs could be widely distributed with the click of a button, rendering the potential to be widely printed by countless recipients, considerably increasing consumption (Stern, 1997). With the increased convenience and flexibility combined with a greatly reduced cost, and incredibly enhanced manipulation of digital photography and printing, the incentive to take and print more photographs has been tremendously amplified. New storage drives are continuously growing in capacity, precisely to save the increasing numbers and size of multimedia files. The increased ease, convenience, and accessibility of downloading, copying, saving, creating, and manipulating digital files, photographs, and videos now means the genie bottle has been uncorked, allowing creativity—not to mention consumption—to bubble over. Moreover, the direct cost for producing media has plummeted due to the efficiencies of digital media formats.

Other examples of concern include that of Reichart and Hischier (2001), who calculated in a Swiss study that, to read the same amount of text, the environmental impacts generated from twenty minutes of Internet use would be equivalent to those generated from newspaper production, given the Swiss electricity mix. However, if any of the information is subsequently printed, resource consumption could rise dramatically.

Advocates of digital media insist that the filtered access to enormous amounts of information will open new doors and new possibilities for learning about what interests us. The case is made that with the application of digital filters, our personal capture of only the stories and information that are of interest to us will enable seamless screening of only that information we desire.

This raises the potential dilemma of blinding the reader to a tremendous amount of information that may (or should!) be of interest or relevance: in effect, a digital filter could function as a controlling agent, creating a myopic input of information. One cannot escape the image of an Orwellian, dictatorial society where essential information can be subverted, or is even chosen to be ignored, in order to fulfill a narrowly defined perception of reality. This future may perhaps already be emerging, exposed by popular Internet searches.

Besides, let's face it: with search engines capable of conveniently and immediately delivering information from a diversity of electronic media, the rate of information overload has risen spectacularly. This often leads to brief thirty-second sound bytes of information being even more briefly reviewed in our relentless pursuit to stabilize our ever faster world. Articles deserving attention rise exponentially, followed by our increasingly unproductive drudgery to pursue their meanings.

The environmental benefits of digital media appear to depend on a number of social and behavioral factors. This reinforces Hesse's (2002) conclusion that consumer behavior is a greater determinant than the ICTs applied.

This finding is further reinforced by Gard and Keoleian (2003). Their life-cycle analysis of digital libraries' journal capacity to reduce environmental impacts employed thirty model parameters, ninety variable inputs, and numerous fixed inputs. Results indicated that the energy consumption characteristics were highly influenced by the number of readings per article, the networking infrastructure generated a small effect on energy consumption, the personal transportation effects considered were significant energy-consumption factors, and the impacts from personal copies varied. Interestingly, photocopying always increased energy consumption, but laser printing actually reduced energy consumption when it substituted for on-screen reading. Given this diversity of possible outcomes, social choices seem to be critical factors in determining the ultimate effects of digital media on sustainable consumption trajectories.

Housing and Households

Aebischer and Huser (2000) examined the impacts of various networking technologies in households on energy consumption. The study considered applications in the following three categories:

1. Process control technology: remote control, telemaintenance, and automation of systems for basic requirements (for example, heat, lighting, and security)
2. White goods: remote control, telemaintenance, and documentation (operating instructions)
3. Multimedia services: telephone, Internet, information technology, TV, video, and audio

The study notes that the third category is the primary driver for the adoption of any application, as these provide the necessary connections to permit functional, value-added services.

For process-control systems, findings suggest that (without networking of white goods), the standby power consumption is approximately seventy-five watts—equivalent to an additional annual electricity consumption of 657 kilowatt hours, or 16 percent for an average Swiss household. Overall, additional energy consumption as a result of networking represents an increase of about 30 percent by 2020, compared with current consumption. Approximately 25 percent of this increase is attributed to standby-mode power consumption, suggesting a key behavioral factor affecting energy consumption. (Similar behavior factors are observed by Kawamoto et al. [2001] discussed in the following text.)

Similarly, Aebischer and Huser (2000, 2003) measured total electricity consumption in the "intelligent home" and found it to use more than three times the amount of electricity used in an ordinary home in Switzerland. They conclude that the additional electricity demand for networking purposes is substantial and may cause a significant increase in nationwide electricity demand in the coming years. However, they also identify the potential for enormous electricity savings—in the range of 80 percent in the equipment used for networking—with rather simple measures, such as operating the equipment without the use of an uninterruptible power supply, and by applying efficient power management of the equipment and components. These results reveal critical insights into conservation opportunities and suggests several key policy options. The simple measures recommended here, for instance, suggest a return to the issue of behavior change, steps as simple as unplugging always-on components when not in use and re-engineering these components for zero loads when turned off.

A more important finding is that, after considering the impact of e-commerce and remote workstations (teleworking), Aebischer and Huser (2000) note that it is anticipated that both applications will reduce energy consumption in the industrial, transportation, and service sectors. However, they caution that these benefits may be "(at least) a scale lower than the maximum additional electricity consumption . . . in private households" (2000, 4). Their conclusion should be quite concerning, given the previous discussions on e-commerce and telework.

E-Learning

Education is increasingly being conducted at a distance. The expectation is that this provides greater access to educational opportunities than might otherwise exist. For some time, distance education has been conducted utilizing print and audiovisual materials. ICTs now offer the capacity to further dematerialize distance education by delivering courses and tutorials electronically. Despite being primarily a service, a substantial portion of standard postsecondary education involves high resource costs resulting from the transportation between residences and family. Distance learning has been promoted as holding the capacity to, among other benefits, greatly reduce these costs.

Herring and Roy (2002) calculate, however, that e-learning does not appear to reduce total energy and carbon dioxide emissions compared with conventional print-based distance learning. Indeed, under certain conditions, the electronically delivered and tutored course appears to involve more energy and emissions per student than the print-based alternative. In this situation, it appears that effects such as printing from the Internet site and additional home heating counterbalance the reduced need for printed matter and travel to tutorials. The energy and material demands of distance-based learning are further compounded by the incredible energy demands of servers, web-based platforms, and video- and audioconferencing.

PRODUCTION

Packaging and Marketing

Marketing through the Internet permits the potential to vastly reduce packaging since the marketing function of packaging is much less significant. This could displace large amounts of plastics, papers, and other materials, not to mention toxic dyes and inks. The production of catalogues could also be greatly reduced as the Internet could offer versions that could be easily updated to reflect current pricing and product options, including a wealth of other product and retailer details. Shipping costs dictate that packaging size and weight be reduced to a minimum. Such incentives would promote the use of recyclable and refillable containers.

Product and company information can also serve the sales and profit goals of marketing. Internet marketing could direct consumers to a wealth of images and branding techniques to sell products for which conventional packaging and advertising cannot compete. Ready access to commercial products through online search engines would simplify and quickly guide consumers to products. "Pop-up" images, advertisements, new techniques, and new applications are regularly embedded into Internet search engines and websites to advertise products and services to consumers—perpetually evolving in the savage battle for Internet eyes by newer technological applications as the old are circumvented or become stale—enormously increasing the market exposure of these products and services. Possible now are online surveys, contests, questionnaires, credit and debit card scanners, as well as server statistics and enormous amounts of data-mined information and sites detailing consumer information about individual's uses, preferences, and desires, and potential marketing groups that are automatically captured, filtered, analyzed, and categorized. Internet traffic shaping and other techniques have the ability to direct web users to specific sites for advertising and marketing purposes, and restrict competitors' sites. Company or product contests, exhibitions or participation in company or product chat rooms, and interactive websites can create "consumption enhancement" by allowing the consumer to participate (sometimes actively) in the value-creation process (Sindhav & Balazs, 1999). Clearly the Internet serves as a powerful medium for advertising and promotions and the capacity to tremendously increase potential target audiences and sales and shape global marketing strategies. Although the consumption of product packaging sold through the Internet and catalogues may decrease, actual consumption could be highly stimulated and greatly increase the volume of products and services sold, targeting a more diverse and extensive range of global consumers. While companies might be able to reduce some costs through reduced packaging and more effective marketing techniques, this may only be complemented—boosting the corporate bottom line—by dramatic sales increases made possible through innovative Internet- and ICT-based global marketing strategies.

Internet sites in fact target very young children—a lucrative, vulnerable, and impressionable consumer segment—worldwide, employing their enthusiasm to help design both sites and the services and the products global corporations peddle. It took federal intervention to limit corporate data mining from children as young as two, three, and four on their families' spending and buying habits, and on their own preferences—exploiting children's inability to differentiate between advertising and fictional role playing. Despite the profusion of similar tactics currently being exploited, the global market doctrine of consumerism scored huge points by indoctrinating many children into the ideology before this form of exploitation was recognized and regulated.

Even more compelling are the consequences, as Naomi Klein (2000) and Benjamin Barber (2007) have pondered, that result in a global consumer economy in which marketing techniques must conform to differentiated cultures to sell generally uniform goods and services. The consequence Barber turns to is the response James U. McNeal provides: children love to play, snack, and generally love just being children, suggesting the viability of relatively standardized global marketing techniques directed at children, and the homogenous culture of play, or, as Benjamin Barber suggests, infantilization. This effectively creates a global, casual, frivolous, and relatively carefree and careless, if not indifferently driven and excessive, consumer culture. What better platform to execute such a global marketing strategy than ICTs that especially appeal to children and youth, who are also exceptionally adept at using these devices and services, and who command and effectively control billions of dollars of discretionary spending that is matched only by the spending power of marketers and advertisers themselves?

Sindhav and Balazs (1999) note that in order for consumers to engage in online shopping, they require both the desire for this type of shopping as well as the ability to do so. Preferences for online shopping might include such factors as a dislike of shopping or a lack of time. In this context, it is interesting to note Binswanger's (2002) observations of a rebound in time-use in which households may not "save" any time at all, although they constantly invest in time-saving devices and consumption patterns, such as computers, mobile telephones, and high-speed data connections. It is also important to note the potential energy-consumption implications of such time-savings devices. Ironically, the desire to shop online because of a lack of time for some may simply reflect the consequences of their choice that gave them the ability to do so (such as through their investments in computer and Internet access)! Indoctrinate the youth and children into this belief and value structure early, and you have a captive market for life, always off balance, dazzled, and anxious to adopt the next time-saving or trend-setting opportunity.

Product Design and Development

Design for the Environment and Eco-Design

ICTs have the potential to greatly improve the design efficiency and, subsequently, the resource consumption of product and process developments. Computer modeling and simulation can eliminate the significant amounts of energy, materials, time, and labor applied to such tasks as the testing of aircraft dynamics. No longer, for example, is the extensive use of wind tunnels required for the design of aircraft. Packaging can be made much more efficient, reducing waste, bulk, and environmentally toxic substances. Information can be shared and new and innovative processes and design techniques can be rapidly deployed and adopted globally.

Despite these possibilities, Nuij (2002) observes there are four barriers to eco-innovation improvements. The first is that environmental considerations are omitted in the initial phase, which is creatively essential. Instead, in this phase, innovations are technologically and market-driven and therefore do not necessarily lead to more sustainable consumption. This is also observed by Arnfalk (2002), BT (2001), and Sonntag (2000), who note that economic forces are key drivers for the adoption of ICTs. The second barrier relates to the need for increased organizational complexity and stake-holder participation. Next is the need for large investments in technology and changes in marketing approaches. Finally, there is the requirement to identify current and future consumer needs. While the potential exists to improve design efficiency, it seems significant barriers remain.

Mass Customization

The introduction of products that the consumer does not embrace, overproduction, shifts in fashions or styles, and new technologies that create product obsolescence are all examples of inefficient, yet largely unpredictable, phenomena. These all lead to unnecessary consumption, imposing additional environmental impacts and costs at all levels of society. The production technique of mass customization can offer consumers products specifically designed for their individual wishes and exact specifications such as jeans cut to personal measurements, computers assembled to customer specifications, and preferred musical selections.

These opportunities appear to greatly reduce the potential for waste and inefficiencies, greatly reducing resource consumption. Reduced stockpiles of unwanted consumer goods and reduced warehouse needs are but two of the obvious advantages. These alone have the potential to avoid an enormous amount of unnecessary energy and materials consumption from the building, heating, and cooling of warehouses to the production of toxic chemicals and energy for processing. They also offer the added benefit of improved profit margins.

Despite these benefits, the hidden risk is the enhanced ability to gather data on customer behavior and tailor information specifically to the individual consumer, providing a tremendously more powerful marketing technique than previously available. More powerful marketing opportunities combined with customization may induce consumers to purchase what they may previously have neglected. Faced with the prospect of a selectively recorded music set chosen by the consumer, consumers may decide to greatly expand their collection of music. Similarly, selecting a computer with the precise hardware and software needed at a price also determined by these selections may induce many consumers to purchase a computer that may otherwise have been judged too expensive or unnecessary. Might mass customization merely open a new chapter on the elusive, materialistic pathway to well-being?

NETWORKING AND ELECTRICITY CONSUMPTION

The materialism of the information revolution embodied by ICTs comes to light with the energy demands of data servers and data centers. Data are essentially tiny electrical impulses that flash across semiconductor chips, switching millions of microscopic transistors on and off. This creates electrical resistance—and requires energy to move the electrons—at the smallest scales that, when magnified by trillions of switches, generates considerable heat inside massive data centers. The energy to push those electrons and cool those buildings and their internal machineries is ballooning almost as fast as the data centers themselves, as demand for data surges globally. The costs are driving companies to seek solutions—

from locating near energy sources to virtualization (software to squeeze more efficiency out of the data servers)—to bring down those costs. Roughly $4.5 billion was spent to power U.S. data servers in 2006.

Kawamoto et al. (2001) measured total energy use by office and network equipment as of 1999. Although their results suggest it is a small percentage, about 2 percent, of total electricity use in the United States, this represents about seventy-four terawatt hours (seventy-four trillion watt hours) per year (Department of Energy, 2008). This is a tremendous amount of energy, a new electricity demand not extant prior to the introduction of the ICT sector. (Whether and to what degree this new electricity consumption has substituted for, complemented, created anew, or induced other forms of energy and materials consumption remains largely unquantified.) This study specifically excluded major segments of the ICT sector—home computers, cellular phones, and so on—that acutely influence demand for networking equipment. Also, electricity consumption by the measured devices is expected to grow as more applications and users adopt ICT applications.

Another study by the same group calculated that the 2 percent figure only rises to 3 percent, or one hundred terawatt hours, when the electricity used by telecommunications equipment and electronics manufacturing in the United States is included (Koomey, 2000). Another study by Hilty and Ruddy (2000) identified that most of the energy and materials throughput of a personal computer's life cycle occurs during production. Between 2 percent and 0.1 percent of the production material actually becomes part of the product. The remainder is production waste. Similarly, the consumed energy for production (five to twelve giga joules), is greater than the energy consumed during its use phase by about a factor of ten (this compares with 2.8 giga joules for a color TV, 13 giga joules used to manufacture a refrigerator, and 83 giga joules for a car). They also note an expected continuing exponential *growth* in the energy and materials consumed in the ICTs market until 2015, resulting in a linear *growth* of the total physical mass that is contained in the ICT devices in operation. This suggests very inefficient production processes for computers. Identification of these production processes is further supported by Federico, Hinterberger, and Musmeci (2002), who calculate the material input per unit of service (MIPS) for the car and mobile telephone devices. Their results show that MIPS for cars (0.2 kilogram/[passenger kilometer]) was of the same order of magnitude as the MIPS for mobile telephone devices (0.207 kilogram/[minute of telephone call] or 0.196 kilogram/[minute for short message service]).

Additional studies by Pout, Moss, and Davidson (1998) and Fawcett, Lane, and Boardman (2000) show similar values for electricity consumption by ICTs in the service and domestic sectors respectively in the United Kingdom. Pout, Moss, and Davidson (1998) estimated that ICTs consumed 6 percent of electricity used within the service sector in the United Kingdom in 1994. Fawcett, Lane, and Boardman (2000) estimated that in the UK domestic sector in 1998, the ICT equipment only used about 1 percent.

The electricity consumption of Internet servers alone were estimated to have doubled in the period between 2000 and 2005 in the United States. This increase has been attributed primarily to a growth in servers, accompanied by a small increase in the power use per unit (Koomey, 2007).

In 2005, server electricity demand was equal to 0.6 percent of total U.S. electricity consumption, a value that increases to 1.2 percent when cooling and related infrastructure is included. This is equivalent to twenty-three trillion watt hours and forty-six trillion watt hours, respectively, in 2005.

Although admittedly very difficult to predict, this report concludes, "If power per server remains constant, those trends would imply an increase in electricity used by servers worldwide of about 40% by 2010" (Koomey, 2007, 8). Were power use per unit to increase as expected by 2010, electricity use by servers would be 76 percent higher than in 2005.

The power demand in 2005 for these servers would translate into five 1000-megawatt power plants. Globally, all servers were estimated to consume the equivalent capacity power of fourteen 1000-megawatt power plants. From any perspective, this is an incredible demand, which is definitely not immaterial.

Mills and Huber's (1999) numbers suggest a higher value for the electricity consumption in the United States due to the Internet, moderately higher than that found by Pout, Moss, and Davidson (1998). Mills and Huber's calculations suggest the Internet absorbs some 8 percent of the U.S. electricity supply, rising to 13 percent when all related equipment is included. The study concludes that the growth of the Internet would rapidly exceed the efficiency improvements in electronics, resulting in increased absolute energy consumption. However, their numbers have been criticized, based largely on the generous assumptions attributed to component energy consumption.[3] These criticisms have argued that the report numbers may possibly be

---

[3] An extensive summary of the Information Technology and Resource Use Project of the Lawrence Berkeley National Laboratory and related resources can be found at enduse.lbl.gov/Projects/InfoTech.html.

as much as an order of magnitude too high, considering the significant overestimates of power consumption attributed to the final results. As with the Kawamoto et al. (2001) study cited previously, however, causal links between ICTs use, the growth in electricity consumption nationally, and economic growth can only be speculated upon.

On the other hand, Aebischer and Huser (2002) predict an increase in additional electricity consumption in Switzerland attributable to the constantly growing number of networked household devices and their higher degree of use. This increase is from approximately 323 kilowatt hours per household per year to 1,393 kilowatt hours per household per year by the year 2020 for Internet applications. Put another way, the study projects the average household in Switzerland will consume an additional amount of electricity equivalent to 400 kilowatt hours per annum in 2010, rising to an additional 1,500 kilowatt hours per annum in 2020 as a result of in-house networking, primarily resulting from ICT applications.

While some have criticized the Mills and Huber report, even when the numbers are reduced by a factor of ten, it is difficult to remain optimistic since Internet traffic doubles every six months (Roberts & Crump, 2001). Diffusion rates of the Internet are tremendous and rapidly changing. Only 4 percent of the world population had access to the Internet in 2001 (Reisch, 2001). By 2009, that number had risen to 24 percent, and grew at a rate of 342 percent between 2000 and 2009 (Internet World Stats, 2009). Moreover, and to contextualize the Kawamoto et al. (2001) study, according to testimony from Mark Mills before the Subcommittee on National Economic Growth, Natural Resources, and Regulatory Affairs in February 2000, in a communication exchange with the Lawrence Berkeley National Laboratory group, this group stated "that the NET effect of the Internet on electricity and energy use (which is really what matters) cannot be estimated accurately without assessing the associated indirect effects of the Internet on resource use in the economy" (Mills, 2000, 5).

Dürrenberger, Patzel, and Hartmann (2001) identify that behavioral changes can lead to substantial energy savings that may even be higher than the savings achieved through technological progress alone. Conversely, one might expect that behavioral changes may lead to substantial energy increases. If aggregate consumption growth exceeds the rate of energy efficiency gains, overall energy demand is likely to rise. Dürrenberger, Patzel, and Hartmann (2001) identify that significant rebound effects occur when the annual energy consumption growth exceeds 0.3 percent. Their findings, however, may represent a low estimate of rebound effects, since they did not account for either income effects or product longevity, both critical factors of resource demand, affecting many variables from personal behavior to institutional structures.

The results from Aebischer and Huser (2000) indicate an annual growth rate in electricity consumption of 1.3 percent per year in the Swiss housing sector as a consequence of ICT applications. This level far exceeds the 0.3 percent threshold level identified by Dürrenberger, Patzel, and Hartmann (2001). Consequently, the actual rebound effects could significantly exceed those from the efficiency gains above the 0.3 percent threshold level identified, despite the potential that a 0.3 percent energy consumption growth rate may be an optimistically high threshold level below which rebound effects may not occur.

Aebischer and Varone explain that "Information Technologies (IT) are overwhelmingly applied for entertainment, increasing productivity, and gaining access to new markets. A significant increase in energy use is expected, though the degree of the anticipated increase is debated" (2001, 394). Clearly, in addition to the rebound effect, there are more fundamental forces driving consumption growth. We discuss the productivity-efficiency paradox (rebound effect) in chapter 5. More fundamental drivers for consumption growth are considered in chapters 6 and 8.

Discussion of Networking and Electricity Consumption Studies

In a global marketplace, advanced production may actually exhibit externalizations. These have been termed *ecological shadow* (MacNeill, Winsemius, & Yakushiji, 1991) and *ecological footprint* (Wackernagel & Rees, 1996). Furthermore, it has been observed that "modern high income economies are actually becoming increasingly indebted to nature" (Rees, 1999, 26). Clearly, a country-specific analysis in quantitative terms will serve little value in a global world, weighing in on the low, perhaps quite low, side of aggregate consumption for advanced-economy countries.

Consider the following example to illustrate this point. Kawamoto et al. (2001) calculate that the total energy consumption of the Internet and associated products in the United States were equivalent to 3 percent of all U.S. electricity consumption, including the electricity used by telecommunications equipment and electronics manufacturing. This applies U.S. data "to create an upper bound to the amount of electricity used to manufacture office equipment and network equipment in the U.S. for all purposes" (Koomey, 2000, 19). Koomey then calculates, on this basis, that the total electricity used for manufacturing the relevant electronic equipment is roughly twenty-one terawatt hours. Then he asserts, "The actual total is almost certainly lower than this, because our assessment of the percentage of each SIC code that is applicable is overly generous, as a conservatism" (Koomey, 2000, 19).

Suppose, however, that some of that equipment were manufactured in another country. Its embodied energy of manufacture and transportation might be exceedingly large. Given the short life span of such products, the resource consumption of the Internet might indeed be closer to the values proposed by Mills and Huber, albeit for different reasons. Nevertheless, resource consumption and environmental impacts would be substantially greater under such assumptions, versus complete local manufacturing of office and network equipment. This represents the complexity of calculating electricity consumption in a global marketplace. It should also serve as a caution for policy makers: at present, limited weight should be afforded quantitative studies of these types, and they must be interpreted with discretion, given the current quality of available data and methodological design. Moreover, given the 2007 estimates of Koomey on server power consumption, unless servers alone represent the lion's share of ICTs' electrical consumption, one would be hard pressed to conclude that all ICTs consume a mere 2 percent of electricity.

Riding the environmental wave of the latter years of the first decade of the new millennium, this massive power consumption has raised considerable debate in terms of the carbon footprint of the Internet. The contributions from Internet operations and data centers to global ecological challenges seem to be tremendous. Recall the reported, albeit somewhat socially mediated, energy demands of Google searches. Considering that there are some three hundred million searches daily, that adds up to a considerable level of energy and materials demands, and pollution and carbon dioxide emissions annually, simply from the use of search engines. While the brilliant observer might suggest this is still far better than hopping in the car to chase after information in a library, it assumes the car would be the preferred mode to access a library repository, and the library would be the preferred destination to gather the desired information. More importantly, would one even be inclined to seek the information if its search were somewhat less convenient than an always-on computer sitting in the next room? Would someone actually hop into a car to go to the library to learn about Sarah Palin, the definition of a word, or what one's favorite musical group did yesterday?

The cost of providing power to thirsty high-tolerance seeking data centers has prompted many bizarre schemes, alongside the existing ventures such as constructing data centers beside their own dedicated power supplies.

Every time someone watches a video, downloads music or stores an e-mail, accesses medical records, makes a credit card transaction, or executes an Internet search for information, computing power at a data center is required to process the action.

So urgent became the problem, amidst the growing environmental sentiment, that following the 2007 report by Koomey, a consortia of technology companies launched the Green Grid collaboration in an effort to improve the energy efficiency of data centers. Beginning with a standard set of measurements for industry to apply, energy efficiency management is expected to improve. Virtualization, for instance, maximizes the efficiency of data center servers to reduce their associated costs: the technique applies technology to solve the problems of technology. Applications and services such as peer-to-peer and web 2.0 can be deployed to achieve new network efficiencies. Without a doubt, in very short order, one would expect the manifold problems created by virtualization to need solving—once identified. First and foremost, because virtualization employs software techniques, no servers are displaced, freeing space instead for future growth in data needs and profits alike. Given future computing power at reduced cost, one should expect that demand will rise. Ultimately, the benefit of virtualization is to reduce the power requirements of servers, routers, networks, switches, and computers below business-as-usual scenarios. These are relative reductions, not absolute. Well, at least they're trying. As we'll see in the following chapter, efficiency is a double-edged sword. Despite this concern, I suspect the collaboration is more about improving corporate bottom lines as the energy demands of data centers isn't a cheap business. One cannot help but question what some of the costs—social, economic, ecological, and environmental—are in terms of virtualization? Little known is that the rebound effect with respect to energy also has a related cousin: the rebound effect with respect to cost. They're still trying.

Similarly, Google, along with the World Wildlife Fund, launched the Climate Savers Computing Initiative in 2007. Their goal is to reduce carbon dioxide emissions from the operation of computers by fifty-four million tons per year by 2010. The initiative claims that simply using the power management features of a computer can save almost half a ton of carbon dioxide emissions annually—equivalent to turning down the home thermostat two degrees Fahrenheit during the winter, washing your clothes only in cold water, and giving up your car two days a week. This is a shocking reminder of how simple it is to achieve more sustainable consumption.

While it is uncertain whether this initiative will derive any substantial reductions in carbon dioxide emissions, it does appear their advertising and communications efforts and their organized events have considerably increased their own emissions. Ultimately, their goal reductions are measured relative to baseline projections, so "reduction" is really misleading—the stated goal will instead be a lesser increase than expected. Quite a difference. Sound familiar? We might just need to replace web 2.0, 3.0, and 4.0 with values 2.0, but we'll save that for later chapters.

The problem, as we will discuss, rests with the massive data centers, speed and convenience of searches and ICT tools, and other factors rarely if ever considered in studies promoting the environmental benefits of ICTs. Despite the neglect of these factors, they likely contribute significantly to the ultimate impact on sustainable consumption.

SUMMARY AND DISCUSSION

The application of ICTs at the micro level appear beneficial, reducing the consumption of specific products or processes. However, this is not so clear at the macro level. For instance, Ory and Mokhtarian (2005) identify that the contextual role of an automobile in an individual's life will be a strong determinant of how much he or she travels and how much he or she wants to travel. If the individual expresses a strong sense of the freedom, mobility, and control provisioning from private automobiles, or identifies strongly with the status symbolism of private automobiles, for example, he or she is likely to relate strongly with the desire to travel. "[T]hose with a strong sense of curiosity or adventure-seeking, and those who need to escape or need to connect with their surroundings, will probably voluntarily engage in travel beyond the minimum required to conduct a set of activities" (Ory & Mokhtarian, 2005, 20). They further note that those who employ travel as a buffer between certain activities or are simply able to use travel time effectively "will have a smaller disutility for travel than would be predicted by the conventional measures of travel time and cost alone," suggesting that this would reduce, as a minimum, "their incentive to reduce their travel, and at the extreme could prompt them to increase it." Similarly, Jackson (2005) notes how the automobile performs various social roles beyond simple functionality. This suggests that the role of ICTs in, for example, mobility could be quite complex, and their capacity for reducing private automobile travel—along with the associated energy and material consumption, and global ecological, and social consequences—whether through e-commerce or telecommuting, could be most ineffective in groups that identify strongly with the favorable aspects of private transport. The same might be said for freight transport, or virtually any other substitutable functions attributed to ICTs. This also reveals the tremendously complex nature of consumption decisions, the role of the social context of those decisions, and the influence globalization and ICTs can have on both the consumption decisions and the social context of those decisions. Many, if not most, optimistic assertions of the benefits of ICTs seem too narrowly conceived and overly simplistic. In fact, Statistics Canada unequivocally states that these "and numerous other such proclamations have all been grossly exaggerated with quantification at this point in time proving them faulty" (StatsCan, 2006b, 11). Indeed, while this is predicated on the acknowledgment that ICTs and society are co-evolutionary ("at this point in time"), the report notes "that many forces are at work simultaneously, many of which concern people's behaviour."

The results of a European Commission study to investigate the future impact of ICTs on the environment were released in August 2004 (Erdmann, Hilty, Goodman, & Arnfalk, 2004). The objective of this study was to explore and assess how ICTs will affect environmental sustainability until 2020. Five indicators—transport volumes, modal split, energy consumption, greenhouse gas emissions, and municipal wastes generated—served to measure the impacts. The results illustrated the tremendously variable possibilities exhibiting very divergent outcomes depending on the input assumptions from three scenarios developed utilizing four uncertainty factors. Whether ICTs further developed or froze at current levels of technological progress mattered little in most scenarios. For instance, ICTs may decrease the environmental impacts on the five indicators from total freight transport by 15 percent to increase them by 168 percent in the progress scenario, indicating a mostly unfavorable contribution. In the freeze progress scenario, the results were very similar, suggesting a decreased environmental impact on the five indicators from total freight transport by 25 percent to an increased impact of 160 percent. The study clearly reinforces the essential nature of policy development, better information, improved predictions and modeling, managing cross-cutting issues, and confronting the rebound effect and social issues. The study also reinforces the very real potential that, even if the policy decisions are the right ones for environmental sustainability, they might not be enough to prevent significant undesirable environmental consequences.

Clearly, ICTs alone will not spontaneously provide a marked improvement in environmental sustainability, and, even under the most favorable of conditions, may generate considerable impacts.

Ultimately, some fundamental questions about the application and adoption of ICTs must be asked. For instance, do ICTs ensure reduced resource consumption in the aggregate? If not, what are the necessary and sufficient conditions to ensure ICTs will help move us in this direction? The environmental impacts of ICTs have been somewhat neglected (Tulbure, 2002), despite the recent commotion of activities and reports seeking to green—or reduce the carbon footprint of—the Internet (Brahic, 2007; Dworshcak, 2008; Global Action Plan, 2007; Global eSustainability Initiative, 2008; Hamm, 2008; Miller, 2008; Pamlin & Szomolányi, 2008). These efforts have largely been, perhaps unfortunately, centered on the efficiency of the Internet. Numerous authors have argued that an increase in the efficiency derived from technological applications does not implicitly lead to a decrease of energy use or reduced environmental stress (Binswanger, 2001; Rees, 1995; Ropke, 2001). It has been demonstrated that the "rebound effect," which is largely a result of changes in lifestyles and behavior choices and the co-evolutionary nature of society and technology, typically exceeds the benefits achieved from efficiency gains by providing numerous alternative outlets for less sustainable consumption.

The ability of ICTs to achieve more materially sustainable consumption in the various applications explored remains very uncertain. While there may be much potential, the application selected and how it is applied are essential ingredients. Important elements of this recipe are the behavior, social, and institutional arrangements driving ICT selection and application. The following chapters intend to broaden the scope of enquiry along these lines.

First, it would be instructive to consider the role of efficiency, since this is a significant argument favoring the potential benefits of ICTs and, indeed, how much of the dialogue—including greening and carbon footprint reductions—has been framed to date. It also lays essential foundations of the social aspects of ICTs and sustainable consumption to be covered in subsequent chapters.

5

The Efficiency Paradox: Intensity and Consumption

INTENSITY AND EFFICIENCY

As we saw in the previous chapter, an important aspect of ICTs is their ability to more efficiently perform certain processes. Often this objective of improved efficiency has become an end goal in itself, driving the advance of ICTs. Paradoxically, efficiency by itself has been recognized for centuries as a catalyst for growth, and this reason, as we discuss in this chapter, helps explain why it is so actively pursued, and so devastatingly disruptive. If a primary objective of ICTs is to achieve more sustainable consumption, this fundamental desire for growth and the ability of ICTs to contribute suggest a dilemma, a fundamental contradiction: while ICTs can improve efficiencies, given the prevailing desire for economic growth, will their adoptions ultimately achieve more sustainable consumption—de-linking—or simply contribute to additional physical growth and the accompanying social problems? This is perhaps in part why, notwithstanding the incredible opportunities to improve the efficiency of processes, analyzing the ultimate consequences of ICT applications, as reviewed in the previous chapter, is an incredibly difficult challenge. Despite the potential for this line of thought to extend well beyond simply the material aspects of sustainable consumption, we confine our discussion to resource consumption for now.

Many different definitions of intensity and efficiency exist, and these warrant some elaboration. *Intensity* is a term used most commonly to describe the amount of energy or materials used per gross domestic product (GDP) (European Environment Agency [EEA], 2002).[1] Fischer-Kowalski and Amann (2001) define *material intensity* as the

---

[1] Similar terms include *resource efficiency* and *economic efficiency*.

mass of material input per dollar value added, where material productivity is the inverse of intensity.

The energy-to-GDP ratio has declined since 1950 in many industrial nations. It is the interpretation of this decline that generates controversy, however. Many have argued that the decline indicates a weak relationship between energy use and economic activity, and they cite this indicator as an important measure of sustainability. Others argue that this interpretation overstates the ability to de-couple energy use from economic activity because the analysis ignores the effect of changes in energy quality. Cleveland, Kaufmann, and Stern (2000) analyze the energy-to-GDP ratio by accounting for energy quality and conclude that, among other results, growth in GDP has indeed not been de-coupled from aggregate energy consumption. Accounting for energy quality reveals a strong relationship between energy use and economic output. They observe that this "runs counter to much of the conventional wisdom that technical improvements and structural change have decoupled energy use from economic performance" (Cleveland, Kaufmann, & Stern, 2000, 313). The shift toward higher quality energy from lower quality energy through technological changes and substitution now means that the higher quality fuels and their associated energy converters embody these technical changes. "These changes have increased energy efficiency in energy extraction processes, allowed an apparent 'decoupling' between energy use and economic output, and increased energy efficiency in the production of output" (Cleveland, Kaufmann, & Stern, 2000, 313). They caution that this process should raise concern since "decoupling is largely illusory."

This is precisely the same conclusion reached by Krenz (1984). Similarly, Huber and Mills (2005) assert a general trend toward more refined energy forms. This in itself, they suggest, will lead to a prevalence of advanced technologies, including ICTs, that contain significant embodied energy.

The concept of intensity may have been useful at the beginning of the nineteenth century when the world was rapidly expanding its arsenal of consumer artifacts and was limited only by human and physical capital. However, today the limit is more often natural capital (Daly, 1996). Intensity has since been replaced by other measures more appropriate to sustainable consumption (EEA, 2002).

There are at least two distinct problems one can draw from these relationships. One is that the GDP measures monetary transactions. Daly calls money a "rubber yardstick," prone to flexing as necessary to suit the economic argument, and shift over time. The other problem is that this approach isolates efficiency gains as an end objective in itself.

To better understand this dilemma, consider the mathematical representation of intensity. $I = x/GDP$, where I is the measured intensity and x is materials or energy consumption. To reduce intensity, we can either decrease x or increase GDP. Both factors are variable, and depend on wider social determinants. Thus with such a rubber yardstick, all that is needed is to increase GDP faster than energy or materials consumption to create the illusion of sustainability. Since increasing GDP offers no information about the sustainability of the action, decreasing x becomes essential to achieving development, which is, at the least, less environmentally harmful, all other factors being equal. In addition, in a world limited by natural capital, this approach is essential. Therefore, rather than speak of ambiguous formulae, replete with value judgments and arbitrary biases, a more appropriate approach is to consider opportunities for ICTs to decrease x.[2]

In fact, the European Environment Agency explicitly notes that indicators of energy intensity are "relative to the overall growth in the economy measured in GDP and [are] not in relation to their environmental impact. A positive score on these indicators therefore does not necessarily mean that the environmental impact of these sectors is decreasing" (EEA, 2002, 3).

Much literature exists challenging the assumptions upon which the environmental Kuznets curve is predicated—a fundamental premise for increasing GDP—to reduce environmental impacts (see, for example, Czech, 2001; International Society for Ecological Economics, 1998; Novek & Kampen, 1992; Stern, 2000). As is discussed in chapter 7, increasing GDP seems to offer little benefit to human health and well-being beyond levels far below those of industrialized nations. Despite these shortcomings, both intensity improvements and GDP increases offer remarkably valuable insights into the social or human features of consumption activity. These too are explored in later chapters.

To better understand how changes in GDP can influence consumption, we need to take a closer look at the possible dynamics involved, how they are influenced by globalization, and what a more intensive, efficient, or service-oriented economy, such as supplied by ICTs, might generate in terms of aggregate consumption. An important distinction must first be made between relative de-linking and

---

[2] A similar confusion arises when differential equations used by scientists to describe environmental phenomena are communicated to the public. Typical examples here include media statements of successfully achieving objectives when the rate of growth of ozone loss is reported to be slowing or the rate of growth in greenhouse gas (GHG) emissions are slowing. In each case, success is ambiguous. The rate of growth of ozone loss is just that: a *rate* of growth. Slowing simply implies a slower *rate of change*. If the loss is slowing, it is simply not as fast as during the previously measured segment of time. Similarly, slowing the *rate* of growth of GHG emissions (i.e., intensity-based targets) does not mean a reduction of emissions; it means only that their positive *growth rate* has declined (relative to profits or GDP, for example) since the previously measured time interval.

absolute de-linking. The former is represented by a reduced impact per unit of GDP. That is, the change in ratio of GDP-to-impact decreases. This may be achieved in three obvious ways: GDP may increase at a faster rate than the environmental impact, GDP may remain steady while the impact may decrease, or GDP may fall more slowly than environmental impacts decline. Clearly, in the case of relative de-linking, there is tremendous flexibility in the actual dynamics of how people and the environment are affected. Setting aside the variations in calculating GDP and environmental impact for the moment, we see that little information can be gleaned from this measure alone, since, in even a beneficial outcome, environmental impacts may be increasing, as might aggregate consumption within a country (global effects—that is, the impacts from globalization—are discussed in the following text). Absolute de-linking, on the other hand, exists where economic growth continues while the absolute amount of resource use remains steady or declines. Whereas relative de-linking has been observed under certain conditions, absolute de-linking is much more difficult to identify.

DOMESTIC AND GLOBAL ECONOMIC STRUCTURE

The structure of a domestic economy can be an important determining factor in national consumption. The role of a service or information economy in de-linking economic and physical growth is important. As a national economy becomes less intensive, several changes occur. First, the goods and services they consume reflect greater distancing and shading (Princen, 1997). The inputs may be derived from less-developed nations, refined, and enter the more-developed nation as already highly energy- and materials-intensive products and services. These are then used to add value, and, as the processes continue, greater value is distilled from less consumption than in previous stages of production. Yet paradoxically, less consumption, reflected as increased intensity or productivity, incorporates greater "hidden" or embodied inputs as these processes continue. Secondly, greater integration within the global economy—globalization—means that these countries depend increasingly on the institutions and structures that support and advance globalization. In its current format, this form of globalization is market-driven. Therefore, as an economy becomes less nationally intensive, it also becomes more growth-dependent. This suggests that the *national* economy will become more materials- and energy-intensive at the *global* (or aggregate) level, and ever more dependent on increasing this form of growth. The impacts of this growth are "outsourced" to less-developed nations. Thus, as a nation moves toward a more value-added and information economy, its domestic intensity and productivity increase at the expense of a global increase in aggregate consumption. In this manner, industrialized countries export their ecological footprints to support their affluence (Rees, 1999).

Fischer-Kowalski and Amann (2001) note how several industrial countries' (Austria, Japan, the Netherlands, Germany, the United Kingdom, and the United States) growth has increased, both in GDP as well as in direct material input (although less slowly than GDP). In other words, in all the countries studied, the material input did not grow proportionally with affluence; thus relative de-linking appears to have occurred during the time period investigated (1975–1995). They note that the "material intensity in terms of tons of material input per unit of GDP is declining" (Fischer-Kowalski & Amann, 2001, 18). They also observe, accordingly, "Nowhere, however, do we find a case of 'absolute delinking' in the sense of absolute reductions of material input occurring while the economy continues to grow" (Fischer-Kowalski & Amann, 2001, 18). These results thus far, however promising, fail to include domestic waste outflows. When these are considered, a similar result is obtained. That is, there is a decline in outflow intensity, yet an absolute increase in outflows. This makes a case for relative de-linking for the countries under study in the given time period, but it does not support absolute de-linking. Both relative de-linking and material productivity appear to be beneficial outcomes from the structural changes in these countries over the given time periods, but does not translate to the global level.

Overall, this effect should not be unexpected. As industrialized countries trend toward more value-added economies, they increasingly rely on extracted materials (often from nonindustrialized nations) as the inputs for more advanced manufacturing, services, and processes. For example, Giampietro and Mayumi (1998) conclude that the high rate of deforestation in Indonesia has been a direct consequence of the expansion of Japanese forests over the last twenty years. Similarly, it has been found that a microchip has substantial embedded energy and materials (Hilty & Ruddy, 2000; Williams, 2000; Williams, Ayres, & Heller, 2002). This phenomenon also reflects an important characteristic of globalization: the distancing and shading of local decisions and national policies can have profound global consequences. As value is added in each step of the production process, energy and material intensity increases, allowing lower mass with greater value. The provision of services is expected to follow a similar path. Eventually, at the consumer stage, the mass or energy consumption is lowest, but their embodied value is highest. This embedded energy and materials can be quite high. On this basis, the earlier findings that the majority of energy and materials consumption for a computer are consumed at the front end—the extraction, processing, and distribution of the unit—simply makes sense. The closer a product is to the extraction stage, the more materially and energetically intensive it becomes. Agriculture and mining, for example, will always be more intensive, directly, than the service sector. However, the "weight" of the latter is substantially greater when the embodied or "hidden" materials and energy are considered. A country more oriented toward a service economy or information economy will appear to have a very low material and energy intensity. This result will be consistent regardless of the standard of living, or material affluence, of the population (Fischer-Kowalski & Amann, 2001). Globalization effectively shrouds these effects.

Moreover, since 80 percent of the energy and materials consumption for a computer are absorbed during its manufacture, it simply does not seem plausible that incremental energy efficiency improvements are likely to offset the total energy and materials consumption of a product that has a remarkably short (three-year) anticipated life span. Likewise, other ICT devices offer similarly stunning results, such as the cellular telephone that has an even shorter expected life span of eighteen months, leading to the astonishing disposal rate of 426,000 cell phones per day in the United States alone, a partial testament to the probability that other factors drive the adoption of ICTs. In fact, as efficiencies increase, the energy and materials costs also tend to increase during the manufacture stages, as in the case of liquid crystal displays versus standard cathode ray tubes. Taken together, end use efficiency improvements simply pale in comparison to the increasing consumption advances in ICTs that are generated, especially during manufacture. Technological efficiency improvements generate a powerful consumption reducing illusion: embodied energy demonstrates that, despite the improved efficiency during the useful life of these technologies, consumption of energy and resources actually rises considerably as a result of those technological efficiency gains. Unfortunately, as we shall see shortly, the efficiency derived during the useful life of these technologies also turns out to be very deceptive.

As countries follow the path from subsistence to agriculture to extraction and mining to industrial to information economies, they are exporting and importing tremendous global debts of energy and materials to support the advancing economies and affluence.

The extraordinarily low and still-dropping level of per capita material input in the United Kingdom has been attributed to their cessation of raw-material extraction and their shift from industrial to service income (Schandl & Schulz, 2002). At the same time, Jackson and Marks (1999) note that consumption levels—and even intensities—have not necessarily been lowered as they increasingly satisfy their utility through imported commodities. "Such a scenario must automatically result in the reduction of domestic material intensity, since imported commodities contribute to Direct Material Input (DMI) by their weight at crossing the borders, leaving behind all the material loads (hidden flows) involved in producing them" (Fischer-Kowalski & Amann, 2001, 29).

This effect also has implications for more socially sustainable consumption. While Williams (2000) noted little evidence that the silicon production chain that supports ICTs had shifted to nonindustrialized countries, other industries that support ICTs may very well have. In particular, extractive primary industries can be simultaneously socially and environmentally disruptive and economically empowering. These are issues that need consideration as industrialized countries take a collective deep breath and congratulate themselves on achieving more productive economies. The expectation is that all countries may be able to accomplish the same result concurrently. That would be a dangerous extrapolation. Even more dangerous would be the anticipation that this form of development would necessarily usher in more socially sustainable development. While this in itself might appear to be wishful thinking, current political and global agreements and institutions place tremendous weight in these leaps of faith as witnessed by the limited flexibility built into global mechanisms such as the Kyoto Accord for greenhouse gas reductions. These are some of the issues that must not be dismissed in national-level assessments of economic intensity gains attributed to ICTs.

Clearly, between structural domestic economic changes and globalization, productivity has improved in some industrial countries at the expense of other countries, ultimately with global consequences. Managing these consequences and reducing their impacts will be very challenging since, as noted previously, local and national decisions can have profound implications globally—even when (sometimes especially when) those decisions are favorable toward local or regional environmental or health objectives. Global governance, improved global mechanisms and processes, and institutional changes are needed to confront this challenge.

MICRO- AND MACROANALYSES

As we have seen, efficiency improvements in some situations at the micro level clearly generate reduced consumption *at this level*. However, aggregating these reductions fails to account for many macroeconomic forces, even after factoring for any rebound effects (Herring, 1999). Consider, for instance, consumers priced out of a particular market until prices drop as a result of improved efficiency. The sum total of individual savings stimulates economic growth (the income effect), ultimately increasing consumption in the aggregate. "Overall, macroeconomic analysis leads to the conclusion that even if the economy is made more energy efficient the eventual outcome is for it to use more energy" (Herring, 1999, 222). This does not bode well for sustainable consumption given the previous discussion on embodied energy.

Mills observed the same occurrence in the United States over the last decade where the "consumption of electricity has risen by 650 billion kilowatt-hours . . . despite dramatic improvements in the efficiency of electric appliances, lights and motors" (2000, 3).

Indeed, Stanley Jevons argued in 1865 that "it is wholly a confusion of ideas to suppose that the economical use of fuel is equivalent to diminished consumption. The very contrary is the truth" (1866, 123). He identified that as coal consumption per ton of iron was reduced by one third, total consumption climbed by a factor of ten between 1830 and 1863. Also noted was the corresponding accelerated growth in coal-consuming industries derived from the reduced cost of iron.

Over a century later, Harry Saunders similarly concluded that "energy efficiency gains can increase energy consumption by two means: by making energy appear effectively cheaper than other inputs; and by increasing economic growth, which pulls up energy use" (Saunders, 1992, 139).

Moore's Law offers some insight and a practical example in this respect. This law states that electronics should be expected to dematerialize by a factor of four every three years. In fact, electronics have constantly become increasingly more efficient. Yet despite these gains, there has not been a corresponding reduction of the total energy and material flows generated by this sector. On the contrary, its share of energy and materials throughput consumption continues to increase, and its wastes pose significant environmental challenges worldwide.

It has been widely argued that the aggregate increase of resource throughput in recent years is precisely a consequence of efficiency improvements (Rees, 1995; Ropke, 1999). Cerf observes, "The Internet has a funny effect of increasing the amount of travel" (2000, 10). Similarly, Mark Mills notes how "faxing should have been expected to reduce the use of overnight mail; in fact overnight mail has grown" (Mills, 2000, 6).

The end result is that the embodied energy and materials of ICTs during manufacture rise as the efficiency of the final product does so.

The more efficient final product also generates macro, or structural, economic adjustments that also increase aggregate energy and materials consumption during its useful life stage. In both cases, as technological efficiencies are adopted, consumption of energy and materials, quite counterintuitively, rise, and this rise can be dramatic.

Despite this evidence, widespread belief—or perhaps political hope—that the service sector can contribute significantly to dematerialize the economy through this efficiency mechanism remains (James and Hopkinson, 2002). For example, goods transport can be organized and coordinated much more efficiently by applying ICTs (United Kingdom Department for Transport, 1999). An important question is whether the more efficient organization of economic activity derived through the application of ICTs will result in positive or negative net environmental effects (Ellger & Scheiner, 1997). Heiskanen and Jalas (2000) discuss why the efficient reorganization of the service sector may not lead to dematerialization. They identify four distinct classifications of services (nonmaterial services, result-oriented services, product-oriented services, and eco-design with a service approach). The nonmaterial services do not directly replace products. Instead they are new products that contribute to less material-intensive economic growth. Result-oriented services at least partially replace products or materials with information and labor inputs, providing customers with a specific result, rather than a specific product (e.g., energy-saving contracts). Product-oriented services (product take-back, rental, and management) offer consumers the use of the product (potentially accompanied by additional services) for a specified time, and thus may reduce the number of products needed. Finally, the eco-design approach focuses on designing new products based upon consumer needs. In this sense, eco-design services are understood as a flow of satisfaction derived from the use of durable goods.

Energy and materials consumption of the service sector is a function of the classification or type of service provided and its specific properties. Clearly, nonmaterial and eco-design services do not optimize or substitute for existing products or services. While result- and product-oriented services have the potential to reduce consumption, a large part of the service sector is necessary and integral to physical consumption.

In fact, Jespersen (1999) concludes that the service sector is no less energy-intensive than the manufacturing sector. This clearly contradicts conventional wisdom, which states that a switch away from manufacturing toward the service sector should reduce the consumption of, or otherwise dematerialize, the economy. Jespersen concurs with Krenz, who concludes that "variations in energy requirements per dollar value of goods and services are not very great, [and] total energy consumption is not critically dependent upon the mix of goods and services in the economy. A simple reordering of economic activities, for example a growth of the service sectors, would probably have only a minimal effect on total energy consumption" (Krenz, 1984, 474).

Herman Daly (1996) observes that the economy cannot continue to grow while being de-coupled from the physical environment. In effect, this would be equivalent to achieving x equal to zero or GDP approaching infinity in our previous equation. He notes that it is impossible to "save the 'growth forever' paradigm by dematerializing the economy, or 'decoupling' it from resources, or substituting information for resources. We can surely eat lower on the food chain, but we cannot eat recipes!" (Daly, 1996, 28). Ehrlich et al. agree with Daly when they assert that "people can't eat or drink services, information, or knowledge" (1999, 275). Despite the fact that there are numerous manufactured goods for which service-type substitutes simply do not exist (Cohen & Zysman, 1987), rarely a day passes in which yet another advocate of ICTs is lulled into the efficiency illusion. Including a marked increase in the "energy efficiency of its products and services, ICT's largest influence will be by enabling energy efficiencies in other sectors" with anticipated savings of significant carbon emissions (Global eSustainability Initiative, 2008, 10). Despite these reassuring assertions, efficiency as an end goal in itself will fail to achieve the results anticipated. "Nothing can be produced without labor and capital. But equally, nothing can be produced (not even information) without some transformation of natural materials, expenditure of energy (exergy) and production of entropy" (Ayres, Ayres, & Warr, 2003, 220). The expectation of substituting physical reality with efficient services indefinitely will encounter barriers. As the substitution process slows, so too will efficiency improvements (Cleveland, Kaufmann, & Stern, 2000). As explained by Cleveland, Kaufmann, & Stern, three primary factors that might limit future substitutions to higher quality energy exist. First, there are limits to the substitution process—at some point, only the highest-quality energy would remain available, preventing further substitutions. Although the discovery of a yet higher quality energy is possible, it would be unwise to rely on the discovery of new physical principles. Second, different energy sources are not perfect substitutes, and economic limits could prevent full substitution. For example, it would be difficult to imagine an airliner operating on electricity. Finally, it appears petroleum supplies have peaked in many oil-producing nations and are beginning to decline in some. Therefore, relying on efficiency improvements may generate serious future economic impacts.

Confusion between improvement in the efficient use of energy and materials with reductions in aggregate consumption of energy and materials and their social and environmental impacts portends a serious policy collision course where the need for more sustainable consumption will be in direct conflict with conventional interpretations of the benefits of efficiency improvements. At that point, weak sustainability will be confronted by strong sustainability (Gowdy, 1994). The ideological baggage of the term *sustainable development* will have to be dealt with one way or another, and we will be unable to postpone some inevitable decisions. The longer we wait, the fewer options we will have to deal with those struggles.

Although there has been a significant increase in energy efficiency, particularly since the mid-1970s, this has had, at best, a marginal effect on total energy consumption. Without these improvements, however, total consumption would likely have been greater, given all other factors remaining equal. Nevertheless, since demand continues to exceed the gains from efficiency, we must look elsewhere to understand the processes driving throughput consumption. Such an investigation forms an essential precursor to identify opportunities for ICTs to achieve the following two distinct, yet intricately related, goals: (1) to reduce aggregate throughput consumption, and (2) to avoid contributing to increased energy and materials consumption.

Noting the insufficiency of efficiency, Hilty et al. suggest that "a *quantitative restriction* is also needed on the input and output side" and will also be required to reduce aggregate consumption (2005, 123). They advise that "an efficiency strategy must always be accompanied by a sufficiency strategy; otherwise well-intended measures may have the reverse effect. This effect is known as the rebound effect."

The thinly shrouded veil of efficiency is even more starkly revealed by Heinonen, Jokinen, and Kaivo-oja, who note that the environmental benefits of ICTs should not be considered self-evident since ICTs "are constantly increasing the productivity of the economy of tangibles" from which the benefits "are mainly directed towards increasing total production" (2001, 322). They suggest that, as a result, aggregate consumption may increase more than is reduced through efficiencies. Despite the decreased consumption per unit, the key measure of aggregate consumption may increase due to the rebound effect.

Novek and Kampen (1992) studied the case of two proposed Canadian pulp and paper mill projects. They investigated the apparent contradiction between economic growth and environmental sustainability. They concluded that nonpolluting economic growth in the ICT sector is not supported. Indeed, they agree with others that the spread of ICTs are, above all, part of the commodification process, and that ICTs promote the consumption of products, such as paper.

Similarly, Heinonen, Jokinen, and Kaivo-oja (2001) observe that, "although ICT promises ecological benefits, in reality the 'information society' is still stuck with commodification processes" (2001, 320), citing the example of the paperless office. "Instead, as a response to the needs of information services, more sophisticated technology has made it ever easier to print out and copy more sheets of paper" (2001, 320). They also cite the example of printing reports and other materials derived from surfing the Internet.

Statistical evidence now supports the failure of the paperless office. Paper consumption in Canada between 1983 and 2003 more than doubled. Taking into account population changes, "per capita consumption increased by 93.6%" (Statistics Canada, 2006b, 7). The report notes that this trend is reflected in the United States and worldwide.

ICTs may be able to increase efficiency, and thereby accommodate more demand. However, when that demand continues to exceed supply (in an ecological context), the real issue is the demand, not the supply. Improved chip-manufacturing processes and lower product costs will have little effect on the excessiveness of the demand for chips. They may, in fact, inspire greater demand. ICTs applied in this manner could be dangerous, should there be no external motivation to ultimately reduce demand—sustainable consumption and efficiency are not the same. Sufficiency would serve sustainable development and sustainable consumption more appropriately than does efficiency

Efficiency (in place of more sustainable terms such as *sufficiency*) is only one metaphor that supports specific objectives of the prevailing social structure. Similarly, the inequitable distribution of wealth and power suggests, rather simplistically, that applying a process to raise living standards should solve distributional shortcomings. Quality of life (arguably the ultimate objective of human endeavor) and standard of living are not the same. Emphasizing living standards does, however, serve specific objectives of the prevailing social structure. The role of metaphors in society can apparently be powerful, and it is to the underlying assumptions of these that we now begin to shift our attention.

6

From Social Meanings to Global Conformity: ICTs and the Global Commons

In chapter 4, we introduced some of the various expectations and arguments for applying ICTs to help achieve more sustainable consumption. It seems painfully obvious that, despite these utopian visions, the slippery nature of human behavior introduced many complicated, unpredictable effects that radically alter the anticipated outcomes. Theory and reality are often clouded when the dynamics of systems that are poorly understood are assumed, such as human behavior or social processes. Emerging research results reveal some striking insights. This is where we now turn our attentions. In this chapter, we explore well beyond the life-cycle assessment, cradle-to-grave-to-cradle contributions of ICTs. Here we squeak open the expansive Pandora's Box ever so slightly to peer into the social dimensions of ICTs: their adoption and adaptations; forces driving and influencing their development; social processes, norms of behavior, and institutional arrangements that help determine how ICTs will be used; and, ultimately, implications for sustainable consumption.

Arguments about methodological issues and data quality and quantity aside, this chapter also intends to demonstrate why, in all likelihood, the impacts from ICTs are apt to far exceed those of any other industry. Imagination can be a powerful motivator. ICTs *can* interact with society in incredibly complex and unpredictable ways. Taking the lead from how they already are interacting with society, this chapter begins to reveal the potentially enormous implications of ICTs. These devices are being applied to supercharge the velocity of globalization, enabling information and communications at literally the speed of light. This chapter begins to explore how ICTs are affecting consumption activities. This leads into our later discussions about the possible consequences of these trends.

ENVIRONMENTAL IMPACTS OF ICTS

The impacts of ICTs can generally be categorized as (1) direct impacts resulting from their life-cycle use; and (2) the indirect (or systems) impacts resulting from the substitution, optimization, or complementarity they offer to existing products, services, and processes, and their creation of new products, services, and processes. These indirect impacts can be significant, conceptually challenging to understand, and methodologically complex to measure.

Technological Expectations

Both the increasing volume of ICTs (adopters) and their more diversified applications (adaptations) have significant implications for energy and materials consumption. The resource extraction and manufacturing of ICTs is not unlike most other extractive and manufacturing processes. As we have seen, these can be highly material- and energy-intensive activities (for example, see Williams, Ayres, & Heller, 2002). The total material inputs along the life cycle of a personal computer can be as large as sixteen to nineteen metric tons. As little as only 0.1 percent of these inputs is the resulting computer's mass (Hilty & Ruddy, 2000). Many elements of ICTs contain toxic materials, which all eventually end up in the waste stream and have recently come to public light (Aubrey, 2002; Bodeen, 2002; Canadian Broadcasting Corporation, 2002; Lazaroff, 2002; Tew, 2002). Shocking as these results are, should the story end here?

The Silicon Valley Toxics Coalition (2000) reports that a six-inch silicon wafer requires 8.6 m^3 of deionized water, 9 kg of hazardous chemicals, and 285 kWh of electricity. Similarly, the production of an eight-inch chip used for Pentium central processing units requires 11.44 m^3 of deionized water, 120.8 m^3 of bulk gases, 12 kg of chemicals, and produces 0.82 m^3 of hazardous gases, 14 m^3 of waste water, and 4 kg of hazardous waste. The ratio of manufacturing inputs to output calculated for a single DRAM chip is 800:1 (Williams, Ayres, & Heller, 2002; see also Anzovin, 1997). For comparison, the input-output ratio for a car is 2:1.

In the user stage, Frey and Harrison (2000) calculated a personal computer footprint close to 1,800 square meters, and a footprint energy consumption nearly 1,000 times as great for the remainder of the life cycle. The deployment of faster communications networks have contributed to the demand for computers to utilize faster speeds and stricter tolerances, contributing to an increase in energy and materials consumption (Kelly, 1999). Additional energy-intensive equipment, such as servers, amplifiers, routers, filters, storage devices, and communication lines compound consumption demands as the sizes of networks and numbers of users expand. Due to the very limited tolerance, server farms or data centers demand one hundred watts of power per square foot of building space (compared with an office tower at four to six watts per square foot). One such server farm, which is located in the Nevada desert and is labeled the world's densest, sucks an astounding "1,500 watts per square foot—almost eight times the industry standard" in order to house and safely store over seven thousand data storage units (Vance, 2008). However, utility planners estimate only forty to fifty watts per square foot based on a number of assumptions (Grahame & Kathan, 2001; Mitchell-Jackson, Koomey, Blazekc, & Nordman, 2002). The need for extremely reliable power supplies are a hallmark of this infrastructure and its components. Talk about an energy demand-supply collision course compelling server farmers to install massively overbuilt systems (Kawamoto et al., 2001; Grahame & Kathan, 2001). An improved utilization of power management features would clearly help (Kawamoto et al., 2001), despite the looming perception that this might serve only to construct a fence to stem the flow of a tsunami—a tsunami whose raw power is derived as much from factors such as "always-on" behavior as from technical engineering constructs.

In the waste stream, Goldberg (1998) estimates there are fourteen to twenty million computers scrapped each year; 10 to 15 percent of them are reused or recycled, 15 percent end up in landfill sites, and the remainder are stockpiled by users. In Canada alone, estimates from 2000 suggest approximately 34,000 tons of computers were disposed of, 16,000 tons were recycled, 25,000 tons were reused, and 6,000 tons were placed into storage. This estimate consists primarily of personal computers and monitors, quite a limited selection of ICTs. It excludes the vast array of new devices that have since entered the market, mainframe computers, large electronic equipment, and anything beyond the scope of computers, such as televisions, cellular telephones, and other ICT devices (EnvirosRIS, 2000). The end-of-life phase of a growing number of ICTs presages considerable impacts on the environment and human health. The toxic materials contained within ICTs are an increasing source of concern. Personal computers, for which the most data is available, not only occupy significant volumes in landfill sites, their toxic constituent parts also pose significant health risks. Personal computers are the largest source of heavy metals, toxic materials, and organic pollutants in municipal trash, superseded only by pesticides (Silicon Valley Toxics Coalition, 2000). Unfortunately, most ICTs are discarded and considered obsolete long before they cease to function, suggesting that social rather than technological forces are driving these trends.

Key to understanding the impacts of ICTs will be these social forces. The relentless pursuit of ICTs is spreading rapidly around the globe, characterized by these very rapid replacement rates, enticing new consumers, advancing niche markets, and enslaving seasoned consumers. New and innovative applications are constantly emerging, further stimulating their development, adoption, and, as we shall see, incorporation into social practices. These practices function to establish and reinforce social norms that further drive their acquisition and application (Ropke, 2001). These processes in turn tend to further stimulate their evolution. This is clearly evidenced as ICTs have materialized in virtually every sector (Plepys, 2002). Let us now turn our attention to these larger social forces.

Social Reorientation—Macro Level

Chapter 4 suggested many ways, beyond the expected, in which ICTs might be applied to affect energy and materials consumption. From that discussion, the following five categories of how ICTs may be expected to influence consumption activity can be identified:

1. Substitution	ICTs replace an existing product, process, or activity.	
2. Optimization	ICTs optimize the efficiency of an existing product, process, or activity.	
3. Induction	The application of ICTs induces the greater use of an existing product, process, or activity (old "extended" use).	
4. Supplementation	A new ICT product, service, or process supplements or complements (adds to or enhances the utility of) an existing product, service, or activity (new application).	
5. Creation	ICTs create a new niche or application for a new ICT product, service, or activity.	

The first two categories relate to direct expected effects from the adoption of ICTs and represent the primary pathways that ICTs can help achieve more sustainable consumption. Alternatively, the primary risks that ICTs may generate less sustainable consumption are through induction, supplementation, and creation. These effectively disaggregate the rebound effect, which is discussed in the following text. Furthermore, there is a multilayer level associated with rebound effects. These categories are commonly manifest as both direct and indirect, or systemic and structural, effects.

Substitution and Optimization

Theories concerning the environmental benefits of ICTs are typically based on two interrelated structural ideas. The first idea is that it is assumed that the production, transformation, and exchange of information will replace, or substitute for, the production of physical goods as the primary focus of economic activity: societal immaterialization. Structural economic change is assumed to lead to the reduction of the most polluting sectors of the economy, such as agriculture and manufacturing.

The second idea is that ICTs are assumed to promote pollution abatement and prevention through the efficient use of energy and materials. ICTs may lead to dematerialization through the optimization of processes and products. Clearly, as in substitution, there is a potential role for ICT.

Both of these ideas assume that environmental problems should decrease regardless of the level of economic growth.

ICTs make communications more efficient and allow faster and more flexible interaction among different agents, facilitating cost savings (Traxler & Luger, 2000). The result is that more businesses have greater and faster access to more diversified information than ever before. Real-time, better quality, and remote information distribution offers business tremendous opportunities to reduce costs, improve efficiencies, and enhance product and process quality. ICTs transform cheap inputs of energy with cheap inputs of information.

Induction, Supplementation, and Creation

Induction refers to the increased consumption or use of a product, process, or service induced by an ICT application. For example, a satellite dish resulting in an increased availability of content might induce increased television viewing.

Supplementation is the addition to an existing product, process, or service derived from an ICT application. For example, a printer or wireless technology would supplement a computer or Internet access, providing an outlet for their increased use. This differs from induction in that the ICT application represents new or additional consumption. With induction, use of an existing product, service, or process is increased.

It is important to note how the dynamic interaction between induction and supplementation may function to amplify consumption. For example, the availability of a printer supplementing a computer would also create increased consumption of paper. Thus, not only is consumption of the complements and their impacts created, but upstream and downstream effects are also added to the consumption process, thus amplifying overall consumption.

Finally, creation refers to the adoption of a new ICT application or a new application for an existing ICT product, process, or service for purposes both foreseen and unforseen (this latter effect is fundamental to the co-evolution of technology and society, and some processes by which it is derived are discussed in the following text).

As with induction and supplementation, complex dynamics might be expected to arise between all three of these processes (induction, supplementation, and creation), thereby offering numerous possibilities to dramatically amplify consumption. The challenge is to apply ICTs to maximize the benefits from substitution and optimization effects while minimizing the potential for induction and supplementation from these applications, and minimizing the creation of new applications where they are not a substitute for an existing application.

These latter three categories are fundamentally dependent on complex social processes, making them inherently challenging to predict. Conceptualizations, methodologies, and models to assess their effects are scarcely apparent in the literature. This suggests a gaping research deficiency and policy vacuum that urgently needs to be filled.

Ultimately, dependence on the substitution effect and its expected benefits reflects a fundamental misunderstanding of the importance of the co-evolution of technology and society. Initially, a new technology or variant is given meaning based on existing technological contexts. For example, the first cars were called "horseless carriages," and the early telephones were considered a specialized telegraph. ICTs often fill numerous roles, depending on their specific applications. For instance, data storage was initially considered a form of virtual or paperless storage. This result is to be expected, since all the properties, potentials, and new meanings of a new technology have yet to be fully discovered and realized. In the case of paperless storage, this would require a complete shift in social practices and expectations of indexing, reading, transforming, and communicating data processes. Ropke (2001) and Rip (1995) term this the *co-evolution of technology and society*, and Green (1992) has called it the *process of societal embedding of a new technology*. Learning and adapting processes occur as the new technology is developed, applications are discovered, and new meanings are attributed to it.

Geels and Smit (2000) identify that the expected benefits from the adoption of ICTs neglect the generation of new activities as a consequence of their introduction. This is attributed to the assumption that the introduction of ICTs is exogenous to existing social processes and needs. From such a perspective, it may seem logical to assume the substitution of certain social practices. For example, teleworking, telecommuting, telepresence, and video- and audioconferencing were expected to reduce transportation as the virtual option substituted for physical mobility. While some substitution effects are possible, increased social and recreational trips; the increased use of a "free" vehicle by other members of the family; the resulting increased travel distances (urban sprawl) when the need arises to attend meetings, be in the office, or attend social engagements; extended business relationships; and the social context of physical proximity may contribute to offset or exceed the anticipated reduced travel.

Future expectations from ICTs are also typically biased by conventional reductionist thought. For example, the substitution of physical shopping by ICT alternatives is largely based on the assumption that shopping is a purely functional activity of purchasing the required goods. That is, functional equivalence is assumed. *Functional equivalence* is the term given intensity improvements, such as those achieved through eco-efficiency or dematerialization, intended to maintain the output ("functional unit" or "service unit"), while reducing the physical input to the process of providing the output. Not only is this an imprecise term, which therefore makes it very difficult to compare alternatives, it is also misleading because it is assumed that different alternatives (such as e-commerce versus shopping in a mall or telework versus working in the office) are assumed to be comparable. Rather, the choices we make between alternatives is done so *precisely because they are different*, not functionally equivalent! It should be intuitively obvious that consumption serves many purposes that are not simply functional (Jackson, 2005; Jalas, 2002). These can be subjective and incredibly complex. Reductionist thought that simply treats consumption activity as a utilitarian objective neglects other, arguably more important, social and psychological, or human, factors. In the case of shopping, Sindhav and Balazs (1999) outline a number of other factors that suggest the continued relevance of traditional retail practices despite the growing prevalence of e-commerce. The social interaction of shopping and the cultural phenomenon of shopping are also key factors determining the importance of physical shopping (Cook, 1999).

Therefore, from a purely reductionist perspective, ICTs may appear very appealing, as they may promise to fulfill a certain function in a more efficient manner. The obvious questions should arise: just how does one socialize efficiently, and why would we want to substitute for an activity that confers benefits? By neglecting the complexity of social processes and their interactions with the natural and physical world, future expectations about the role of ICTs in achieving more sustainable consumption may be overly optimistic, simplistic, and dangerous.

While many decision makers seeking more sustainable consumption might have simplified, misunderstood, or neglected these processes, advertisers and marketers appear to have grasped at least some of these intricacies, manipulating consumption activity in the process. This knowledge has been used as a leverage to propel consumption according to fashions, styles, and trends. Branding and brand loyalty have enabled manufacturers to maintain a growing supply of willing consumers to discard perfectly functioning products and adequate activities in exchange for the latest and newest versions, styles, trends, and fads. Ironically, the public sector is increasingly adopting these strategies for similar purposes. More and more municipalities are undertaking to "brand" themselves and public buildings and services, presumably to attract global investment. Similarly, major infrastructure projects have been aligned with corporate advertisers to generate necessary investment. One cannot help but marvel at this stroke of genius. By the same token, one must question what is to become of these communities when brand loyalty dissolves or those municipal "consumers"—residents—discover the latest and newest versions of municipal brands. Will the municipal leopard simply change spots when it becomes convenient to do so? What manner of identity are these municipal initiatives generating by attempting to conveniently align themselves with global market imperatives?

Is economic growth the *raison d'être* for these forms of marketing? Many researchers have suggested an inherent social bias for economic growth and commodification (Ayres, 1995; Clark, 1995; Cogoy, 1999; Durning, 1992; Heinonen, Jokinen, & Kaivo-oja, 2001; Hoogendijk,

1993; Manno, 2000; Milbrath, 1995; Myers, 1995; Princen, 1999; Ropke, 1999, 2001). Are ICTs merely a tool to advance this bias? That ICTs offer considerable business advantages for growth suggests they are already being applied in this capacity. For example, Reijnders and Hoogeveen conclude "that as increased business efficiency that is characteristic for e-commerce in general leads to economic growth one should not be optimistic as to the overall environmental effects of e-commerce" (2001, 281). Hilty and Ruddy (2000) observe that it is unlikely that ICTs could ever fully substitute for the conventional practices, as there will always be some advantages and some disadvantages. It is more likely that ICTs will be applied as a new "layer" of human activity, building upon and supplementing existing activities and creating new ones.

These challenges and pathways are poorly understood in the sustainable consumption literature. Despite this limitation, advertising and marketing appear to effectively leverage these limitations. It serves no purpose from a sustainable consumption perspective to proclaim utopian visions based on the same reductionistic isolationism that plagues our limited understanding of the mechanisms and dynamics involved (Rattle & Kwiatkowski, 2003). Intervention toward more sustainable consumption must overcome these limitations, or more precisely, leverage them to transform powerful social biases.

THE REBOUND EFFECT

Originally identified in the energy sector, *the rebound effect* refers to an effective increase in the consumption of an energy service after its price decreases due to the higher efficiency of the production of the service. If technological progress makes certain equipment more energy or materials efficient, less energy or materials are needed to produce the same amount of products or services. As the cost per unit of production and operation falls, demand for that product or service may rise. Increased consumption in the aggregate may limit or surpass the gains made through efficiency. Ayres, Ayres, and Warr describe this "growth engine" as "a positive feedback loop involving declining costs of inputs and increasing demand for lower priced outputs, which then drives costs down further, thanks to economies of scale and learning effects" (Ayres, Ayres, & Warr, 2003, 219).

Greening, Greene, & Difiglio (2000) describe the process as follows: at the micro-level, direct rebound effects may be attributed to pure price effects. This results when increased energy or materials efficiency leads to a reduced price by decreasing the amount of energy or materials needed to produce a commodity. The decrease of price, if no other changes take place *(ceteris paribus)* will increase (induce) the demand for such a commodity, whether product or service.

In a complex system, however, demand may shift to other products and services. Thus the direct effects for consumers could be further decomposed into substitution and income effects. Clearly, a consumer will not continue increased use of the "price efficient" product or service indefinitely. Consequently, consumption may shift to other products and services (supplementation or creation). As the real income of consumers is increased, additional, or second-order consumption effects may emerge. The preceding effects (price effects and substitution and income effects) are micro-level effects.

As these results are scaled up, economy-wide effects may also appear, resulting from price and quantity readjustments across economic sectors in a nonstatic situation. This effect builds on the interrelationship of prices and outputs of goods and resources in different markets, which form a unique equilibrium state. The prices of commodities, such as energy, affect the price equilibriums of other commodities across many sectors of the economy. Energy price is a very important determinant of supply–demand equilibriums for essentially all products and services across the economy. As a product or process is made more efficient, its cost decreases. As secondary effects increase the demand for other products and services, their prices would be expected to increase. However, provided that the other commodities are highly energy-dependent, increased efficiency will reduce the production costs and therefore their final prices. The new market equilibrium will be a function of both factors.

Finally, transformational effects are a consequence of changes in consumer preferences, social norms and institutions, and the organization of production. These effects are the most obscure, abstract, and analytically challenging since both theory and empiric data are in their genesis.[1] Ultimately, these effects result from fundamental social forces.

---

[1] Until the twentieth century, man-made, rather than natural, capital was considered the limiting factor of productivity. Thus it was logical to identify ways to increase the former. It was not understood until the late twentieth century that the shift toward natural capital as the limiting factor had occurred—the need for sustainable development, or, at least, sustainable scale. Consequently, most economic theory identifies ways to increase man-made capital. Little research to understand how to increase natural capital, or sustainably decrease man-made capital—sustainable economic degrowth—within economic models has been conducted. Consequently, both theory and empiric data are embryonic.

Binswanger (2001) observes that there is both general agreement that the rebound effect exists, as well as disagreement about the degree of its influence. He contends that this disagreement results largely from the strong assumptions of the single-service model from which the rebound effect is derived. Studies based on this model neglect substitution and income effects, and can therefore be misleading. He also argues that efficiency increases can induce behavioral responses, which can *significantly further* increase energy and materials consumption. He also notes the strong time-savings effect derived from efficiencies of time (time-saving devices, such as faster modes of transport), which also tend to increase throughput consumption (such as correspondingly greater travel distances). Indeed, others, such as Ropke (2001), also observe this phenomenon, whereby energy and materials consumption can be stimulated to accommodate conflicting social demands, such as time constraints (see also Jalas, 2000, 2002). This effect can be particularly strong when high wages, representing the opportunity costs of time, encourage the increasing use of time-saving, consumption-intensive devices and activities. The irony is that, although—or, more accurately, since—households may invest significantly in time-savings appliances, time is actually not saved due to the "rebound with respect to time" effect (Jalas, 2002; Linder, 1970; see also Burch, 1995; Elgin, 1993; Schor, 1991, 1998 for very different perspectives on this phenomenon).

The adoption of ICTs has likely increased labor productivity and contributed to rising personal incomes (standard of living). While there has been no concomitant reduction in working hours (Rifkin, 1995; Schor, 1991), consumption must nevertheless increase at an ever greater rate to offset capital substitution for labor in the production process (Schnaiberg, 1980). Higher incomes and the time-saving effect of ICTs function to increase consumption. It is worthwhile to note that beyond a certain threshold level, there appears to be an inverse relationship between standard of living and quality of life (Max-Neef, 1995). It is also insightful to note the relevance of different approaches to this paradox by such authors as Hochschild (1997), Rechtschaffen, (1996), Dominguez and Robin (1992), Burch (1995), and Elgin (1993). Also of importance in this context are the observations of Schor (1998) and Rowbotham (1999) that people are consuming more and becoming bound by debt, and thus are compelled to work and contribute to the production process more than if not indebted. This debt-bound productive process further contributes to increased consumption and is extensively considered in chapter 8.

Social Reality

The rebound effect presents a paradox for national governments, particularly in advanced economy countries. Increased efficiency has led to both economic growth and at least the illusion of more sustainable development. Yet, simultaneously, energy and resources demand continues to increase. At a global level, beyond the jurisdiction of national governments, economic growth has exceeded the rapid dematerialization and gains in efficiency achieved in part by ICTs. This suggests that, in terms of sustainable consumption, efficiency gains may be insufficient and possibly deceptive. The role of long-neglected social processes, such as market forces and human behavior, in energy and materials consumption must now be confronted.

Hilty and Ruddy conclude "that technical progress in the direction of eco-efficiency or dematerialization is a necessary, but not a sufficient condition for approaching the goal of sustainability" (2000, 7). Similarly, Langhelle (2000) concludes that technological progress such as improved efficiency is a necessary, but insufficient, condition for sustainability. Sufficiency (Reisch, 2001) may instead be a more appropriate objective, which ventures a radical shift in values.

The beneficial transformational effects of ICTs are a function of their potential to improve efficiency through dematerialization, e-substitution, production optimization, and product efficiencies. These benefits will only be realized if they are accompanied by the necessary social changes (ASSIST, 2002; Commissioner of the Environment and Sustainable Development, 2001; Dürrenberger, Patzel, & Hartmann, 2001; Hesse, 2002; Hilty & Ruddy, 2000; Jokinen, Malaska, & Kaivo-oja, 1998; Matthews & Hendrickson, 2001; Matthews, Williams, Tagamic, & Hendrickson, 2002; Rees, 1995; Reisch, 2001; Ropke, 2001; Schauer, 2000; Simmons, 2001; Sui & Rejeski, 2002; Tulbure, 2002). This suggests that particular attention must be given to the social processes and institutions from which these needed changes will be derived. ICTs can perform a critical role in each of these objectives.

For example, the Internet offers, among other things, a set of powerful marketing tools with which conventional approaches cannot compete. It is able to target, direct, and guide specific consumers and consumer groups; affect perceptions and lifestyles; and tempt consumers into the trap of the "illusion of control" over consumption (Reisch, 2001). Yet the Internet might just as simply facilitate education and empowerment and promote more sustainable lifestyles, targeting, guiding, and directing more sustainable shifts. However, the latter is very unlikely to spontaneously emerge, and will therefore require significant investment and effort by (national and global) governments

(Greiner, Radermacher, & Rose, 1996; Heinonen, Jokinen, & Kaivo-oja, 2001; Malaska, 1997; Radermacher, 1996). Governments must pay particular attention to the social conditions from which the necessary changes will be derived.

These social conditions are profoundly woven throughout human–environment relationships, which are themselves characterized by complex, self-organizing systems—they exhibit thresholds, lags, discontinuities, and nonlinearities nested across temporal and spatial scales (Folke, Pritchard, Berkes, Colding, & Svedin, 1998). Objectivity of social phenomena is determined by the observer's perceptions—assumptions are based on the "facts" chosen. ICTs both derive from and help shape these conditions.

A new social reorientation as a condition for more sustainable consumption is to consider immaterialization as a function of lifestyle change and to shift from the individual orientation (substitution and optimization) "to a more aggregated approach based on an individual's patterns of consumption behavior and deriving from their perceptions of values—i.e., moving away from resources and towards lifestyle issues" (ASSIST, 2002, 8). As we shall see, this fits remarkably well with the social-determinants-of-health approach. Similarly, Plepys illustrates the complexity of environmental impacts derived from ICTs, and underscores the crucial "role of human behavior in determining their significance" (2002, 509). Geels and Smit state that a key recurring theme from the historical future expectations of the role of new technologies is "that expectations may be biased by the broader cultural concerns of the time" (2000, 877). Culture profoundly shapes the lens through which people perceive the future, which may also help "explain why certain future images gain widespread popularity."

Clearly, a technology itself does not determine how it will be applied. Technologies are never neutral. They reflect cultural values and biases (Milbrath, 1989, 232; Smyth, 1990). The societal and institutional dynamics that emerge from these biases and values are key to better understanding the social conditions within which ICTs coevolve.

SOCIAL PROCESSES OF CONSUMPTION

Identity formation is an important social process that helps shape consumption behavior—it helps define who we are and makes social statements about our values. In Western culture, identity formation is closely connected to materialism. It proceeds in ways that encourage increasing consumption of material artifacts, intensified further by the renewal process (Baudrillard, 1988; Klein, 2000; Penaloza, 2001). The artifacts we own tell of who we are and communicate complex messages with the rest of society.

This knowledge has been used effectively to increase consumption and enhance the consumer ethic. Advertising, marketing, branding, subtle messaging, and promotions have become effective tools used in a variety of combinations to elicit product and company loyalty and overcome consumption barriers. Corporate and government entities have used these tools, perhaps unknowingly, to modify behavior, institutions, and social mechanisms in support of greater consumption, profit growth, and economic growth. Consumers have both openly and unconsciously embraced these processes.

Through brand loyalty and other processes of commodification, innovation and craftsmanship have been significantly reduced. Since innovation and craftsmanship previously served important social functions, those functions soon needed new outlets. The growth process that has displaced traditional experiences has become highly creative, and, subsequently, a very important element of identity formation—perpetual consumption and renewal offers opportunities to contribute to this process (Ropke, 2001).

Domain conflicts, where contradictions occur as people shift domains, also represent another important social process that helps shape consumption behavior. Ropke (2001) has demonstrated how conflicts between family members might arise in their use of products, services, and space. Family members resolve these interfamily conflicts by providing for each others' needs for both personal and family engagement. Consumption growth is manifest through the increasing number and renewals of such products as televisions, compact disc players and stereos, telephones, computers, personal digital assistants, and so on. In addition, specialty uses might drive the acquisition of more than one type or style of product—such as a computer for home use, one for home-based business, and another for travel; or a separate cell phone for each member of the same family. Finally, as products become obsolete, they are replaced with newer varieties offering similar experiences (e.g., for computer information and data storage the computer cassette tape and tape player were replaced by the $5\frac{1}{4}$ floppy disk and disk drive; which were replaced by the $3\frac{1}{2}$ floppy disk and disk drive; which were subsequently replaced by the compact disc/DVD and CD/DVD player and the writable CD/DVD and read/write drives; which were eventually replaced by memory keys and USB ports and new internal and external hard drives and a gradual shift toward virtual, online document storage, manipulation, and retrieval from server farms). Simultaneously, new uses are being devised to extend, enhance, and improve convenience and flexibility, and better express, or associate, identity. (For example, the cassette tape replaced the vinyl album and record player and supplemented the compact disc and CD player; which was replaced by writable CDs and players; which gave way to MP3 players and digital music and the purchase, download, creation, and manipulation of music electronically and through the Internet.)

Cellular telephones offer an interesting case study. These devices have become smaller, more compact, and more versatile. Their list of functions has grown considerably. They can now produce photographs and movies. Product transitions have motivated a constant renewal of older technologies with newer versions. In many situations, the growing trend is simply to accommodate fashion and styles of cell phones. However, functionality is rapidly expanding, further driving new acquisitions. The ability to master and own the latest and newest functions and trends conveys important social signals to peers and others. Yet there is also a "pull" from the technology. As conventions and institutions change, so too must their tools of implementation. When upgrades and changes are made to any technology, older variants may no longer prove functional or practical.

This has serious implications for leapfrogging and reusing older technologies that, while fully functional, can no longer be supported by modernized networks and institutions. In addition, new options and conveniences further act to push the adoption of newer variants. There may be even more practical reasons that leapfrogging will be unable to deliver the astonishing results some posit. Given the remarkable increase in telephone calls, length of calls, telephone lines, calls per line and per capita, and time spent on the telephone, a certain amount of this usage must be attributed to modem use, which began to rise in the late 1980s. Yet as Internet access grows in new areas, much access will utilize conventional land-based telephone lines. While cell phones can displace land lines for voice and other communications, they cannot displace many of the other utilities or the social and institutional needs ascribed to land lines as readily. While there are options, they tend to add layers of technologies dependent upon previous technological layers. The sustainable objectives leapfrogging alleges to offer may simply be untenable.

These issues point to the important role social institutions perform. While individuals might select their preferred mode of access and tool—like their preferred consumer brand—this decision is heavily influenced by the institutional structures society has provided.

In addition, as the social infrastructures transform, so too must the tools applied for those infrastructures in many cases. The digitization of cellular technology or television signals comes to mind. Interestingly, these and similar shifts seek to access additional transmission capabilities and features that will contribute to and extend economic growth processes. This is further discussed in chapter 8.

Returning to domestic technologies, Ropke (2001) explains that once a new product or service has been acquired, the "consumer" must incorporate it into his or her lifestyle. Initially, this will require shifts in behavior, and eventually it becomes a part of routine. These shifts are viewed as inevitable and essential due to their social construction as a necessary "production" approach to accommodate the various family and social tensions, and to serve essential social roles such as identity formation. The product then becomes intricately woven into daily practices and therefore intrinsic to quality of life—severing the product and its associated activities would create a significant disruption, interference in conducting daily tasks, and even perceived hardship.

Finally, Ropke (2001) further identifies how complex relations between these products and services may both separate and unite family members (to satisfy both family cohesion and individual needs), reduce frictions, and satisfy domain conflicts. Clearly there are strong forces encouraging the adoption and replacement of ICTs. These social processes generate behaviors that may be extremely intractable as they manifest powerful family, consumer, and relational bonds, and social expectations and norms. Once widely adopted, they reflect and reinforce firmly established institutions and social protocols that are layered upon and integrated with previous successive levels.

Consider that during the last couple of decades, there have been dramatic increases in both the frequency of telephone calls as well as their length (Statistics Canada, 2006b). Substantial increases in the number of telephone lines also occurred between 1983 and 2003 in both Canada and the United States. Simultaneously, both the average number of calls per line and per capita *increased*. Time spent using the telephone also rose, tripling from 1.7 trillion minutes in 1980 to 5 trillion minutes in 2001 in the United States.

What is interesting is the magnitude of spending and willingness to spend on these services and technologies. Household spending patterns have demonstrated significant growth in the percentage of expenditures going to ICTs. Both absolute spending on and the proportion of household expenditure directed at ICTs has increased. The degree of social ICTs infusion is most remarkable in that the absolute expenditures by households on ICTs rose during a period when prices for ICT products and services tumbled. Given their present ubiquitous nature, these ICTs may serve some utilitarian purposes, but it is astounding just how much utility we happily survived without for millennia prior to the arrival of ICTs. Clearly ICTs serve many other social purposes.

Increased usage does not necessarily mean the derived utility from a process or product has simultaneously increased. Consumption can serve many purposes, and social processes and institutions often can drive consumption without regard to utility. The gradual shift to electronic bill payment and banking, for instance, establishes numerous barriers to conventional financial transactions and simultaneously motivates continuous upgrading. This trend functions to increase spending on ICTs simply to maintain a previous level of utility. Consider also the increasing use of the Internet to supply (supplement) previously printed information. Despite the potential financial and environmental savings (which are questionable since many hardcopy versions are prepared, maintained, and distributed too), the choice to print the electronically provided information is expanded to a far greater (global) audience. In an ever expanding number of situations, costs (environmental and economic) are simply downloaded from corporate and institutional entities to global citizens and the global environment. They become commodified and linked to a system that continuously reinvents and upgrades itself. Indeed, this hypothesis may be supported by the fact that lower income groups seem to be dedicating a greater proportion of household expenditures to ICTs than do higher income households—they appear to be driven to maintain pace with the technology, despite the (albeit declining) maintenance of many earlier patterns of provision. This suggests a minimum level of ICT use is now being driven by newly created and emerging social processes and institutional arrangements. While "companies [may] have little direct impact on the natural environment, as is the case with banks or insurance companies, their indirect influence (e.g., on logistics, shopping habits, lifestyles) may be substantial" (Fichter, 2003, 36). These effects may be amplified by the degree of control over the production chain the company exerts, and its integration with various social processes. As accessibility, flexibility, and conveniences are afforded newer products and activities, their older variants rust and seize. New meanings ascribed to the new products and activities help propel the renewal and consumption process. While the proportion of spending is greater for lower income households, the time impoverishment might be much greater. As ICTs usage increases, much less time can be directed at other activities. However, for a lower income household, more time must be devoted to earn the marginal income necessary in order to acquire and maintain the ICT products and services. On the other hand, greater debt loads may simply represent the alternative to more time working, higher incomes, or overall increased consumer spending.

In a global world, these trends know no boundaries. Consider the mountain farmers in Laos and Myanmar, or the Nigerian who purchased the one billionth cell phone. Transforming these complex driving forces and social relations to accommodate more sustainable consumption won't be easy. Dramatic changes to some fundamental values and social processes nested across geographies increasingly embedded into cultural understandings and practices will be required.

As modern social life has become fractured, people participate in society under varied roles—domestic, labor force, leisure, consumer, and so on. People have differing roles in different places and at different times (Ropke, 2001). Expressed values in one role may not even translate into another role or be consistent across roles. Accordingly, consumption activity in one role may exhibit anomalous results if shifted between social contexts. Similarly, domain divisions imply that people might often experience domain conflicts. Emerging global social forces support the institutionalization of consumption practices to resolve these conflicts. In other words, markets, now global in nature, have displaced traditional institutions used to supply our essential material artifacts and needs. A good example is the purchase of labor-saving devices (Warde, Shove, & Southerton, 1998; see also Binswanger, 2001; Jalas, 2000). Consider the use of the cellular telephone and portable computer. These products promise to optimize time by packaging activities and lifestyles as densely as possible, making them convenient, versatile, increasingly accessible, and applicable to such needs as resolving domain conflicts. These processes establish global social transformations, in this case to densely package as much as possible into a given time and place, and apply new commodified consumption to resolve conflicts.

Alternatively, it is important to note how Rechtschaffen (1996), Burch (1995), and Elgin (1993), for instance, recommend a "slowing down" and less tangible or less commodified approach to enhance quality of life. Various similar "slow" movements have expressed concern about the fast pace of the commodified, tightly packaged global world, advocating instead recapturing the intent and dreams of specified social engagement. These approaches focus on broad determinants to satisfy welfare and sustainable development goals, particularly reduced consumption or demand approaches that center on their social nature. Slowing down or emphasizing quality of life curiously contradicts the more conventional approaches—approaches that apply production techniques to meet rising demand (Manno, 2000; Warde, Shove, & Southerton, 1998). One might even argue these new approaches and movements advocate more with less.

META-LEVEL IMPACT

Ropke (2001) demonstrated that the behavior of adopting new domestic technologies forms an integral part of several dynamic forces behind increased consumption and accelerating rates of consumption. These activities can counteract the environmental improvements from those technologies. The pervasive renewal process renders older products obsolete (nonfunctional), and feedback processes stimulate new production. The social and value conflicts generating the pervasive renewal processes rippling through global economic systems evident at the domestic consumer level can also be identified at the business and sectoral levels.

By adopting advanced manufacturing technologies—such as ICTs—in response to competitive market forces, businesses exhibit similar renewal processes intended to improve efficiencies. Faster product cycles presage new product variants and faster product obsolescence (Sonntag, 2000), justified on the basis of increased product volumes and reduced price per unit (Traxler & Luger, 2000). Traxler and Luger cite MacKie-Mason and Varian, who state, "This outcome constitutes an economic mechanism toward expanded use of networks like the Internet" (Traxler & Luger, 2000, 288). This resonates with broad social and market trends toward increasing demand, and accommodating that demand through increased efficiency.

Such strategies create the dilemma of technological equipment cost recovery—without the increased product volumes—over reduced product and process lifetimes. Thus the faster cycle times and speed to market assumes strong market growth. To justify investments in these technologies necessary for economic growth and competitive success, companies must realize immediate sales growth (Agility Forum, 1997).

The economic rationale underlying increased product diversification and market fragmentation—accelerated product cycles generating new product variants and more rapid obsolescence linked with consumer desires—counteracts the problems of market saturation and over-capacity. The inevitable result, as Schnaiberg notes, is not only increasing consumption, but an ever increasing *rate* of consumption.

Novek and Kampen (1992) conclude that the information society model fails to provide a panacea for nonpolluting, nondepleting growth in the industrial world. They specifically note the predictions of a paperless information society and stress that this is representative of a technocentric ideology. The information society requires paper products at increasing rates, pressuring pulp and paper industries to increase their production.

Many of these social processes and institutions have become fundamentally dependent on consumption activity (Sanne, 2002). Institutional and policy mechanisms have evolved to accommodate these social processes. Legal, educational, social, and other frameworks have been established to globally unleash these forces worldwide and minimize the capacity of states to restrict access to markets (Manno, 2000; McMurtry, 1998; Rowbotham, 1999).

WHAT WENT WRONG?

Geels and Smit suggest that many technological shortcomings are a function of several factors, most notably the "performative role of expectations and future images in technological development" (Geels & Smit, 2000, 879). In this sense, expectations function as an intervention to affect the direction and speed of technological developments. Due to the risks of developing new technologies and their initially low performance characteristics, they are unable to immediately compete on the market. Development therefore requires advocates to establish specific "niches" in order to further develop the application. These niches consist of networks of actors such as funding organizations and technology developers. The groups share common beliefs in the future value of the technology and invest significant resources in further developments. Future expectations represent generalizations of the technologies' potential. This is intended to influence the relevant actors, such as policy makers or scientists, to invest resources in the technologies' development and establish a process of political and technological agenda setting. By obscuring the social factors that may take these developments in unexpected and unintended directions, decision makers can easily be persuaded. As specific goals can be established, resources become available to achieve those targets. Outcomes are assessed and new, more specific goals are established. This cycle may be repeated many times. Geels and Smit (2000) conclude that as this process continues, optimistic expectations are shifted toward more pragmatic expectations. This is not too dissimilar to what is now being discovered in the application of ICTs. Initially, optimistic expectations function as a strategic activity to attract the needed actors (financial) to stimulate the agenda setting process (technical and political) and establish niches.

Ayres (1998, 2001, 2002) has argued that energy and materials consumption function within the economy as much as a driver of growth as a consequence of growth. This growth mechanism, or growth engine, is a feedback process. Declining costs lead to declining prices, which drive increased consumption. This in turn triggers investments in new capacity (resulting in increased economies of scale) or research and development aimed at cutting production costs. "Learning by doing" also increases production efficiency. All three of these phenomena push costs down and complete the cycle. "The falling costs per performance unit increased the cost–utility ratio and made computers more valuable to substitute for other commodities as well as increased their use in new applications. The effect is increased energy and material consumption in ICT hardware in total" (Plepys, 2002, 513).

Economic forces are primarily responsible for driving the development and adoption of ICTs, and these forces clearly do not consider their sustainability (Heinonen, Jokinen, & Kaivo-oja, 2001). The initial, and creatively essential, phase of the development of ICTs neglects environmental considerations. In this phase, innovations are technologically and market driven (Arnfalk, 2002; Garrison, 2000; Nuij, 2002). There currently exists general agreement that the majority of economic development is not ecologically sustainable (Daly, 1996; Ekins, 1996; Kaivo-oja, Luukkanen, & Malaska, 2001).

Ropke (1999) and Nuij (2002) stress that the ultimate objective of product development is to increase sales, and they are not, in general, motivated to achieve more sustainable consumption. Profits can easily be generated within this global value structure by targeting lifestyle aspirations, dreams, and fantasies. All one need do is to buy the dream, despite the product's generally complete failure to satisfy those dreams (Simmons & Leevers, 2001). Little doubt remains that the heroic efforts by industrialized nations to sow the seeds of these dreams across virtually all cultures in order to support this growth imperative have succeeded. How has this affected those peoples and cultures who, until recently, have not participated in the processes of economic expansionism?

GLOBAL HEGEMONY OR CULTURAL GENOCIDE?

Through the physical transformation of their lands, many Aboriginal peoples, sometimes through their own participation in formal wage economies, are now discovering that their previous traditional practices have become increasingly difficult, if not impossible, to sustain. Many cultures have discovered it to be exceedingly difficult to elect out of the formal global economic system. "The end result is a form of cultural genocide" (Manno, 2000, 364).

In addition to their lands being degraded, sometimes, but not always by their own participation in the "commodity economy," global market forces present serious challenges to traditional economies. The long-range transport of pollutants, climate change, ozone depletion and loss of biological diversity, intrusion of "development" into subsistence lands, and arbitrary reshaping of political boundaries have extended the reach of global consumption activity to every corner of the planet. This has had a profound impact on the way of life of traditional peoples. Novek and Kampen (1992) cite the conflicting relationship between economic growth and sustainable development. They argue that the distancing and shading of consumption from resource harvesting conceals the distributional and ecological impacts. As a consequence, the environmental and social effects of resource extraction are unevenly distributed. They argue that the inclusion of foreign industry in the competition for a limited resource base threatens the traditional activities of Aboriginal populations.

Alienation of traditional lands endures through the sanctioned licensing by national governments of major resource exploitation projects. Confronted by these global economic forces and coerced to frame the problems in the context of dependency reduction, Aboriginal communities pursue new and creative resource tenure and governance structures. This new context exploits Aboriginal populations as much as their environments by framing the questions to reflect issues of territorial and resource ownership and to identify the most efficient regimes and authorities to develop them (Scott, 2004). These arrangements for resource tenure and governance constitute a form of cultural genocide, imperialism, or colonialism in which concepts such as ownership and land tenure completely transform traditional cultures, understandings, and beliefs. A similar phenomenon occurred when Canadian and U.S. residential schools removed Aboriginal children from their communities and exposed them to alien and harsh experiences. Whether resource exploitation, global economic forces, forced territorial, land tenure or ownership discourse, or residential schools, the resulting effect has been to replace dramatic disruptive cultural transformations with a form of increasingly subtle, pervasive metamorphosis that is no less culturally disruptive.

Should we be surprised when different peoples forced to live to-gether within arbitrarily defined political borders, themselves shaped by global political events, become violent? The fact that many of these cultures were stripped of their most visionary and healthy members during colonial, imperial, and slave trade eras is deplorable. That their resources, livelihoods, and spiritual lands and ecosystems were plun-dered and reshaped in the name of development, and continue to be so, is outrageous. The fact that they were and continue to be exploited by development ideologies is tragic.

These effects are fundamentally a result of our increasingly less sustainable consumption trajectories and their globalization. A basic understanding and application of how different cultures exist and how different cultures might coexist so as to cultivate varied social frame-works and inspire naturally resilient and diverse societies is urgently needed.

ICTs continue to play a central role in these trajectories. For example, in an attempt to counterbalance censorship, open source software is widely adopted and spread to nations where repressive re-gimes manipulate information and communications. In some cases, this censorship has been adopted to protect cultural beliefs. In many cases it represents simple power and control ideologies. But one re-ally needs to ask, "Where is censorship being applied, who is doing the censoring, and, ultimately, what ideologies are being protected?" Is it the nation that censors the exploits of one hedonistic economic globalization approach the one invoking censorship? Or is it the na-tions that conceal and overtly repress thousands of distinct cultural ways of knowing within a single global monopolistic cultural ideol-ogy that has been elevated to the status of religious dogma, and is zealously defended as "too big to fail"? What about the nations that bring—often by military intervention—a flood of global economic information to a fledgling country subsisting on long-held beliefs and customs?

Despite the many different cultural ways to satisfy human well-being, these are rapidly disappearing through the processes of global-ization (Erdal & Whiten, 1996; Goehring, 1993; Maybury-Lewis, 1992; Rowbotham, 1999). Their wisdom offers vital opportunities to help achieve more sustainable consumption. Sustainable consumption will require that this disappearance—in effect, the loss of socialization of different values and social practices—be prevented. However, extreme caution must be taken in doing so: we must avoid the impulse to sim-ply disaggregate and disassemble distinctive cultural practices. The context—ecosystems, social structures, worldviews—within which they have co-evolved must not be dislodged (Clark, 1989; Erdal & Whiten, 1996; Goehring, 1993; Maybury-Lewis, 1992).

The role of ICTs can be simultaneously empowering and constraining. There are countless examples of how ICTs can and do empower low- and middle-income countries and traditional cultures and communities. Yet the adoption of ICTs demand a particular set of social processes, institutional arrangements, understandings, and experiences. Absent of any experience with ICTs, there is likely no appropriate social context. On the one hand, this can avoid a nasty encounter with old values and the need for change. Conversely, the context within which to introduce the ICTs would need to be created. "In both situations, new rules will have to be learnt and accepted" (Davison, Vogel, Harris, & Jones, 2000, 5). They can transform the user if these needs are culturally different from their own. The application of ICTs to empower and learn from other cultures manifests a tangible likelihood that they may draw these peoples into the consumer society with all its cultural baggage: consumer and producer lock in to materialistic growth processes and structured inequality.

How should this profound predicament be resolved in the case of introducing a leapfrogging technology, for example? Leapfrogging assumes the value of technological rationalization and economic growth. This may not necessarily be shared by the culture it is being introduced into. How confident can we be that this change is necessarily appropriate and sustainable? What are the implications of uniformly redirecting a chorus of cultures: in effect, creating a set of globally conforming cultural values, institutional structures, and social norms—a new global worldview within which only minor aberrations are permitted?

Nor should we tolerate intimidation that squarely situates this trajectory on the path to dissecting, cataloguing, and displaying cultures as museum relics. Consider the case of traditional ecological knowledge (TEK). To satisfy the uncompromising laws of capital in search of ever more scarce resources to feed the growth of global development models, TEK serves as a convenient tool in the "development" process to placate "underdeveloped" nations and indigenous communities. Sustainable development under these models dictates that TEK conform to existing ideals of globalization. "Surviving the way Indigenous people have for thousands of years is not given serious consideration. . . . TEK research and implementation in support of sustainable development is arguably another form of colonialism. . . . We have been down that road before!" (McGregor, 2004, para. 9). ICTs perform a firmly established role in the development processes and the use of TEK. These processes can all too readily be applied to further the historical transformations indigenous peoples endured through guns and cannons in the past.

Consider the residential schools program in Canada. The program, which predated Canadian Confederation, included a variety of schools in all except one province, and was intended to separate and isolate Aboriginal children from their cultures and train them for assimilation into a Western market economy. The Royal Commission on Aboriginal Peoples framed it as an ambitious yet tragic program to assimilate First Nations, Métis, and Inuit cultures. Initiated in 1849, the program eventually included both boarding schools and industrial schools to train children to function in the wage economy. Lessons were taught exclusively in English (except in some schools in Quebec where they were taught in French) and students were subjected to influences that would "effect a change in [their] views and habits of life" (Royal Commission on Aboriginal Peoples, 1996, 58). In part motivated by economic and commercial natural resource interests seeking to secure agricultural and industrial profits through expansionary settlement, the program attempted to remove the indigenous barrier that "inhabited and claimed title to vast stretches of land."

Compare this to the act of surfing Internet websites: "Although communications technologies permit the cross-fertilization of ideas, they are currently dominated by the English language and by American perspectives around them" (O'Meara, 2000, 141). Since the majority of information is English, different ways of perceiving and understanding the world are being lost and transformed. Phrases, words, and concepts do not always readily translate into different languages. McGregor (2004), for example, explains that the concept of sustainable development is alien to the indigenous worldview—in a manner of speaking, it *is* the indigenous worldview. To identify a corresponding term or even a similar meaning requires the reconstruction—the distortion—of indigenous knowledge in different ways so as to make the process itself somehow boorish, offensive, and profane. "Coercive processes that force Native people to think and operate in non-Native terms frequently result in loss of meaning" (McGregor, 2004, "From an Indigenous Perspective," para. 4). Activities as "simple" as surfing the Internet, using a cell phone, or watching television may create, or necessitate, a whole new set of meanings. It will, as Ropke has demonstrated, establish new and transform existing domestic, social, and cultural practices. Beyond the horizon of language differences, consider the extensive constellation of social artifacts and institutions supplementing ICTs that will also be rising on this final chapter of culturally diverse landscapes—reorganized spaces, displaced practices, altered relations, and new norms and expectations of behavior. For better or for worse, from need or from necessity, globalization has ushered in a new set of tools and practices that have rendered traditional activities obsolete.

Compelling one culture to function like another can lead to a form of cultural homogenization. Should everyone adopt the same belief structures, war and conflict might be crippled—so too would our resiliency and creativity to overcome future hurdles. If Hamilton (2007) and Monbiot (2006) are even remotely accurate, these future hurdles—such as climate change—will not be solved through the application of the Internet. "By giving the illusion of individual power to desk-bound revolutionaries, the internet has in fact only hastened the erosion of real democratic participation" (Hamilton, 2007, 12). A seemingly innocuous suggestion to apply ICTs to learn from other cultures becomes a potential weapon to further colonialism and hamper our future resiliency and creativity—to effectively discard a cultural evolution of options. This is not to suggest traditional knowledge is not being applied. That is not the case. TEK is being applied—to foster less sustainable consumption by splicing cultural adaptations onto conventional development practices. How might we fashion our tools to avoid this dilemma?

Global economic growth and increased material wealth enable an increasing number of people to have access to global communications technologies and media. This transition appears to enhance social processes that contribute to unsustainable consumption. Therefore, ironically, instead of educating high-consuming societies about the benefits of more sustainable worldviews, the converse may be occurring—ICTs may function as a medium to draw low-consuming societies into the world of high-consuming practices, and inspire global aspirations for the consumer ethic.

Many very populous countries have until recently exhibited relatively low ecological footprints (Wackernagel & Rees, 1996). If the social processes we are exporting through ICTs do in fact contribute significantly to generating high-consumption behaviors, the potential level of consumption from these countries should be taken very seriously. A small increase in growth by a very populous country such as China or India would be and, indeed, has been equivalent to an enormous leap in growth levels in a comparably low-population country. At the same time, the extended social norms, behaviors, lifestyles, and institutions would be that much more pervasive and entrenched—and historic options will have been lost. The approaching tidal wave of consumption could be disastrous. Certainly we—as a species—are intelligent enough to envision, discover, or recover ways to enable a high quality of life with a low footprint.

SUMMARY AND DISCUSSION

The velocity and momentum of globalization help define prevailing social processes—principle factors defining how ICTs can be applied. Conventional applications of ICTs may implicitly embody the very social processes responsible for over-consuming lifestyles and activities. The social and cultural determinants of ICTs are critical elements defining their ability to contribute to more sustainable consumption. Efficiency gains from ICTs may simply be overwhelmed by the sheer volume of products and services made available, and the social transformations adopted by a growing population. Ultimately, the benefits from ICTs depend on people and social choices, factors much more difficult to predict than the energy demands of Internet servers, material demands of factories, or pollution from cars. "In the end, people matter, and when we leave people out, our technological aspirations often fall prey to the mundane forces that shape our everyday lives" (Sui & Rejeski, 2002, 160).

A key feature in the development of ICTs is neglect of their societal roles. Identifying the needed preconditions for the intended functioning of the application is inherently unpredictable, and, beyond increased sales, rarely the intent. Clearly, this is a critical omission resulting in an overestimation of associated benefits, and underestimation of possible deviations. There is justifiable cause to not treat all new ICTs as "an indisputable good, as is often done, for instance, when the new information technologies are discussed, and when public policies are decided upon in this field" (Ropke, 2001, 420).

We are still missing an important piece of the puzzle: what are the forces shaping these social processes, and is there a role for ICTs here as well?

Considering aggregate energy and materials throughput globally, we continue to move in the wrong direction. Continuing to assault both natural ecosystems and human health in the process, potentially including our long-term survival, is certainly unproductive. Technological and production efficiencies have not succeeded in reducing the scale of the global human economy. Classical economic growth clearly has not reduced inequalities. Perhaps it is time to consider the framework from which these tools have been derived. We need to explore the forces shaping our social processes and institutional structures. What is ultimately guiding behavior and lifestyle choices?

Before we address this question, the following chapter considers an approach that might help our analysis.

7

Pathological Tendencies:
The Health Link

POPULATION HEALTH AND THE SOCIAL DETERMINANTS OF HEALTH

It could well be argued that any activity people engage in is motivated by a fundamental desire to improve their quality of life and well-being. This has three important implications. The first is that human well-being is a basic goal that connects people, societies, cultures, and understandings—the human environment—across space and time and with the natural environment. Connecting this concept with sustainable consumption implies that the latter does not then simply reflect an environmental "tree hugger, nature lover" phenomenon that is easily dismissed or criticized. This approach can avoid the simplistic philosophic debate over nature's "value." The second implication is that, if we are to pursue this line of reasoning and use it to set objectives and direct policies and activity, we need a reasonably accurate description of well-being and quality of life. This chapter intends to link well-being with health, and argue that this forms an essential basis for understanding and directing consumption activity—population health has intrinsic value and importance to sustainable consumption as well as the converse. The final implication, which actually follows from the second, is that the health sector has already considered many issues of sustainable consumption, although not in that context nor even necessarily recognizing the linkages. Despite substantial social, economic, and global forces that often function at odds with public-health objectives, health promotion and disease prevention have achieved remarkable success in the last century. Moreover, such success contributes to global health, both human and ecosystem, and it is from this perspective that sustainable consumption might gain new and meaningful insights.

In no way should a health approach be interpreted to criticize the philosophical debate—it simply seems likely that this form of rational thought is more apt to convince decision makers than are philosophical debates, which very much hinge on values. Nevertheless, for this very reason, this approach does hold certain limitations, precisely because a "rational" debate also hinges on values. However, hopefully these are the values that those with the greatest social planetary power and influence—the rational ideology—retain. It is also limited in that behavior is rarely motivated by rationality, despite the globally prevailing fictitious precepts much of conventional economics are fabricated upon.

Health is more than the absence of disease—the biomedical or epidemiological perspective. In fact, health care facilities, while an essential part of ensuring healthy populations, function as an end-of-pipe intervention. Disease treatment facilities such as hospitals investigate, diagnose, manage, and treat the outcomes of diseased states. They house tools and facilities that can be used to respond to and intervene in normally perceived departures from health.

The World Health Organization (WHO) defines health as "a state of complete physical, mental and social well-being and not merely the absence of disease or infirmity" (WHO, 1967). This includes "the extent to which an individual or group is able, on the one hand to realize aspirations and to satisfy needs, and on the other to change or cope with the environment" (WHO, 1984).

The Lalonde report observes that "the organized health care system can do little more than serve as a catchment net for the victims" of environmental and behavioral threats to health (Lalonde, 1974, 5). Following this report, development of a determinant of health model began to take shape. Today, it is widely recognized that there are numerous determinants that affect the health of populations. These include relative income and socioeconomic status, education, employment and working conditions, social support networks, health practices and coping skills, healthy child development, culture, gender, physical environment, biology and genetic endowment, and medical services. To most, it might come as quite a surprise to see almost any of these determinants, with the possible exception of the last. In reality, the last, while important to mitigate the effects of poor health (not causes)—sickness care—is an ineffective level at which to promote health and prevent disease. The first eight determinants are what we shall call the *social determinants of health*, while the last three are the *physical determinants*. While the urge might be to consider each determinant in isolation, in reality there are complex synergies between them all, and no one determinant functions in isolation.

For example, evidence suggests that relative income and socioeconomic status are significant health determinants—people are progressively healthier the higher they are on the income scale. This seems counterintuitive in countries that provide universal or virtually equal access to health care. As wealth distribution becomes more equitable, the population becomes healthier, regardless of the amount spent on health care.

Studies also consistently identify a social gradient apparent in health status. What is important about these studies is the obvious social meaning, expectations, and desires associated with material affluence rather than the absolute level of material affluence. It "seems unlikely that comfortable 'middle class' people in Britain are suffering from the effects of material deprivation" (Marmot & Mustard, 1994, 203). Yet as is consistently and dramatically illustrated in studies such as the Whitehall and Whitehall II studies, each social stratum exhibits improved levels of health as job seniority increases and control over employment and income conditions improve (see, for example, Marmot, Davey Smith, Stansfeld, Patel, North, & Head [1991] or the Whitehall II study website at www.ucl.ac.uk/white hallII/). Simply put, "[A]n individual's 'free choice' and all lifestyle decisions are influenced by the socioeconomic environment" (Canadian Public Health Association, 1997, 5). While greater education may improve employment opportunities, income, and job security and satisfaction, and enhance knowledge and skills for problem solving, educational opportunities vary within and between socioeconomic status. Similarly, social participation and work experiences can enhance health status. Unemployed individuals may experience increased psychological distress, anxiety, and other health problems. Stressful jobs and unsafe working conditions—which may be influenced by educational and socioeconomic factors—may increase health problems. Volunteer, community, and other forms of social participation develop social networks, skills, and relations, and these too may be affected by other social experiences and opportunities. Social support networks, healthy lifestyle and behavior choices, and early life experiences all contribute coping, management, and problem solving skills, and help improve resilience, yet are all highly affected by other social, economic, and cultural conditions and opportunities.

AN EXPANDED VISION OF SUSTAINABLE CONSUMPTION

One might expect sustainable consumption to be largely about the natural environment and the implications from human activity on ecosystems and the environment, or the impacts on population health derived from epidemiological factors. Taking a more comprehensive approach by applying a determinants-of-health approach within an ecosystem health framework, the natural environment only represents one element of a multidimensional interactive framework. Ultimately, philosophical debates aside, human activity seeks to improve human well-being and quality of life. By situating the discourse of sustainable consumption in a population-health approach, the consequences of and for human activity can be more clearly articulated. A sustainable consumption approach based on these properties reveals how sustainable consumption is as much about the human, social, and cultural consequences of consumption activity as it is about physical consumption and the interactions between the human and natural environments. This also interfaces quite effectively with globalization, linking physical geographics across different cultures and social activities, transgressing conventional conceptualizations of space and time.

SOCIAL DETERMINANTS OF HEALTH AND SOCIAL FACTORS DETERMINING HEALTH: CRITICAL ISSUES DEFINING BEHAVIOR AND THE HEALTH GRADIENT

The human dimensions of global change are critical elements of human and ecological driving forces and their impacts. Social forces are responsible for establishing the institutions and structures that facilitate human activity. In turn, this activity has consequences for both the human and natural environments.

Health experts have now recognized the pivotal role of the social determinants of health. The confluence of social theory and population and public health models identifies some very interesting bonds between health and sustainable consumption. Jackson (2005) describes various viewpoints of the role of consumption. These include consumption as well-being, as a social pathologic condition, as an evolutionary adaptation, as industrial "lock-in," and as symbolism.

The simplified view that consumption represents well-being and that increasing material affluence correlates with improved well-being is altogether idealistic and simplistic. This view was based largely on the neoclassical model of *Homo economicus*. In a society where wealth is heterogeneously distributed and growth both an implicit and explicit objective, relative material affluence becomes an important determinant of population health (Soskolne & Bertollini, 1999).

For instance, child poverty in Canada during the late 1990s was close to 15 percent. On the other hand, Denmark experienced a child poverty rate of just over 2 percent during the same period. Yet, based on measures of gross domestic product (GDP), Canada is a wealthier nation (Raphael, 2007). How could a wealthier nation come to have higher levels of child poverty than a poorer nation? Higher levels of wealth as measured by poverty levels do not necessarily lead to improved population health. Clearly wealth distribution and scale are important determinants of health.

It should not be surprising, then, that so many people have begun to question the role of consumption—materialism, the consumer ethic—in well-being. Equating well-being with consumption, and in fact increasing levels of consumption to satisfy our supposedly insatiable wants, lends itself to policy and practice with a focus on efficiently allocating resources with little regard for scale and distributive concerns. In this way, the emphasis is on market function—ensuring market efficiency, incorporating costs in prices (internalizing external costs), ensuring the provision of information to consumers—and employing measures of success such as the GDP. Evidence supporting a positive causal relationship between well-being and material consumption beyond certain "threshold" levels is limited. Despite the limited evidence and rationale, economic growth has been widely invoked to guide development—raise the tide and all ships benefit. The obvious failure of such policies (United Nations, 2005) suggests neither more sustainable consumption nor improved population health can be achieved simply by turning to conventional economic theories and market-driven practices that merely encourage increasing levels of material affluence.

The social framework within which the determinants of health function can be, and often is, an extremely powerful motivational and behavior-shaping force. While this social framework will be further explored in the following chapter, there are certain more general features that can be considered here. First, health determinants do not simply shape an individual's health status. Since populations are more than aggregations of individuals, health determinants also include the patterns and trends experienced by the exposures and outcomes of groupings of people. Thus "the determinants of individual differences regarding some characteristic within a population may be different from the determinants of differences between populations" (WHO,

2005, 5). This interpretation raises some fascinating questions and provocative possibilities. How are individual causes of health outcomes related to the causes of incidence within populations? What are the underlying causes of the health gradient—the relationship between socioeconomic status and health status that affects people regardless of their socioeconomic position? How does this gradient shift across time and vary between cultures? What are the roles of consumption activities—changes in material affluence—for population health (and well-being), and how do these roles vary between different individuals and populations?

SMOKE AND MIRRORS

We know that knowledge weakly correlates with behavior change. Health information simply does not elicit the necessary behavior change for improved population health in many situations. Let's briefly consider tobacco consumption. Informing smokers of the risks associated with tobacco consumption does not necessarily motivate a smoker to quit or to seek opportunities to quit. Many other social factors override informational messages. In the case of tobacco, this might include the significant time lag between tobacco consumption and disease onset; the social meanings attributed to tobacco consumption, such as identity formation and associations; marketing, advertising, promotion, and normalization efforts of the tobacco industry; and others.

Identity formation in the tobacco industry has been used as an effective tool to increase the consumption of tobacco globally (Amos, Gray, Currie, & Elton, 1997; Choi, Ahluwalia, Harris, & Okuyemi, 2002; Dalton, Tickle, Sargent, Beach, & Aherns, 2002; MacFadyen, Amos, Hastings, & Parkes, 2003; McCool, Cameron, & Petrie, 2001; McCool, Cameron, & Petrie, 2003; Pucci & Siegel, 1999; Saffer & Chaloupka, 2000). For example, Lynch and Bonnie observe, "Tobacco use is a learned and socially mediated behavior. Experimenting with tobacco is attractive to children and youth because of associations they learn to make between tobacco use and the kind of social identity they wish to establish" (1994, 71). Identity formation, through branding and group associations, for example, have been effectively used to market tobacco products to all demographics.

By employing concepts in their youth campaigns such as "smoking is an adult choice or decision," and neglecting any mention of the health consequences or the addictive nature of nicotine, tobacco companies have effectively promoted smoking. These mandated yet ineffective campaigns (from a health policy perspective!) actually function to encourage youth to smoke by linking an image of authority and freedom to the smoking decision. Simultaneously, by launching marketing campaigns intended to appear responsible, tobacco companies have been portrayed as the "good corporate citizen." Notice the health and corporate outcomes are diametrical opposites—what is beneficial for population health is harmful to tobacco corporations and vice versa.

In the tobacco industry, brand advertisements focus on particular identity formations. They apply such images, words, and phrases as *individualistic, independent, self-assured, lifestyle, confident, secure, successful,* and *femininity.* Note the similarity to conventional marketing metaphors, linking independence with individualism, security, and visions of success, for example. Even the use of terms such as *health conscious* and *full flavor* is common practice. The application of globalization as an opportunity to market an "international" or "American" image has also been widely employed. Many of these phrases are strategically intended to appeal to youth worldwide.

Interventions to reduce tobacco consumption—and its health consequences—have been pitted against powerful social forces. Tobacco consumption reduction activities have had to move toward denormalizing the activity of tobacco consumption—a far, far greater challenge than simply conveying information or economic incentives for reducing tobacco consumption, particularly given the fact that large transnational corporate interests consistently act to increase the normalization of the activity in order to enhance profits. Denormalization requires the political acceptability of widespread institutional changes—no-smoking areas, spaces, or buildings; legal changes; transformed social preferences; and so on.

More than simply the unrelenting assault of powerful transnational corporations, tobacco reduction advocates have been and continue to be confronted with the persistence of the entire marketing and advertising industry, and, perhaps, even the incessant tidal wave of global capitalism. Tobacco corporations, some of the largest players in globalization, also wield significant economic clout, a fact low- and middle-income countries (LMICs) are beginning to encounter in the global war on tobacco. These and other social meanings and determinants influence in tremendously complex ways the consumption of tobacco, as they do other consumption activities, and therefore population health. The social framework, norms and practices, institutional arrangements, and values and expectations within which (tobacco) consumption occurs form complex social health–determining mechanisms.

Let's expand upon this for a moment by way of revisiting the social processes we discussed previously. The corporate image of the tobacco industry has been a strategic policy of tobacco companies. The Pan American Health Organization observes that the tobacco industry "developed plans aimed at improving its corporate image by making itself an integral part of the communities in which it operated" (2002, 23). This effort included community development programs, contact with government officials and the media, donations to universities, scholarships, educational sponsorships, and donations to government ministries. The document also notes these same strategies are applied globally. At the same time, the tobacco industry also appeared to be acutely aware of its image in its campaigns and activities. It is noted in Tobacco Documents Online that "we are presented with a dilemma in developing markets where the total market is growing and advertising expenditure is rising accordingly. How can we reconcile this?" (1989, 1).

As part of their public relations efforts, the tobacco industry included activities to "fund healthy community pilot programs with municipal authorities, which include smoking cessation seminars" (Pan American Health Organization [PAHO], 2002, 25). Not only was the corporate image bolstered by this approach, the activity itself, by focusing on an intervention at the individual level, would have minimal effect. In doing so, the tobacco industry was able to ineffectively (again, from a health policy perspective!) address the problem of smoking, and, moreover, bolster its image, thereby potentially increasing tobacco consumption. In effect, similar "smoking cessation funding" activities by the tobacco industry function to *increase* tobacco consumption—they become an effective strategy to leverage promotional (media) funding.

The tobacco industry has been intensely sensitive to trends in the social acceptability of tobacco consumption. The tobacco industry has stated, "'It is our opinion that the single most important issue facing our industry is the erosion of social acceptability of smoking. . . . In the absence of a well-coordinated international campaign, we feel that this is an inevitable trend which will lead to continued assaults on the industry—and the smoker—in the twin areas of taxation and public smoking'" (PAHO, 2002, 50). Industry programs to counter youth smoking effectively guarded against eroding the public image of tobacco companies while preventing meaningful regulation of tobacco promotion. "The rationale is that, if the industry is already trying to discourage youth from smoking (albeit through weak and ineffective campaigns), there is less reason for governments to develop their own, and typically stronger programs" (PAHO, 2002, 62). Campaigns strategically manipulate threats of marketing restrictions, social acceptability, corporate image, and branding and marketing to capture, maintain, and expand markets. They create, express, dispense, and reinforce social behavior to serve the interests of profit.

The shameless application of tobacco tactics has become increasingly obvious in the climate change debate, among others. Controversies about the existence of human-induced—anthropogenic—climate change have only very recently begun to yield to the more repressive obstruction by certain global actors: assuring the public that "things are under control," statements to suggest "climate change is everyone's individual responsibility," funding for carbon offset and other guilt-assuaging schemes, and rampant unfounded technological optimism. This dangerous game perpetrated by capital interests represents a potent social paralysis (Union of Concerned Scientists, 2007). While there exists a kernel of truth to these techniques, the social message tends to confound the necessary action, as demonstrated in the tobacco war. Despite the important roles for individuals, the key technologies already available, and the good policies in existence, many important factors lie beyond the control of individuals that affect how, where, when, and what actions will and can be taken. Moreover, these techniques seem to suggest that these are the limits of actions that need to be taken. Like the social determinants of health, there are social determinants of environmental responsibility and of our consumption choices and activities. Recycling programs, modes of travel, reasons for travel, energy consumption—indeed, most of our daily behavior—are all socially mediated, generally well beyond the control of individuals. The same social factors that determine our health are also important factors determining our level of environmental responsibility and participation. Just as health care, schools, community centers, social resources, jobs and working conditions, and income supplements affect our health, many socially defined structures affect our consumption decisions. While there are many things we can each do for the environment, unless the social mechanisms, networks, institutions, and norms of practices exist, they simply will not occur. Jobs or capital markets couldn't even exist without the social agreements, institutions, regulations, and mechanisms, and technologies that make them possible. Nothing functions in a vacuum, and neither do our environmental actions as individuals or society. Like the ecosystems we depend upon for survival and the social determinants of health, factors largely beyond the control of individuals (and if Benjamin Barber,

Chris Hedges, and others are correct, moving increasingly beyond the perceptual acuity of most individuals) determine our consumption decisions.

Global market interests boast an impressive arsenal of tools geared toward nothing less than expanding markets—chemical and pesticides, pharmaceuticals, resources, and fossil fuel industries all employ these tools. These interests are merely doing as the market dictates. Why should the ICT sector be any different? The reduction of tobacco consumption is, at its very nucleus, fundamentally antithetical to "free" market expansion. Naturally one would expect this to be challenged despite the rational arguments in its favor. Why has this approach not translated—as has the application of tobacco tactics to expand global market penetration—to many other unsustainable consumer goods, services, and activities? Despite the continuing tobacco battle, progress has been made reducing tobacco consumption within certain limits.

SHAPING SOCIAL BEHAVIOR

Margaret Mead has observed,

> Human nature is almost unbelievably malleable, responding accurately and contrastingly to contrasting cultural conditions. The differences between individuals who are members of different cultures, like the differences between individuals within a culture, are almost entirely to be laid to differences in conditioning, especially during early childhood, and the form of this conditioning is culturally determined. (1963, 280)

Similarly, the social framework of global market-based capitalism compels people, institutions, and society to behave in particular ways, and forms incentives for those behaviors and barriers to others. Historical developments, existing infrastructures, legal and regulatory mechanisms, political structures, educational institutions, and other factors well beyond the reach of individual decisions shape the social framework within which people must make daily consumption and health decisions. These factors can guide and restrict individual agency considerably—they hide some choices, promote others, and simplify significant segments of individual day-to-day decisions. As Raphael (2002) notes, factors outside personal control are largely responsible for determining health status.

An individual may choose to smoke, but that choice is profoundly influenced by the individual's social environment, over which he or she has little choice. At the level of everyday consumer decisions, "the ordinary consumer will have little or no control over most of this decision architecture" (Jackson, 2005, 29). Our free choice is not as free or objective as we might think, and this has profound implications for population health and sustainable consumption. Individualism, as just one of many "values" inherent in our prevailing social structure can, apparently, contribute powerful messages and motivational incentives for social choice.

The role of governments is viewed as active interventions in disease diagnosis, treatment, and management, rather than active interventions in promoting healthy behaviors and their supporting social policies. In policies, programs, and strategies that span the full spectrum of government roles and responsibilities, except for a tremendously limited set, healthy living is assigned little active intervention.[1] This often leads to conflicting government policies, such as regressive fiscal prudence and tax policies disproportionately affecting lower socioeconomic incomes, simultaneously undermining population health and the financial and resource bases needed to support disease treatment. Fundamentally, governmental intervention in the health-impeding social structures that prevail is nonexistent. Policy conflicts are, or at least should be, widely apparent when the needs of existing social arrangements and institutional structures collide with health objectives. An example is the promotion of national tobacco industry interests for trade purposes by the same governments explicitly intending to reduce national tobacco consumption (Ontario Trade and Investment Mission to China, 2005). Similarly, many governments are scrambling to attract medical professionals to accommodate ballooning national disease burdens and health care demands. In so doing, at each step on the international wealth ladder, governments are enticing medical professionals from lower income countries. Some of the poorest nations are investing disproportionate amounts of resources to train critically needed medical professionals, simply to see them drawn away by wealthier nations by the promise of better working conditions and more modern medical equipment. This globalization of labor disproportionately harms the poorest. At the same time, these very governments pay lip service to the exploited countries in the form of development aid, up to 80 percent of which never leaves their national borders. The list of contradictions is lengthy.

---

[1] I say *active* because through both action and inaction, societal decisions influence specific values and social processes, institutional arrangements and lifestyles that are regularly intervened upon and promoted or concealed as the case may be.

While a sad testament to the conflicting values expressed by many governments, this example is also illustrative of the powerful motivational forces many sustainable consumption activities must now confront. One need look no further than the events of September 11, 2001, and the ensuing plea by the U.S. administration to spend for the sake of the economy. Similarly, in 2009, following the rapid and continued decline in global stock markets, the swift and consistent infusion of funding of unprecedented magnitude by all governments worldwide was intended to "stimulate" the economy—facilitate and expand the money supply, loans, and lending; motivate consumer spending; and encourage business growth to "get the economy growing" again. With more than a staggering $7 trillion (Jackson, 2009), governments around the world implored global actors to get credit flowing; to float, underwrite, and sustain unsustainable investments for short-term expediency in a deeply regressive effort to buoy our growth-addicted society. The capacity of these forces to compromise and undermine ecological and social sustainability and decision-making architectures is why they are both so dangerous and incredibly attractive.

Moreover, any decision to allocate scant resources to ICTs in the development process requires either the redistribution of limited resources or the identification of alternative resources. Canada and the United States have a combined 2005 GDP of $15 trillion, and spent a combined $700 billion on software and services in 2005. Yet a meager $40 billion per year would be needed to achieve the first seven Millennium Development Goals—which falls far short of the almost $700 billion spent on software and services by commercial and government interests in 2005 alone. Leapfrogging, for example, might offer a tremendous opportunity, if appropriately developed, to avoid some of the resource-intensive and socially disruptive earlier stages of technological development. Redirected resources can also provide an advanced base for health services, functioning to keep nationally trained health care professionals or draw international professionals. On the other hand, this process reinforces complex social and cultural changes, issues we previously discussed. It also foreshadows a critical entry point to the compromising future investments and resource allocations demanded by this specific development path.

These health and development examples are seen in most consumption activities. Blaming victims of illness and placing the role of disease prevention on the individual is consistent with the prevailing social framework that promotes a particular set of values. The emphasis on the individual means that society and social policies have no role in guiding behavior. Behavior is a genetic predisposition. This is biological determinism, an approach certain dictatorial leaders have employed through history to wrest control of national agendas. It has been thoroughly discredited, yet lingers on in policy circles. However, as should be evident, social policies, both implicit and explicit—both active interventions and passive complicity—have a tremendous influence on behavior.

Since health inequities emerge from social stratification (WHO, 2005), the social stratification "serves the interests of the established and powerful" (Raphael, 2002, 57) and permits illness to be defined as an individual lifestyle choice. This means that government attentions can be diverted from policies and actions that support population health because it is assumed there is no role for institutional frameworks and social organizations to support population health if it is an individual responsibility. Besides, what government agency in their fractured reductionistic manner would be foolish enough to consider it part of their mandate to confront and transform an entire social structure?

GLOBALIZATION, ICTS, AND THE SOCIAL ENVIRONMENT OF POPULATION HEALTH

Globalization affects social networks, connections, and flows as well as infrastructures, institutions and power structures, stratification, and modes of interaction. The World Health Organization's Commission on the Social Determinants of Health (CSDH) notes that "the most relevant aspects of globalization for the work of the CSDH are: market access, trade barriers and liberalization, integration of production of goods, commercialization and privatization of public services, and consumption and lifestyle patterns" (WHO, 2005, 25). The consequences for population health from globalization are unquestionably important. What is the role of ICTs in this nexus?

In a largely market-oriented society, one in which the velocity of globalization has intensified, public policy has increasingly important roles, from the individual to the population level, to cultivate health-enhancing social environments. As we have seen, health policy and improved population health is much more than medical care facilities and disease interventions. ICTs, insofar as they reflect and reinforce social values, reinforce the individual aspect of health, and, as we have seen, this can be problematic.

New advances in technologies and genetic engineering are both exciting and important as they hold promise to better understand and treat specific diseases. Yet, "however important *individual* genetic susceptibilities to disease may be, the common causes of the ill health that affects *populations* are environmental: they come and go far more quickly than the slow pace of genetic change because they reflect the changes in the way we live" (Wilkinson & Marmot, 2003, 7). In fact, environmental factors, rather than the advance of new medical technologies, are largely responsible for improved life expectancy and population health over the last century. It explains why some countries have improved their health and others have not; why, as socioeconomic conditions change, so do health differences between different socioeconomic groups.

Another risk of the genetic (individual) approach, is the growing emphasis on the diagnosis, management, and treatment of disease. "The 'technological fix' ideology reaffirms the unfortunate belief that 'human survival is independent of nature'" (Soskolne & Bertollini, 1999, iii). The role of medical technologies, including ICTs, is clear here, and in this way they serve an important role in advancing the prevailing social framework.

Medical technologies and an emphasis on the biomedical or epidemiological nature of health are more than simply the application of a *technofix*. They represent an important transformation along the nexus of market ideals toward commodification. Manno observes, "Diagnostic equipment to support a physician's observational skills *(products)* are highly developed while the observational skills themselves *(processes)* grow increasingly and comparatively underdeveloped" (2000, 360). Value has been clearly situated on the physical, tangible, marketable product. Similarly, Rees observes, "For the first time in human history, it seems necessary for some to put a price on the biophysical structures and functions that make higher life possible on Earth. Until now, the essentials to life have been free" (Rees, 1998, 49). The assumption is that if nature or technology can be commodified, its contribution to human well-being is better understood and may be more efficiently exercised. Like the smoke and mirrors used by the tobacco industry, this assumption can be controlled and manipulated by vested interests. Manno also observes that this obsession to "value" social activity and processes systematically seeks to select goods and services with high-commodity potential "over noncommodity, noncommercial, means of satisfying human needs and aspirations" (Manno, 2000, 351).

Paradoxical, given the diverse determinants of health (Federal, Provincial, Territorial Advisory Committee on Population Health, 1994) and the social determinants themselves, is the emphasis on high-commodity-potential products readily evident in the health care sector. High-commodity products such as pharmaceuticals and genetic engineering, hospital and health care supplies and equipment, vaccines, diagnostic equipment, vitamins and herbs, health books and magazines, exercise equipment, and the emerging field of eHealth are consistently privileged. A much reduced emphasis is given to health processes and skills with low commodity potential such as disease prevention, health maintenance education, therapy, doctor-patient interactions, exercise and outdoor play, personal hygiene and sanitation, and counseling. Despite the lip service afforded these latter, the institutional structures that benefit commodification dominate. Underlying social values make it very difficult to encourage the absence of something, such as in disease prevention, particularly when disease can be quantified through treatment products and measured through accounting techniques such as the GDP. Applications of ICTs, such as telehealth and telemedicine, provide an outlet to contribute to such measures of progress. ICTs benefit measures of well-being, such as the GDP, despite—or in fact because of—their greater expenditure of resources.

Global health expenditure growth largely reflects our increasing resource expenditures to diagnose, manage, and treat the symptoms of diseases and diseased states. People continue to become ill from entirely preventable causes. Is this a good trend? We consider this a positive contribution to the economy simply because our accounting mechanisms treat all costs as positive contributions to the economy. Ultimately, if these undesirable costs in society were subtracted from the GDP as expenses (which more accurately describes their economic role), our national and global ledgers would look very different (Coleman, 2004).

HEALTH AND SUSTAINABLE CONSUMPTION

Electronic health records and health information can help ensure accountability, and they can provide greater access to health information and relevant health knowledge. This can empower patients with "a more active role in maintaining their health and making decisions about their medical care" (Romanow, 2002, 77). The emphasis in this model clearly remains on the individual and commodification, diagnosis, treatment, and management. Telehealth systems can ensure greater access to health and medical help in remote areas of the world. Records management and eHealth can effectively help manage drugs and equipment, so supplies are available where they are needed when they are needed. ICTs offer new and effective ways to manage the disease burden in both industrialized countries and LMICs.

However, the consumption effects from new technologies, particularly those not specifically intended to achieve more sustainable consumption, remain largely unknown. ICTs in any sector will cause fundamental changes in the way people work and interact; the institutions and mechanisms for service delivery; and the structures, processes, and decisions made. This is no different in the health sector. Health care workers have experienced difficulty maintaining pace with changing technologies. Cultural and sociospatial differences have raised concerns for telehealth applications and their efficacy (Heaton, Kishchuk, & Picot, 2004). Serious social, legal, and ethical concerns have also been raised. The costs of many eHealth applications and programs can be substantial, diverting tremendous human, financial, environmental, and other resources (Balka, 2003; Peddle, 2004). Finally, the assessment of new health technologies has been problematic and ineffective, and assessment resources have often been disproportionate to the developments themselves (Romanow, 2002).

The impacts of this trend are most starkly evident by contrasting the values of Aboriginal communities with those of the social institutions that evolved ICTs and generated many of the diseases they seek to treat in the first place. In one approach to diagnose diabetes, individual Aboriginal community members are isolated and subjected to noninvasive tests that enable health practitioners, both locally and in distant locations, to evaluate the data. A mobile van—packed with ICTs—serves as the focal point for screening and educating the individual about diabetes (Health Canada, 2003).

Diverting attention away from the source of community health problems, this approach arguably contributes to further reinforce the health problems within the transforming social tapestry. Successes are cited as increased screening, treatment, and awareness of diabetes, and increased sickness care. Other successes are cited as more employment and training—subtly shifting the cultural fabric toward wage income, precisely that to which traditional (health-enhancing) cultural practices are falling prey (although not as overtly, abruptly, and forcefully as with historic colonialism). The capacity for private profit and capital growth through eHealth reflects the commodification of health care. Is it possible to retain, promote, or enhance cultural identity, language, and lifestyles under such unrelenting and subtle persuasion?

If ICTs can be used to bring such awareness to individual disease, why can they not be used to bring similar awareness to the social fabric that generated these diseases, and to the social changes necessary for disease prevention?

The diversion of resources, in particular, is perplexing, if not disturbing. While it is reasonably well understood that more equitable societies experience healthier populations, we continue to see a shift of wealth from social to private hands. Tax reductions have been substantial in many countries, particularly those of the Organisation for Economic Co-operation and Development, yet funding for health research (indeed, for all social services) to better understand and improve the mechanisms by which equality promotes health and prevents disease, has been trivial in comparison (Labonte, Schrecker, Sanders, & Meuss, 2004).

Global institutions and transnational corporations perform key roles in these trends. Rodrik administers a scathing lashing to the free market assumptions afforded the World Trade Organization (WTO), claiming the WTO is an organization "'that enables countries to bargain about market access'" (Rodrik, 2001, 34). The process actually sacrifices consumer welfare through hegemonic negotiations forced upon competing labor interests by export-driven transnational corporations. The purported beneficiaries (consumers) of free trade are unrepresented in negotiations. The structure of these global institutions are simply inconsistent with more sustainable consumption.

While the societal and population health benefits of ICTs may remain mixed, arguments persist favoring jobs and economic growth. In the latter, there seems to be little supporting evidence that such an approach is either sustainable or healthy. In the former, jobs and increased income can benefit population health, although relative income is a much more important measure of population health. Yet we must reexamine the values and institutions of a society that necessitates the "creation" of work coincident with the advance of technologies intended to reduce work. This is particularly salient in cultural settings where traditional lifestyles are essential for healthy communities and populations. Their disappearance and decline have been documented, accompanied by dramatic reductions in well-being, where wage economies have supplanted and diseases of affluence have undermined entire communities. The division of labor is critical to social stratification and to power and wealth relationships in society. Technological displacement of labor has been proceeding since the division of labor. Why should we expect this process to suddenly and spontaneously atrophy?

ICTs applied in the health sector tend to emphasize the biomedical and individual concepts of health (sickness care, management, diagnosis, and treatment). ICTs are invoking a continuously accelerating rate of change. This will lead to behavior shifts, suggesting that human behaviors will be critical variables in future health outcomes (Jones et al., 2005).

During the nineteenth and early twentieth centuries dramatic gains in life expectancy were widely attributed to improved nutrition and sanitation. Samuel Epstein (1998) notes the institutional focus on diagnosis, treatment, and management of cancer. Epstein's observations are remarkably similar to those of Jack Manno (2000): both have identified the increasing reliance on productive approaches to mitigate and treat the effects of human activity. Epstein questions the political underpinning of this approach. He asserts that cancer is the result of "involuntary and avoidable exposures to industrial carcinogens in air, water, the workplace, and consumer products" (1998, 511). Despite the evidence to support his claims, large cancer institutions and organizations "remain narrowly fixated on damage control—diagnosis and treatment—and on basic molecular research, with relative indifference to, if not always benign neglect of, prevention" (1998, 511). The "cancer establishment," as Epstein calls it, has sunk untold resources into the detection and treatment of cancer while virtually ignoring the prevention of cancer. Annual lotteries now divert millions of dollars to disease research and treatment, despite the knowledge of the effect prevention could have. Moreover, these lotteries contribute in not-so-subtle ways to condone consumerism—the very activities that often generate or contribute to the causes of those diseases in the first place! The optics of a cure is much more apparent than that of prevention—people can visualize, diagnose, measure, monitor, and profit from someone who gets better—and the material contribution (especially to wealth measures such as GDP and balances of trade) is perhaps a powerful motivational force for their adoption. Someone who does not become ill is very difficult to visualize, monitor, measure, and profit from. Market ideals perniciously misdirect prevention, and therefore have a vested interest in diagnosis, treatment, and management of disease, and maintaining the onset and continuance, if not outright expansion of, diseased states (see, for example, Moynihan & Cassels, 2005). Despite the excellent and tireless work of so many people and organizations, we have become fundamentally dependent upon expanding disease and unhealthy populations. The depth and pervasiveness of this condition will become more obvious in the following chapter. Maintaining diseased states is clearly not in the interests of population health. It also contributes to enormous increases in resource consumption, which also does not seem to benefit health.

Nuij (2002) provided the basis of the barriers to more sustainable ICT design (omission during design, organizational complexity and stake-holder participation, investment and marketing, and user needs). The failure to incorporate these features into the design phase of ICTs not only confines their contribution to sustainable consumption, but also limits, or perhaps misdirects, their application to population health. Balka (2003) similarly observes that the design and implementation of health ICTs does not consider health care work organizational changes, or the privatization of care services. These features are considered by computer scientists rather than by end users or policy makers. Global actors—international standardization bodies, legal and trade entities, large technology vendors, and, to a large extent, international health agencies—disengaged from local decision making and the policy processes are imbued with immense power to determine structural conditions that define local policy options and individual decision making (Wagner, 1995). The design, development, and adoption of ICTs, while fundamentally defined by global commodification and prevailing trajectories of globalization, has not been exposed or compensated for, or protected from, these biases—the necessary "guardrails" have simply not been constructed that would empower more sustainable consumption (Information Society Forum, 1998).

Without these compensatory measures, critical benefits may be lost, as current patterns reveal those benefits are unlikely to spontaneously emerge (Alexander & Stafford, 1998). The development of ICTs originates largely from the private sector and global institutional actors, driven largely by profit motives within prevailing global institutional structures, also fabricated for the purposes of the private appropriation of social wealth. The social stratification and wealth differences these processes and actors generate in turn strongly influences the social determinants of health and population health—core to more sustainable consumption trajectories. The resulting ICTs derived consistently fall short of initial expectations and possibilities (Balka, 2003; Heaton, Kischuk, & Picot, 2004).

The success of ICTs, or any technology, fundamentally depends on the cultural relevance of the application. Knowledge—which has historically originated from local contexts—necessarily requires consistent support across institutional and social contexts (Brown & Dugiuid, 2001; Knorr-Cetina, 1999). The resulting—largely unconscious and unquestioned—knowledge sets and operating principles define a culture (Heaton, Kischuk, & Picot, 2004). Globalization and ICTs have dramatically altered this historical cultural landscape. The transformation of different cultural settings as globalization sweeps ICTs through virtually all cultural landscapes worldwide necessarily requires that uniquely defined cultures now accommodate global institutional and social contexts.

The unconscious and unquestioned premises of prevailing social processes form a meta-level of operating assumptions that supports a particular evolution of ICTs. The physician functions as both an individual and a medical practitioner, conforming to and perpetuating a series of specific cultural understandings, practices, and institutional structures, and generating a duality of structuration (Heaton, Kischuk, & Picot, 2004). Yet, by definition, not all cultures incorporate the epidemiological concepts of health in the same context at the same level with the same historical underpinnings and the same institutional and organizational infrastructure with the same worldviews and ways of knowing as those of Western medicine. Introducing new features that depend on these precise supporting frameworks will unquestionably introduce challenges and the need for cultural change to accommodate these new worldviews. Ultimately, if they are successfully adopted by providing the necessary frameworks, they are certain to create profound cultural changes.

Similarly, if social processes form powerful determinants of consumption, they are clearly important factors defining population health. On that basis alone, should we not respect the importance of culturally distinct social processes in our search for more sustainable consumption? Given the global nature of ICTs and the pervasiveness of the changes they have the power to spawn, should we not closely examine and weigh their costs and benefits? This should suggest at least a modicum of caution in our selection of ICTs for sustainable consumption.

It should be apparent that we have not discussed in this chapter the direct health effects of ICTs. Although there is a growing body of evidence indicating health impacts from ICTs as a result of ergonomic, chemical, electromagnetic and other possible causes (including the risks derived from the inattentiveness to surrounding environments during their use), this approach diverts attention toward the individual. The assumption is that if you limit or avoid use of or exposure to a specific product, your chances of contracting certain diseased states is reduced. These studies would better serve us were they to consider the societal influences—why people use the products—rather than heaping all the responsibility onto the individual decision. Granted that the research is attempting to influence policy making and thus serves an important role, these studies still neglect the deeply profound societal embedding of the nature of using ICTs, which is where we will now turn our attention.

8

Incantations and ICTs:
A Global Ideological Pervasion

In previous chapters, we explored how ICTs influence consumption and interact with globalization. One approach is to investigate the potential opportunities of ICTs to help achieve more sustainable consumption by considering the variety of claims and their possible consequences on an assortment of application possibilities. Another approach is to investigate how the application of ICTs influence various social processes, mediate social behavior and decision making, and co-evolve with social institutions. What we are discovering as we proceed is that ICTs interact in tremendously complex ways with both consumption activities and globalization. In this chapter we more closely examine the premise that the prevailing social framework plays an important role in ICTs and in their effect on sustainable consumption and globalization. More specifically, we consider why economic, or, more precisely, capitalist or market-based values are important.

RATIONALITY AND VALUES

It was late 1999. A growing euphoria was developing about the markets, led by savvy technology stocks. "What rises keeps rising" was the growing sentiment. Millions crowded in for a piece of the pie. Then, suddenly, markets began to plummet. Not without warning, mind you. Comments about "irrational exuberance" should have been sufficient to instill widespread contemplation and caution—at least one would have thought so. The technology market indices fell by half, and then to one third of their original values, and remain there a decade later. This shook the very foundations of the physical infrastructure of thousands of dot-com startups, communities, and technology parks, and sent shudders through global markets. The precipitous drop of thousands of points must have made Black Monday—a drop of a mere 407.20 points—seem serene by comparison. Indeed, a decade after the tech bubble, gyrations of hundreds of points, measurable percentages of stock market indices, regularly ripple through global markets. The unthinkable events of September 11, 2001, demonstrated the power and effect external factors can have on the markets, already unstable from an extended sequence of global market shocks and awes. The meltdowns of 2008 and 2009 make even the tech bubble look calm by comparison. Global markets regularly gyrate, shaking off thousands of points weekly, only to rise again the following week, if only briefly, to once again gasp for air as they breach the surface of yet another record or euphemistically labeled "market correction."

Each time these and other similar events occur, new safety mechanisms are instituted and regulatory changes are made—systems management is increased—to limit the extent of future damage. Each time, the modifications fail to prevent or anticipate the next event. Why is this?

Environmental and social research and policy has typically focused on the proximate causes of environmental damage and social inequality. Often these efforts encounter barriers such as inertial resistance, a sense of disempowerment (when the problems as explained seem overwhelming) or irrelevance (when separated spatially or temporally), dependence on and hope for technical fixes, or the fear of sacrifice and reduced living standards.

Increasingly, attention is now being directed toward the underlying social and economic driving forces behind the proximate causes. By shaping the context in which choices are made, values can establish powerful motivational forces that can produce, indirectly, tremendously greater environmental and social consequences (Brown & Cameron, 2000; Kilbourne, Beckmann, Lewis, & Van Dam, 2001; Manno, 2000; Rosa & Dietz, 1998; Vayada, 1988).

Values are the foundations of research. Research is the foundation of theories and models. Theories and models are used to describe and predict outcomes from phenomena, decisions, and objectives under different assumptions. Values help determine both those assumptions and the institutional structures and goals of society. Ultimately, values determine the choices we make individually, socially, and institutionally. These cultural structures, rules, regulations, and other mechanisms shape and guide choice. They simultaneously limit and expand, confine and encourage choice. Together, they shape the choices that enable the functioning of societies.

Unquestioned faith in rational, insatiable, utility-maximizing automatons appears to be faltering. The foundations of consumerism are slowly, almost imperceptibly, yet unarguably unraveling as more research brings to light the dynamics that generate consumption activity. As attention has shifted ever so slightly toward the much ignored demand side of the equation, a better understanding of the dynamic complex forces and factors, beyond the overt, such as marketing, is finally shedding some light on the complex nature of consumption behavior.

Joanne Naiman (1997) explains how the common belief that the world consists of facts that can be assembled into a coherent bundle as the truth is a simplistic, somewhat inaccurate depiction of science, and is often used as the basis for the exercise of social power and manipulation. All "facts" are subject to their initial constraints and assumptions. For example, Newtonian physics function perfectly well under everyday experiences at the macro level. However, if we change these initial parameters and, for example, increase the frame of reference to a velocity approaching that of the speed of light, relativistic dynamics must then be employed to accurately describe observed phenomena—and predict the effects from interventions or external forces. Similarly, if we were to examine particles at the microscopic atomic level, statistical mechanics or quantum physics would then be needed to properly describe observed phenomena. Under a different frame of reference or set of initial conditions (assumptions), different models and theories are necessary to meet the conditions of repeatability, verifiability, and accuracy.

Similarly, there is often more than one explanation or theory for a given set of social phenomena. In social theory, there can be different general theoretical frameworks that explain the same facts in different ways. The framework used may even influence which facts are selected.

Scientists are people, and, like everyone else, feel the pressure to conform and seek approval from their peers. Theoretical frameworks phase in and out of popularity at certain times and in certain places. On rare occasions, new frameworks are proposed and are sometimes even adopted. Practitioners and students of a particular discipline who do raise fundamental questions or challenge or criticize established abstractions are often dismissed or even ostracized. New ideas can be difficult to accept, and introducing them into established forms of thought can be extraordinarily difficult. New subdisciplines may be established, but fundamental transformations to established practices are extremely rare. Eventually, indefensible theories will be exposed and discredited. However, they may persist for very long periods, particularly when structures and institutions exist that both support and depend upon those theories, and where many people or entire societies have become dependent on them. As Upton Sinclair perceptively noted, it's very difficult to get a person to understand something when his or her salary depends on not understanding it.

Our ideas, experiences, and values simply cannot be laid aside to study or convey information. Although unbiased, independent, or value-free information is taught as desirable, all information has implicit values, beliefs, biases, and assumptions attributed to it. The reason most biases are not noticeable is that they usually match our own, and, accordingly, simply seem natural. Biases are most commonly noticed only when they differ from our own views. Capitalism, like all social sciences—and religions—has particular values embedded within it. These are supported by rigid doctrines and intricate and sophisticated institutional frameworks.

This explains why, as John Livingston (1994) observes, Darwin felt compelled to present the theory of evolution in a manner that closely resembled the beliefs of his time. The foundation of the theory of evolution was developed in the social context of Adam Smith's capitalism. This is an exceptional, however unfortunate, example of scientific socialization and cultural conditioning. The result was that evolutionary processes were modeled on Victorian social norms from which modern economic theories were rapidly developing. It was with the cultural baggage of this period that Darwin "felt obliged, intellectually, to make his case as strongly as possible within the accepted rules" (Livingston, 1994, 76). Darwin himself "claimed that the idea for evolution by natural selection occurred to him after reading the famous 'Essay on Population' by Thomas Malthus" (Lewontin, 1991, 9). This reveals insight into the tremendous differences that occur across cultures and societies, and demonstrates the subjective and contextual nature of social phenomena. In reality, the theory of evolution is modeled on Malthusian economics, not the converse, as is often claimed!

As can be seen, ideas both arise out of the social world and have consequences for it. Capitalism is a class-structured social system in which people are situated in different places within the social structure. Since everyone is situated *somewhere* within the social structure, Naiman (1997) explains, there can be no such thing as unbiased or objective social thought. Those at the lower socioeconomic status might consider equality and freedoms very limited. Those in the middle may feel there are reasonable freedoms. Those at the top may feel the social structure is very fair and reasonable. Despite the widening gulf between wealth and poverty across local or global comparisons, what is fascinating is that so many in a lower socioeconomic status may actually consider the social structure to be very fair and reasonable, and often support and engage in actions that might reduce, restrict, or otherwise limit their choices and freedoms. Sophisticated techniques may be employed—conjured through various social institutions and mechanisms—to ensure this message is conveyed. Consequently, a social structure, regardless of equality or sustainability, may prevail for very long times indeed (Naiman, 1997).

Similarly, the perception or belief in the "technofix" suggests that since technology has come to our rescue in the past, it will continue to do so in the future. The problem with this expectation, or form of linear thought, is that technologies are developed within the social system, and are thus influenced by and predicated on fundamental assumptions. For instance, scientific "discoveries" and the institutional structures to develop those discoveries into appropriate tools such that they may be applied at the right places in the right time and order is simply assumed. Moreover, where recent technological disasters—Exxon Valdez, Chernobyl, or the August 2003 blackout, for example—have occurred, it is rationalized that more technology is the solution—double-hulled tankers and monitoring systems, respectively. This simply reinforces the belief in technological rationalization.

These assumptions work reasonably well so long as system parameters, or frames of reference, remain consistent. Many emerging global challenges—climate change and peak oil, for example—greatly distort the frames of reference we must now operate within. We are now confronted by large-scale biogeochemical processes and social phenomena that are poorly understood and exhibit lags, thresholds, and discontinuities. These were never before encountered on such grand scales or with such significant consequences as now.

Alfred North Whitehead observes that modern science's methodological procedure fixates on a set of abstractions—neglecting everything else in the process—to extract detailed information and thoroughly understand what remains. Success is dependent upon the accuracy and rigor of the abstract assumptions: "But, however triumphant, the triumph is within limits. The neglect of these limits leads to disastrous oversights" (Whitehead, 1925, 200). The prevailing social framework of market-driven capitalism, and its widespread dogmatic incantations reincarnated in modern globalization, stand on a rather dubious set of abstractions whose limits are consistently neglected, particularly as far as human and ecological premises are concerned. "One implication is that traditional market forces operating on the information technology realm have not, and will not, automatically result in positive social and environmental outcomes" (Rejeski, 2003, 2). Astoundingly, these assumptions are regularly applied in practice well beyond their original limits, as are those imposed by the models that incorporate them.

Were our social framework concerned with environmental and social problems—scale and distribution—or capable of managing these emergent problems, environmental and social problems would be far less likely to develop in the first place. Conversely, should the prevailing social environment within which technologies are developed not inherently exhibit a propensity for environmental sustainability, social equality, or the management of complex problems, could it be reasonably expected that a new technology, institution, or layer thereof that is developed within or as an outgrowth of that framework, would spontaneously solve the emerging scale or distributive problems? ICTs are developed, largely adapted and adopted, and mainly dispersed, to satisfy market imperatives—profits, sales, and economic growth (Arnfalk, 2002; British Telecom, 2001; Davison, Vogel, Harris, & Jones, 2000; Nuij, 2002; Ropke, 1999; Sonntag, 2000). Technological rationalization has been reduced to a profit motive: the economic incentive must exist—however created—for us to need ICTs. To better understand this phenomenon, the role of economics and the emergence and context of modern market capitalism must be understood.

First, let's take a brief look at where along this economic trajectory we presently reside. Economic theories are primarily generalizations of economic behavior that are in reality conditioned by cultural and social relations and institutional settings (Peet, 1992). In practice, many economic models that inform policy and decision makers are inherently and deeply flawed. Similarly flawed are the modern transmitted and communicated popularized correlates widely dispersed through social discourse. At best, these are only capable of generalized indications of what might occur *within the originally established assumptions,* if all other factors remain equal. However, given the complex and indeterminate nature of socioeconomic systems, "given all other factors remain equal" cannot be held valid in *practice*—in the real world now transformed by global decision making.

Neoclassical, or laissez-faire, economics have been extensively criticized for many reasons. Their underlying assumptions, methodological analyses, application, and institutionalization have been fraught with misunderstandings and outright errors. Though many in number, the imperatives of the prevailing economic worldview count among its beliefs or expectations endless growth, self-interest, competition, rational utility maximization, linearity, discounting, property rights, perfect substitutability—many untenable, if not groundless, assumptions.

The current pretensions of objectivity, rational behavior, and similarly questionable assertions have instituted a perilous idealization of market-driven globalization. In practice, original assumptions should be maintained, which greatly restricts the scope of application of these theories. In other words, economics still has a limited scope of application—the limits of its objectivity must be adhered to. Economics must yet develop suitable theories and models that recognize and account for scale and distribution. Fundamental beliefs and assumptions must be acknowledged. Yet modern economic models are indiscriminately and regularly applied beyond their intended purposes. This precludes the development and application of more appropriate tools. The sacrosanct fervor with which neoclassical tools are fallaciously applied presages not merely national, but now global tragedy. Most important, economics is not an objective science—there are many ideological values attributed to the assumptions and theories that support economic decisions. As such, these should not solely guide or shape decisions, despite their regular dominance in the sustainability discourse.

That they do suggests the inherent and indispensable role of power and influence in Western society—a key feature that has proven resistant to change toward more sustainable consumption. Wood asserts, "Struggles at the point of production . . . remain incomplete as long as they do not extend to the locus of power on which capitalist property, with its control of production and appropriation, ultimately rests" (Wood, 1995, 47).

The current social framework, prevailing economic worldview, or dominant social paradigm is key to consumption decisions and population health. It therefore makes sense to examine the historical developments and decisions that have led to market-driven globalization's current state and global trajectory. Let's have a look at this "locus of power," and how and why it has developed, from an historical perspective.

A BRIEF HISTORY OF CAPITALIST VALUES

Since Adam Smith and the development of modern economics, behaviors have been primarily attributed to biological factors: competition, survival of the fittest, and dominance, for example. These assumptions have fueled the rise of nation states, justified cultural and geopolitical conquests, and produced international development (Goehring, 1993; Maybury-Lewis, 1992). Yet their basis and capacity for representing hominid behavioral predispositions is questionable (Clark, 1995; Eisler, 1987; Erdal & Whiten, 1996; Naiman, 1997; Power, 1991; Sahlins, 1972; Whiten, 1998).

Obviously, there is some need to further explore and better understand human activity and factors that contribute to our behavior. Hunter-gatherer societies represent 99 percent of human existence. Since so many economic assumptions are premised on biological foundations, a closer investigation of hunter-gatherer societies should distill any possible biological predispositions. Strategic modeling of hunter-gatherer societies has identified some common patterns through the utilization of "the enormous diversity of cultures and ecologies associated with present-day" groups (Erdal & Whiten, 1996, 140). This modeling technique has proven valuable in generating vital information about hominid behavioral ecology during which time "the basic human social forms, language, and human nature itself were forged" (Lee, 1979, 1).

Common patterns reveal two key benefits exhibited by hunter-gatherer societies essential to low-consumption behaviors: their compatibility with long-term ecosystem sustainability and therefore human sustainability, and their highly egalitarian lifestyle unobserved in modern agricultural, industrial, or postindustrial societies. In modern ecological economic parlance, this is a sustainable scale and equitable social organization (Gowdy, 1994; Power, 1991).

Erdal and Whiten (1996) suggest that hunter-gatherer societies exhibit egalitarian, cooperative social structures with natural constraints to dominance and competition. For example, food sharing is not conducted only with kin or out of reciprocity; sharing is conducted "according to need, even when food is scarce," even though a selfish strategy may deliver greater returns (Erdal & Whiten, 1996, 142; see also Hawkes, O'Connell, & Blurton-Jones, 1991; Kaplan & Hill, 1985). The observed universality of this behavior where a tension between selfish tendencies and cultural rules favoring sharing "always and everywhere resolved in favor of sharing, with aberrations being minor and rare, is too low to give support to the cultural model" (Erdal & Whiten, 1996, 142).

Another example of such behavior Erdal and Whiten explore is the absence of dominance hierarchies. Contact with agricultural or colonial societies, invasion, colonialism, or the imposition of roles from external government authorities may lead to the creation, to some extent, of leaders or leadership titles (Gardner, 1972; Lee, 1979; Morris, 1982; Turnbull, 1965). Lacking these conditions, hunter-gatherer societies tend to exhibit universally consensual decision making where everyone has the right to speak. In certain situations, those who are generally acknowledged for their particular skill are paid greater attention on those matters and frequently obtain agreement on their positions. However, this is not always the case. Experts may be overridden; in different situations others may be given greater respect and in the identical situation at a different time the same expert may not be respected. The result, Erdal and Whiten argue, is that the absence of permanently dominant positions within the group is maintained. Aspirations for status or dominance are effectively and even harshly thwarted. Erdal and Whiten cite Meggit, who notes that having considerable responsibility one day and perhaps insignificant responsibility the following created "'frequent variation in the extent of authority that an individual exercised from one situation to another [that] militated against the emergence of a class of permanent leaders'" (1996, 146). The goal would be "not so much keeping up with the Joneses, as making sure that none of the Joneses gets ahead in the first place" (Erdal & Whiten, 1996, 148).

Aggressive, dominant, competitive hierarchical social structures only appear with the evolutionarily recent development of agricultural societies (Knauft, 1991). Why, then, did the development of agriculture about ten thousand years ago cause the emergence of chiefs, classes, and eventually our complex institutionalized global hierarchies? Moreover, why are these behaviors still widely promoted and dominant throughout Western capitalist societies, through such institutions as financial and labor markets, educational systems, and sporting leagues? The time elapsed since the emergence of agriculture is insignificant from a biologically evolutionary perspective. This leads to an almost unavoidable conclusion that cultural, not genetic, factors must be responsible (Symons, 1979; Tooby & DeVore, 1987).

Around ten thousand years ago, hunting and gathering societies began to change as the domestication of plants and animals began to serve as the primary food source; this resulted in a shift from a wide variety of wild gathered foods and prey to a relatively few starchy cousins in the form of roots and grasses combined with the suitably domesticated livestock we now endure. We traded quality for quantity in a period that represents, for the first time in human history, an increased control over food supply. Significant changes in social organization also developed during this period.

Notable changes included increased populations, a greater permanence of settlements, and increased surpluses (Lenski & Lenski, 1978). Naiman (1997) traces and explores the cultural significance of these changes, noting they permitted flexibility in social activities as fewer people were required for food gathering and hunting. As specialization and technologies changed, greater surpluses could be realized, permitting further specialization and innovation. The reality of these events, however, meant more work and reduced freedoms (Naiman, 1997).[1] This marked the beginning of a divergence from egalitarian hunter-gatherer societies.

Increased food security, among other factors, seems to have favored the emergence of agriculture and fixed settlements. Social inequalities at this stage simply seemed to work and make sense—greater populations in fixed settlements retaining control over greater surpluses logically required more complex social arrangements to manage the population and surpluses. Formalized political leadership and structures emerged to maintain and improve social conditions in these new environments. People came to accept these structures as a means of insurance in the form of more stable and surplus supplies of food and protection from those who might expropriate those surpluses. Early compensation for that insurance took various forms of tributes and has evolved to complex forms of compensation and taxation in modern societies.

If, in reality, behavior is the complex result of both biological and social forces, why are our modern social institutions, relations, and cultural beliefs predominantly modeled on aggressive biological theories? To answer this question, historical transformations, the emergence of their corresponding social relations of power and wealth, and the roles of prevailing institutions must be considered.

As agricultural settlements became fixed and populations grew beyond the cooperative upper limits exhibited by hunter-gatherer societies, institutionalized hierarchical governance structures emerged, replacing hunter-gatherer egalitarianism. These power structures were early depictions of the culture of fixed settlements. Inequalities became structured. Those with greater surpluses had an increased interest in maintaining, or even expanding, those inequalities. Alternative social arrangements became more difficult to perceive (Naiman, 1997).

Livingston argues that as humans shifted from small-group nomadic gathering and hunting and began to establish sedentary lives "in semi-permanent villages, that an enormously significant repression of our own nature took place" (1994, 19). One can interpret part of

---

[1] In contrast, !Kung Bushmen, for instance, spent only two to three hours a day in activities directly related to subsistence and required only about 60 percent of the population for subsistence work, although the environment in which they lived could often be unforgiving. Hunter-gatherer lifestyles provided ample food, leisure time, and long, healthy lives. Of the two paths to affluence, that of producing much or that of desiring little, Sahlins captures the essence of hunter-gatherer societies when he describes them as exhibiting a low standard of living and a high quality of life (Sahlins, 1972).

that repression as the advent of (and resulting from) a dominant social structure to maintain a stable surplus—in effect, to permit the Joneses, or at least certain Joneses, to get ahead—a cultural, rather than biological, obligation.

This newly created environment required a new set of social rules governing behavior. It also meant certain biological predispositions were no longer needed to be functionally effective. These changes simultaneously led to changed "values, beliefs and behavioural patterns" (Naiman, 1997, 66) through modified cultural components. Once institutionalized, they become "rigid doctrines" employing powerful, often highly sophisticated techniques to eliminate the dissonance between our natural predispositions and the new social environment (Koestler, 1975; Livingston, 1994).

As agrarian societies progressed, so did productive forces, advanced by a series of inventions and discoveries. These in turn permitted populations to increase further, facilitated even greater specialization, and stimulated a greater degree of organization, leadership, and social control.

Naiman (1997) traces this progress further to a complex system of rights and responsibilities between individuals that eventually emerged to form the basis of feudalism. Military threats and economic uncertainties motivated serfs to provide services to feudal lords in return for protective guarantees. The serfs would spend a majority of the week on the lord's land, with the remainder spent on their own or a common apportionment. Virtually everything was consumed locally; the lord appropriated everything produced on his portion while that which the serfs produced was consumed for their own use. Land was not actually owned; it was simply held and worked for someone above, with the Crown the ultimate landholder. The lords, however, maintained effective control over their estates.

Since there was little incentive to produce abundantly on the lord's estate, a system of rents gradually replaced that of agricultural services. In this system, the serfs worked their own lands and provided the lords with a portion of what they produced, thereby compensating the lords for the privilege of producing on their estates. Monied payments and goods subsequently replaced the former systems of payment.

This began to draw everyone into a more formalized market. Lords began to rent their lands and use the income to purchase goods. The serfs sold their products at markets to obtain money for the lords' rents. With surpluses, trade could increase. With a common basis for exchange—money—trades could become complex. Now, with both surpluses and a monied economy, complex trading arrangements could flourish. Since money is the common denominator for land and labor as well as capital, it became a principal contributing factor weakening the landlord class.

Naiman (1997) notes how several other factors contributed to the decline of feudalism. Markets ushered in the growth of urban centers, drawing people away from the rural, more oppressive, agriculture. As wool and leather production became profitable, lords began to recognize the opportunities for greater wealth by evicting their peasant workers in exchange for sheep and cattle. These were known as the *enclosure movement* and the *clearances.* New class relations also emerged. As merchants and craftspeople developed their trades, they began to gain greater control over the productive processes by providing raw materials and tools. The most powerful of this new class were the money merchants, or goldsmiths, as money lending became central to the expanding markets. Wage laborers who migrated into urban centers balanced the growing capitalist class and provided the available labor forces for production. As advances in technologies were made and new forms of power were harnessed, small-scale craft work soon gave way to the manufactory system. Once the capital was available to surpass the threshold cost of developing larger, more profitable, and more efficient machines, labor productivity was greatly enhanced. The Industrial Revolution, launched by the power of steam and the printing press, was underway. Urban centers became a focus for industrial growth, and the need for capital expansion had become established.

Attention was now focused on capital and wages to satisfy the needs of an expanding industrial society. During the days of Adam Smith and David Ricardo, rent was a principal function of economics. As industrialization found a foothold, the economic analysis of the role of rent became "an ideological weapon in the power struggle between the rising capitalist and the entrenched landlord" (Daly & Cobb, 1994, 115). This led to the decline in both the importance of land and resources in economic analysis and the landlord class in society. Whereas capitalists favored cheap resources and food, the feudal lords favored higher prices for food, natural resources, and other products of the land. With a growing number of people moving or forced to urban centers, capital, favoring cheap resources, became the dominant class, followed by organized labor and landlords.[2]

---

[2] As Daly and Cobb (1994) note, the largest landowners, governments, have failed to maintain resource prices, opting for low prices to encourage growth. This policy has maximized the use of resources to raise the productivity and incomes of labor and capital—synonymous with an increasing standard of living. Daly and Cobb question the merit of shifting attention from land simply to reduce the role of rent in the economy.

Capitalism was now firmly established. Today, Western social institutions, values, behaviors, and lifestyles—largely the trajectory globalization has followed—manifest the influences of these transitions. Hierarchical social organization, competition, survival of the fittest, and individualism, among other idealogical values, emerged during these periods. The foundations of economic theory were developed in this social context. In fact, as we have seen, an exceptional, however unfortunate, example of scientific socialization and cultural conditioning occurred when evolutionary processes were modeled on Victorian social norms from which economic theories were developed. Livingston further reminds us these social and cultural manifestations are unique to "the dominant Euro-American exotic ideology; they do not belong to all human cultures" (1994, 82).

As the capitalist class system evolved, it extended its dominance globally. Colonial powers were projected onto every continent under the new ideals of capitalism—expansionism, individualism, and competition. These formative years were probably congruent with the emergence of globalization in its early gestational years.

For most of human history and across cultures, the concept of owning the productive capacity for social well-being did not exist. Class capitalism appears to have created this new environment in which stability with social and ecological systems no longer held. By expanding the concept of private property, some people can appropriate for themselves that which has been produced by others. In capitalist societies, those who own the means of production have substantial influence over the lives and activities of those who must provide the labor for production. Although significantly less restrictive than in the feudal system, freedom of the worker in capitalism remains greatly limited.[3]

In theory, there is no forced relationship between the worker and the employer. In reality, coercion takes an economic form. If wage workers do not sell their labor for income, they will be greatly limited in their participation in the market economy.[4] Of course, as essential goods and services become commodified, they enter the formal market economy. Water and air remain virtually the last bastions of a once free, commonly shared resource pool. As other noncommodified goods and

---

[3] However, as Naiman (1997) observes, the irony is that this less restrictive system has been developed free of any obligations from the owning class.

[4] There are also strong elements of environmental and health coercion. Local, regional, and global pollution compel escape and protection from health risks, increasingly necessitating new forms of insulation and insurance usually derived through market participation (for example, technologies and processed food supplies). This also helps explain why many traditional cultures are experiencing a shift toward market economies (Rattle, forthcoming).

services are valued, they too enter the market economy—food and food services, child care, health promotion, recreation, sports and leisure, mobility—and institutional arrangements shift to accommodate these formal market arrangements. Market participation becomes imperative. Money in a capitalist society is essential for survival. The ability to choose not to participate in wage labor yet avoid subsistence living (a perilous choice, not the least in part due to severe source and sink limitations) requires sufficient capital to gain access to some means of production, an option that is simply out of reach for most people. Ironically, once this option is achieved, the individual begins to shift allegiance toward the appropriating class and its ideals, institutions, and behavior. Conversely, the inability, or even limited ability, to participate in socially mediated materialism can have grave consequences for both individual and population health.

As we explored in the last chapter, the social distribution of wealth is a key determinant of health. It is essential to recognize the important contribution of economic coercion to the social determinants of health. Often this has been invoked as the key argument of groups, such as labor unions, seeking inclusion of their members. In this sense, unions and similar social groups seek a raised level of social inclusion by raising wages and formal benefits. This singular approach is entirely consistent with capital values. It emphasizes participation in the formal economy through wage labor. Neglected are the countless people who are socially excluded by way of their inability or lack of desire to participate economically (Durning, 2006; Raphael, 2004). More important, however, is how this approach conveniently dodges the issues of class struggle. Most governments are delighted to engage labor unions, debate minimum wages, pension plans, and so on simply because it avoids the difficult questions of wealth redistribution or upsetting the Pareto optimum. Debate at the nexus of class struggle is avoided, completely hidden from the labor pool. Class consciousness is high with the owning class, but virtually nonexistent with the working class. Work fairs, retraining, and similar programs are designed to further encourage participation. This approach ensures people must participate in national and global productivity, despite their values, concerns about social equalities, or personal torments about the environmental sustainability of their actions. In this manner, the economy first and foremost directs social activity—people simply must participate in formal market mechanisms. One can choose—within limits—where and how they produce, but they *must* choose *to* produce. (The converse, of course, is that they must consume that which is produced.) Social exclusion through economic exclusion is apparent through each step on the socioeconomic wealth ladder, and it translates into equally divisive health disparities across all steps. Those who choose not to produce or cannot work are both economically and socially excluded. While there are clear health and social benefits to economic participation, the *lack of choice* is neither beneficial nor healthy. That work serves this purpose increasingly less frequently, and instead "comes to be seen primarily as something that allows us to consume" (Naiman, 1997, 123) weighs heavily in the court of social legitimization (see also Schor, 1991, 1998).

A high level of specialization and abstraction characterize capitalism, and the means of production falls under control of the appropriating class. These features reduce work to a marketable commodity. Decisions on work process, product, and surplus are made to satisfy profit and capital growth as we approach a market-based system.

As a result of the immense wealth and power at the disposal of relatively few individuals, they are able to defend specific ideologies and promote certain institutional structures. Advertising and marketing augment worker alienation and convince workers that material goods will improve their lives (Durning, 1992; Elgin, 1993). The educational system imparts the values and norms of class society and capitalism. Through socialization, formal education allocates students to the labor market based on a competitive grading system (Kohn, 1992). There is a reason why bullying has pervaded primary schools and daycare centers. Children as young as two and three learn early from their social environments—books, television, the daycares and schools they attend, computers, mommy and daddy—that "Those who hold power will be most able to have control over the norms, values, beliefs and social institutions within a society" (Naiman, 1997, 72). Ownership and control of the media and technological convergence limits information sources, coverage, depth, and development paths. The goals of advertisers and the media have converged. These maintain the status quo through materialism and capital acquisition. The close associations between political and market elites, the powerful and the wealthy—principle decision makers—is a critical feature shaping society and globalization. A shrinking number of people control global capital—the means to control the productive processes. As Jared Diamond astutely notes, those with the greatest social and political power today regularly profit "from activities that may be bad for society as a whole and for their own children" (2003, 13). Phillips (1998) suggests information freedom (and perhaps availability) is intimately close to the interests of capital, seeking only to sell advertising and attract viewers. Conversely, where information and news is contrary to the interests of capital—advertising, sales growth, profitability—it is deemed irrelevant and not valuable, and is generally omitted.

Despite their far more diverse expressions of information, ICTs remain a key form of information provisioning, the networks and infrastructure primarily confined to private capital interests—it was capital that was essential in surpassing the threshold costs of developing the information networks. A global contest is currently playing itself out over the desire of some actors, for likely very legitimate reasons, to manage or otherwise manipulate Internet and other informational traffic flows, or, as some like to bemoan, interfere in "network neutrality." If powerful global actors, those who own the infrastructures of information provision, are willing to express their privileges in this manner (or is this simply the global market imperative manifesting itself?), in what other ways might they exert their control over social activity? Simultaneously, those who believe the Internet is a neutral, democratic source of power derived through free, unbiased information, need to subject themselves to a reality check: there are considerable inequalities in the provisioning of information and its democratization, even neglecting the substantial biases expressed through the capital interests controlling the infrastructures and a majority of the overt and socially enshrouded messages. The ability to access the Internet free from any intervention raises, and perhaps increases, serious social, health, economic, and environmental costs derived from that use activity. ICTs merely function as yet another layer of technology—an added degree of separation from reality and the distancing and shading of consumer choices. While information confers a certain degree of power, information by itself is not power, and the availability of information depends on a number of other factors, including capital.

In the global economy, the principal form of power is capital and, due to its flexibility, money, which was formerly but is no longer pegged to the gold standard as a store of wealth. With the cost of a mere few seconds of network television air time into the hundreds of thousands of dollars, only the wealthiest can afford to transmit messages to mass audiences. At these rates, it had better be worth their while! This sends a clear yet subtle social message about the value attributed to these media—the message must be tremendously important: look, listen, adhere, follow—believe. It is estimated that as few as five hundred corporations control 70 percent of world trade, and 50 percent of foreign direct investment is owned by 1 percent of all transnationals. "[T]he largest 100 corporations in the U.S. pay for about 75 percent of commercial television time and about half the public television time" (Mayer, 1998, 73). The largest media organizations in the United States have a strong network of direct links to other corporations. This network shares common interests, affiliations, boards of governors, and goals that extend to many Fortune 1000 corporations. Large global transnational corporations (TNCs) also exhibit many direct links and common interests with media organizations (Phillips, 1998). As a result of the immense wealth and power at the disposal of relatively few individuals, they are able to maintain dominant arguments in social discourse. This can function to substantiate their position and defend aggressive, hierarchical, materialistic, and individualistic behaviors. They wield tremendous power and influence in shaping global, national, and local institutional structures—legal, regulatory, educational, and social. Ownership and control of the media and technological convergence shapes ideologies. Limiting the debate to greater participation in the economy shields the debate about the *choice* to participate. Given the immense power ascribed to wealth, a closer examination of the socially agreed-upon form of that wealth is now needed.

THE VALUE OF MONEY

Market transactions in feudal societies were largely characterized by barter or trade of surplus commodities: the exchange of one commodity (C) for another commodity (C*), denoted as C-C*. With the introduction of a common currency, money, and as people were gradually drawn into the market economy, these transactions became more complex, characterized by the use of money as a medium to overcome the trading limitations of barter: the exchange of a commodity for money, which could then be exchanged for another commodity: C-M-C*. This is described as the *use value of money*.

Marx (1867/1965) identified the next critical step: capital circulation, represented by the exchange of money for a commodity, which can then be exchanged for money: M-C-M*, where the goal is to have M* greater than M. The goal in our advanced capital society is to expand *the exchange value in money*: $M* - M = dM$, where dM must increase positively ("dM" indicates the difference in value between the initial and final quantity of money exchanged in the transaction $[M* - M]$).

As money has become more abstract, its creation has been entirely severed from the value it is supposed to represent. Use value has been eclipsed by exchange value. Financial markets have abandoned real production and dismissed the human and environmental consequences of their investments. Daly and Cobb observe that money, as a cultural symbol and measure of wealth, has, as does any abstract mathematical formula, the ability to "grow both exponentially and indefinitely. This lack of symmetry in behaviour between reality measured and the measuring rod has serious consequences" (1994, 408). As the pivotal sustainable development decision maker, economics measured in terms of money has severely distorted our actions and warped our sense of reality. The need for production and consumption to maintain pace with the creation of this new abstract wealth has generated an innate need for increased throughput growth. This exponential growth culture is inherent to capitalism (Marx, 1867/1965). Our cultural representation for value is no longer linked to the real world. We now consider further the importance of this concept to consumption, after which we explore the roles of globalization and ICTs in this phenomenon.

The creation of money, or, more precisely, debt, is key to consumption activity. Our present financial system is often described as debt-based since the great majority of money supplied to national economies is created exclusively by the process of acquiring debt. Contrary to the naive belief that governments create money by printing it, this process only accounts for the legal tender circulating in an economy,[5] typically only 4 percent of the medium of exchange (Rowbotham, 1999). Commercial banks create credit by the process of lending to borrowers.

The shift in prerogative to create money came with the goldsmith-bankers in early capitalism. They accepted deposits of gold and coinage and created the system of transfers from one account to another by notes, developing payment by check. Experience demonstrated that only a fraction of deposits were withdrawn on a daily basis. This revealed that most of the gold could be safely loaned out at interest. The public function of supplying money was now linked to the private benefit of lending at interest. This became a standard business practice with minimal risk to the bank. Private banks do not create legal tender, only the socially contracted means of payment.

Following the lead of Daly and Cobb (1994), the process can be simplified as follows. Banks are legally required to hold reserves against their demand deposits. These reserves are legally determined and generally are less than 10 percent. Letting r represent this reserve requirement, $1 - r$ is the excess reserve above requirement. For each x

---

[5] This misconception is not surprising since as late as 1920 it was claimed that a majority of economists did not believe banks could create money (Schumpeter, 1954).

amount on deposit, $(x/r)(1 - r)$ can be loaned. Total demand deposits will now equal $x + (x/r)(1 - r)$ or x/r. The bank can effectively expand its demand deposits by $1/r$, not, as many may believe, $1 - r$. In other words, at 10 percent reserve requirement and based on $100 deposit, a bank may loan out $900 $[(100/0.1)(1 - 0.1) = (1000)(0.9) = 900]$, not simply $90 $(100 - 10)$ as one might expect. This effectively creates $900 in new money for loan purposes, and generates $1000 demand deposits ($900 in new loans plus the original $100 loaned).

In reality, there is more than one bank. Reserve amounts change as demand deposits are deposited into another bank. In this situation, a bank may only safely lend $x(1 - r)$ on each x amount deposited. As this amount is redeposited by the depositor in another bank, that latter bank may only lend $x(1 - r)(1 - r)$, or $x(1 - r)^2$; the third bank can safely lend $x(1 - r)^3$, and so on. The effective result of this lending, spending, and redepositing in a many-bank case multiplies the new reserves by the same factor of $1/r$.

We now must consider demand deposit contraction as reserves are lost. When people decide to hold more cash rather than check money and when total reserves are reduced by the Federal Reserve, the overall system loses reserves. As loans are repaid, principal plus interest is added to the reserves of the receiving bank. These become excess reserves to the receiving bank and lost reserves to the paying bank. The excess reserves then become available for new loans and are inevitably used for that purpose (this follows from the imperative for growth, as we discuss shortly).

Therefore, the creation and destruction of new money offset each other less the interest charged to the borrower. It is this interest that composes the real revenue generated and does not disappear when the loan is repaid. In other words, private banks are granted the social endorsement to create money, as much and as quickly as they desire or can produce. Banks can afford to pay interest in a competitive environment because they will charge interest on the amount of $(x/r)(1 - r)$ while they will pay interest on the amount of x. Even if the rate of interest paid equaled the amount charged, there would be, in today's reserve requirement environment, considerable room for profit. However, the loan rate is typically much greater than the deposit rate (note that 2 percent on deposits and 4 percent on loans translates into a 50 percent profit for the bank).

Tobin (1965) observes that both physical goods and fiduciary goods, or paper money, are assumed to collectively equal the wealth of a community, which creates the motivation for the gross domestic product

(GDP). GDP was never intended as a measure of well-being; rather, the GDP simply represents the positive addition of all goods and services in a society. Obviously, some of these are interventions to mitigate unsustainable or unhealthy states and social or environmental undesirables. Real wealth actually consists of tangible products and services, and many economists today would argue that wealth consists of human and physical capital. An ecologist would add natural capital to that list, with good reason. Despite their general neglect in prevailing economic discourse, the value of ecological services worldwide have been estimated to be $33 trillion annually—twice that of the global human economy (Costanza et al., 1997). Yet sadly, the intact values are generally ignored in the decision-making processes.[6] Nevertheless, the illusion is that wealth includes both physical goods, capital, and money. This illusion can only be maintained if a society neither attempts to convert all its money into real wealth, nor its fiduciary issue into money.

Hoarding and owning excessive physical goods is inefficient and unproductive. There is, however, no limit to the amount of abstract exchange value one can own—money does not physically deteriorate, and can always be exchanged for use value—so long as the social agreement to do so exists. It delivers both greater flexibility and the capacity to confer power and control over productive processes.

Imperative for Money Growth

As more money is created faster than physical goods and services, it depreciates in value. If money were linked to reality, it would be an expression of the total goods and services, including those that are ecological and biogeochemical in nature. The rapid expansion of money through exchange production and debt has led to a volume increase in money greater than that of goods and services. This is one of the reasons why costs seem to rise over time. This phenomenon motivates all formal market participants to consistently seek more money—profit, income, and wage growth. This depreciation of money should not be confused with the shorter-term fluctuations of inflation and deflation.

As fiduciary wealth increases faster than that of goods and services, its relative value decreases, obliging actors to grow their income just to *maintain the same standard of living*—to compensate for the

---

[6] Yet, as previously discussed, to measure and incorporate these values into a formal market mechanism raises some deeply flawed and ethically challenging issues—namely the incorporation into formal market mechanisms of nature's "value." The process also reflects the absurd attempt to reconstruct nature as an element of our social environment.

diminished value of money. How does a social actor increase income? Increased production and consumption is one obvious way. Capital and profit growth through modern financial markets—increasing exchange value—is another way.

The culturally derived belief in competition maintains that success in the marketplace is dependent on the development of new, faster, better, cheaper, or simply different products (Hoogendijk, 1993). This produces modernized, more efficient, and typically faster production machines (new technologies) and processes. Wage earners are replaced with new production techniques, often developed through their employment, and are obliged to seek income elsewhere, generating new production (Menzies, 1996; Rifkin, 1995). Thus, consumption increases at an accelerating *rate* to satisfy labor needs derived through capital substitution (Schnaiberg, 1980). This generates political action to create work and competition to attract business—the individual, competitive nature of human behavior is substantiated as surely as the wizard can conjure his spells!

Since production needs consumers, there is a strong incentive to provide workers with reasonable wages so they may consume what they produce. In so doing, Hoogendijk (1993) suggests that rapidly improved living standards for the working class has been fueled by the need for physical consumption growth. The educational system is used to effectively maintain control over the working class; more advanced production requires better-educated work forces. A healthy and happy work force would likely better perform what it has been trained for, and be less likely to question the prevailing social framework—so long as they perceive benefits from it. Presto! Capital is able to substantiate the prevailing social framework of structured inequality by employing such techniques.

With a general improvement in living standards, and since labor has become fundamentally dependent on capital and structured inequality, the working class is more than willing to effectively defend this framework. Due to a generally low class consciousness, conflicts are typically only a struggle for better wages and working conditions (Naiman, 1997). People simply accept the premises they are culturally accustomed to, do not question them, and do not observe others questioning them—the media effectively and intentionally impairs such dialogue. Despite the increased informational democracy ICTs afford, these premises remain largely intrinsic and "assumed rather than articulated in discourse" (Milbrath, 1995, 107).

Increasing production requires growing consumer markets. Accordingly, there is abundant motivation to move beyond national borders through international trade and export. However, since most other industrial nations are similarly saturated with overproduction, they must locate or create new consumer markets to relieve the overproduction. New consumers are therefore indoctrinated into the world of higher living standards and mass consumption—new products and product variants; newer, faster, and bolder toys, gadgets, and norms; more stuff and more space—urged forward by the institutional arrangements—legal, advertising and marketing, trade, tax, educational, social, health care—in the name of progress and development, paid for through multilateral transnational global debt programs.

These massive debts of low- and middle-income countries (LMICs)—which largely benefit transnational corporations, donor countries, and advanced economies—must be repaid. In order to do so, these countries must grow their economies. Adoption of economic growth policies simply becomes imperative. If that weren't enough, many international organizations (such as the World Bank, the International Monetary Fund [IMF], and the Bank for International Settlements [BIS]) help encourage this approach through structural readjustment plans. Rowbotham characterizes third-world "debt" as "permanent debt-bondage" and "export aid for the industrial nations" (1999, 16). This process of globalization is in effect transforming other cultures in an attempt to maintain fuel for capitalist growth (Goehring, 1993; Maybury-Lewis, 1992). Blind to the majority of impacts consumer-oriented lifestyles generate, high-income countries "actively encourage the developing world to adopt the same driving values and lifestyles" (Rees, 1999, 26). Culturally embedded discourse substantially limits cross-cultural understanding, frequently leading to contradictory actions (Milbrath, 1995). Traditional strategies for coping in specific environments are being lost. "Cultural patterns have been disrupted and their societies made unstable" (Clark, 1995, 73). Cultural diversity has been not only undermined and seriously compromised, but categorically sacrificed for the cultural and social values, institutions, and forces that maintain mass consumer lifestyles. Public- and private-sector debt problems are resolvable—for instance, by declaring bankruptcy or orchestrating a public bailout, especially when markets function as intended and sectors become "too big to fail." For some reason, we have not translated these principles to LMIC debts in previous decades, and we continue to fail to do so.

Economic growth relies on the production-commodification approach to resolve the social and environmental consequences of an exponentially expanding money supply, in the process further accommodating monetary expansion. Since the emphasis has been on the production process, many measures to confront over-consumption tend to target production-oriented strategies—many applications of ICTs are needlessly thrust and hopelessly forced into this category precisely because these may avoid the thorny and controversial issues of scale and distribution. The dominant cultural values and social institutions of capitalist class relations would necessarily be challenged by framing consumer behavior as a problem that "cannot be solved by ever more economic activity or ever more efficiencies" (Princen, 1999, 361). Sustainable consumption is a fundamentally intractable problem when approached from the production, or growth, side of the equation.

Americans, Rowbotham (1999) asserts, are bound to work, despite their enormously productive economy, due to their enormous debts incurred to achieve the material abundance that surrounds them. Conventional development ultimately depends on satisfying capital and profit growth to generate jobs, stimulate buying, satisfy competition, or create new businesses and innovations for fear of swift global capital withdrawal; this is rational economic performance. Using growth as a roadmap to improve well-being means "[m]any policies used to change consumer behavior are found to be inadequate" (United Nations, 1998, 15). Solutions, it seems, rest with reversing growth. Ouch! This contradicts the fundamental tenets of capitalism, prevailing social values and objectives, and global institutional structures. It has therefore never been seriously considered. The closest we have come is the metaphor of efficiency. Well, we know how far that has gotten us.[7]

A GLOBAL AWAKENING

Supporting this analysis is the salient observation by Scholte on the importance of capitalism to globalization: "Yet no account of globalization and the state is adequate without extended attention to capitalism either, and it is regrettable that so much analysis of globalization has neglected even to consider the importance of processes of surplus accumulation" (1997, 429).

Scholte notes that the critical forces of the framework of structured inequality have been pivotal in the rise of globalization through extending market regions, lowering or externalizing costs (such as labor, taxation, and regulations), and generating new market opportunities such as "information, telephone conversations, and mass media productions that circulate in global space itself" (Scholte, 1997, 429). It

---

[7] Recent events are emerging that do place the emphasis on "degrowth," recognizing the insufficient progress derived from eco-efficiency measures.

is in the final contribution to globalization that ICTs contribute most obviously. These "new opportunities for accumulation," as have been previously explored, mean accumulation not just of those products, but also of the indirect consequences of their consumption and consumption trends.

If one considers the prevailing social framework that shapes globalization to be beneficial to both human and ecosystem health, its globalization will certainly be perceived as a wonderful phenomenon. If, conversely, that social framework inherently manifests certain pathological and dangerous features, its globalization poses tremendous risks. ICTs have an important role either way.

While globalization is not inherently good or bad, it does interact with our values and institutions that shape and are shaped by it. Herein lies the heart of the problem, "for what we have, now, is not a global village, but a global marketplace where the dictates of capital and economic self-interest have made our earlier discourses of dignity and justice somehow obscene or archaic" (Labonte, 2002, 1). New layers of technology are added to support the ideals, expectations, needs, and institutions of the prevailing social framework. ICTs compensate for the barriers of old technologies, affording greater maneuverability, extending the limits of older technologies applied for quantitative growth (Hilty & Ruddy, 2000).

Specific low-level applications such as the mobile telephone are characteristic of this process. However, it is the broadening of such processes to a societal or higher level that reveals dramatic insights into the potential of ICTs in their contribution to supporting, reinforcing, and extending the reach of the prevailing social framework (Wilska, 2003). Analogous to the technological layers, social layers of institutions and decisions are constantly added, buttressing the prevailing social framework and dramatically weakening the distinctiveness of other social frameworks. ICTs are an important tool in establishing the new layers of social institutions as much as they contribute to the technological layers.

Our sustainability crisis is one of a social nature. We avoid solutions through added "social" layers—technological rationalization, economic efficiency, and political liberalism—that function to justify and reinforce the existing framework. Technologies such as ICTs are applied to stimulate growth in economically efficient ways, firmly reinforcing the social framework that ultimately generated their perceived need.

ICTs appear to have enabled a global leap in all economic activity, especially informational economic activity, without a corresponding reduction in conventional economic activity. In one decade—1989 to 1999—the Internet boom propelled the net worth of the world's two hundred wealthiest people to $1 trillion from $463 billion (O'Meara, 2000).

Modern globalization emphasizes increasing trade volumes, capital flows, and market liberalizations. It is dominated by large transnational companies, a few powerful governments, and several international financial organizations, notably the World Trade Organization (WTO), the World Bank, the BIS, and the IMF. International rules are established by these actors to meet their objectives of increased trade and capital flows and greater market access. The power and influence of transnational corporations and global institutions cannot be understated. They define globalization and "control the vast majority of these global flows of capital, goods and services, and information, processes and use global production, marketing, and distribution networks, and can no longer be associated with one specific 'home' country" (Fuchs & Lorek, 2001, 11). "International trade rules apply to countries, but not to large corporations, which have been able to consolidate and to diminish competition in their sectors. They are price makers" (Easter, 2005, 11). TNCs, through their immense power, ultimately influence national and international decisions.

Both profit and capital growth have increasingly become benchmarks of value, with TNCs controlling vast amounts. Following from our discussion on fiat currencies and chrematistics,[8] the role of ICTs in shaping the global capitalist enterprise and modern trajectories of globalization begins to crystalize. Modern mathematical models and tools made available through advanced computers and globally deployed through ICTs have contributed to the enormous growth in financial market activity and chrematistics. Fluid and extraordinarily diverse information, received and transmitted from all points on the globe, feeds these models and the millions of individual actors engaged in financial markets at any given moment. New actors and innovative sources of investment have been procured through space and time in large part thanks to the advanced computational capabilities and information dispersion properties of ICTs—including, of course, the media and their significant power over public discourse. Modern exchange markets are built on, connected by, and accessed through ICTs. As currency markets mushroomed, national governments' ability to

---

[8] *Chrematistics* is defined by Daly and Cobb as "the branch of political economy relating to the manipulation of property and wealth so as to maximize short-term monetary exchange value to the owner" (1994, 138).

establish economic policy vanished. Interest rates and national (fiat) currency values have become largely a function of global financial markets and distant political, economic, and social events. Provided by ICTs, the information that guides national decisions is already truly global.

This information includes the virtually instantaneous transmission of transactions across financial products and national currencies by actors that are globally connected from almost every country. The result can establish, and has established, sufficient momentum to trigger abrupt global cascading events. The connections established between products, actors, currencies, and countries leads to a very tight bonding between all activities as values and events change, are recorded, transmitted, read, filtered, and retransmitted. More often, however, these events lead to the slow evolving of trends within and across nations, helping to shape global market directions, expectations, and values. This is further fueled by the convergence of media and communications technologies, and the various agents that contribute filtered, opined, and scripted messages. The principal message of rapid capital withdrawal is insidiously concealed in a sea of cultural baggage; political, economic, even environmental decisions are unremittingly held captive by the modern sword of Damocles.

These messages conform to specific ideals, and these have come to be controlled and manipulated by fewer individuals as wealth has become more concentrated. This concentration has been achieved through a form of social consent for structured inequalities, a consent given centuries ago, long before its modern apex could even have been envisioned. As the conditions have enabled transglobal corporations to merge with and acquire other corporations, the ability to influence global thought, expectations, values, and social norms has become a reality that directs national policy-making, including the institutions and social organization that, while facilitated nationally, radiate globally. Politicians dare not aggravate perceived reality and value expectations; instead, political entities employ diverse mechanisms, such as polls, to understand the polity—if not to confuse with random informational gibberish and overload[9]—and to respond by setting ap-

---

[9] While ICTs offer a growing number of messages contrary to the established trajectory of globalization, how will people access this growing glut of information, will they access it, and will the social institutions exist to enable them to act on those messages? How much information floating around in cyberspace is just so much presumptuous gossip, filler, inaccuracies raising popular Google searches? Can any information be acted upon lacking the requisite social mechanisms? Global capital, through its competitive and dominant ideologies, will continue to defend its niche, confounding and thwarting change.

propriate policies. Anachronistic, evidence-based policy making has yielded to policy-based evidence making in the shrinking global world of growing info-glut. Global financial wealth and the ability to influence ideals and expectations through informational resources and financial global markets—combined with the institutional mechanisms that firmly support capital growth—represent global power to shape and direct our local, regional, national, and global institutions and social expectations at will.

Paradoxically, the conditions that empower transglobal corporate wealth concentration include the exponential rise in informational financial resources and individual agents participating in the markets, currencies, and other financial products. ICTs have enabled this activity, which has subsequently enabled the entrenchment of capital and the expanding wealth differences globally, nationally, and regionally. It represents an ironic twist on the class distinction of capitalism; individual agents, mostly in the industrialized nations, working to squeeze the maximum from their labor income, typically through large mutual funds or pension plans, as well as individual investing, are contributing to a system that raises some yachts disproportionately. Simultaneously, very populous "emerging economy" countries and Aborigines around the globe are being drawn into the globalized world of corporate wealth concentration through mechanisms that both encourage and compel their participation, magnifying tremendously the numbers and allegiance of individual agents. While labor might be fundamentally dependent upon capital, this relationship has become much more profound with the advent of ICTs and the convenience of access to capital markets they afford. The process that has been unleashed allows wealth—bits and bytes of electronic currencies flashing around in cyberspace—to direct political decisions that favor the wealthy and drive more individuals with greater allegiance into the market, enhancing the process further. Castells observes that the machineries of ICTs taking control of our world, not in the manner that concerned the Luddites, but as "an electronically based system of financial transactions" (2000, 56), seems ever closer to reality. By restricting and controlling governmental interventions and regulatory options, directing and designing institutional frameworks, and limiting individual agency to within the dictates established by global market ideals, ICTs and market-driven globalization are giving birth to a new macro civilization guided by the flows of information in response to market values, or, more specifically, both profit and capital growth in which humans have little control beyond philosophical debates. It subsumes class capitalism, nationality, and, indeed, entire ecosystems.

It is an emergent, self-organizing phenomenon. Commodification and valuation of nature's ecosystems and social goods brings into this brave new world a steady inflow of consumables in terms of physical resources and energy, and thus serves its new global financial masters. But wait: isn't this the information economy, in which information, not resources, becomes the valued commodity; in which equality and democracy are expected to sweep the globe; and in which environmental sustainability is at last within grasp?

Since supply and demand is but one very minor determinant of this macro civilization, the rules of Adam Smith and those laid down by both standard and unconventional economics no longer function. We have shifted from a Newtonian world to a Einsteinian world where the old rules, if ever they were an accurate predictive or management tool, no longer apply. Rational *Homo economicus* has been replaced by the new sources of information delivered to market actors through ICTs in a global world. Global entities, "either directly or through intermediaries—are obeying the implacable logic of capital by creating barriers to entry, stifling local economies, and racing to liquidate finite resources" (Mayer, 1998, 71).

Other information providers directly connected with market ideals, such as market valuation firms, central bankers, and investment firms, focus on specific market characteristics. This has the obvious effect of distorting values, if not overtly excluding certain social and environmental values. Numerous influential decision makers and institutions offer daily commentaries on market events and trends. Taken together, Castells concludes that "largely uncontrolled information turbulences are as important as supply and demand in setting prices and trends in global financial markets" (2000, 56).

There now exists a war for the eyes and ears of the Internet: established transnational interests on the one hand and a grouping of often unified yet independent interests on the other. Where environment, social, or health departments should be making decisions, finance departments transcend. The allocation of resources are determined by the emergent artificial financial imperatives because it is the financial performance of a country that determines its level of investment and growth, and thus determines how effectively it is willing to accommodate market-driven globalization. Increasing standards of living accommodate this dictate, which in turn satisfies capital mobility.[10] Thus

---

[10] This helps explain why, in the war on tobacco, for example, punitive restrictions on smoking in public spaces had to be consistently constructed to demonstrate no net impact on economic growth (Ontario Tobacco Research Unit, 2003; Physicians for a Smoke-Free Canada, 2001; Warner & Fulton, 1994).

finance, a social contract of artificial wealth, trumps reality in this social structure. Virtual wealth defined by chrematistics, represented by a mere social contract, and manipulated by wealth accumulation has become the new master influencing individual and national decision making. As politicians bend incessantly further toward global market ideals, social support mechanisms are being eroded and dismantled, and national environmental protections fall prey to global trade and financial investment imperatives. Combined with the coherent regulation and oscillations of financial markets around the globe, this facilitates greater financial transactions and participation. This has the effect of driving more people into the market, which supports wealth concentration, as well as creating a greater divide, both within and between nations, of wealthy and poor. The consolidation of global wealth and power has serious consequences for local tangible economies. The process also fortifies the prevailing economic worldview in subtle and complex ways. Capital, as a powerful and globally efficient leveraging institution in the form of bits and bytes, has become the anchor maintaining the existing class system and consumer lifestyles. Ultimately, the spiral of financial market energies are enhanced and catapulted by ICTs into a compact set of values that impoverishes communities and ecosystems alike, as a black hole inescapably siphons matter.

Social, environmental, and economic needs become caught in the eddies as global markets ebb and flow with single-mindedness and numbing mindlessness as the value of this wealth sloshes into and out of real goods and services. Witness the financial meltdown in the fall of 2008 that affected first loans and housing, then capital markets. The power at its command cannot be denied. Informational resources will be applied to serve investing principles based on mathematical representations of complex, self-organizing systems, rather than corporate fundamentals, environmental sustainability, physical realities, or social responsibility. It will become increasingly difficult to corral the effects of capital as global market access increases, tools proliferate, transaction costs decrease, and anonymity increases. ICTs are accelerating the global free flow of capital, or, more accurately, abstract wealth represented by bits and bytes that, in turn, represent fiat currencies—a social contract for the store of value created, but not printed, by private, often transnational corporations that are certainly growing in power and control. John Livingston (1994) speculates how other species, birds or fish for example, have an innate ability to communicate seemingly effortlessly and instantaneously—a form of group consciousness. "The flashing angles, turns, slants, starts, and stops are too swift, too fine-tuned—indeed, too erratic—to be executed by

the synchronized separate movements of hundreds of individuals"
(Livingston, 1994, 106). Naturalists, he argues, are unable to imagine
this higher level of entity than the individual because we are so ingrained in our cultural baggage of individualism, our prosthetic ideology of technology, and our mechanistic reductionism, and thus can
only marvel at their synchronous movements, their speed, and their
extraordinary maneuverability—their "oneness." Could it be that we
have re-created this "group-consciousness"—an emergent adeptness—
through our technological outgrowths in servitude of capital and profit
growth? Have the institutions of market-driven globalization and the
role of ICTs given birth to an emergent global superorganism capable
of functioning not as a mere aggregation of individuals, but as a self-
aware, coherently functioning, synchronized single-growth entity?

ICTS AND GLOBALIZATION:
A TECHNOLOGICAL OUTGROWTH OF CAPITALISM

Nicholas Carr (2008) believes the Internet is changing the way people
think and organize information, driving personal thought to distraction; manipulating and managing information rather than absorbing,
contemplating, and reflecting on the knowledge it contains. He explains that in 2007, Larry Page, cofounder of Google, the online search
engine company, revealed to a gathering of scientists that the ultimate
objective of Google was "to build artificial intelligence and to do it on a
large scale" (Carr, 2008, para. 25). Analyzing the thousands of daily ex-
periments and terabytes of information collected by Google through its
search engine websites, Google is attempting to systematize everything
it does by collecting, logging, assessing, and modifying how people find
information on the Internet and extract meaning from it. In doing so,
Google is altering and refining the algorithms that ultimately control
how people use the Internet, effectively normalizing human behavior,
from the information we seek to the way we read and interpret that
information, and the uses and meanings we extract. Maryanne Wolf,
director of the Center for Reading and Language Research at Tufts University, asserts that the processes of reading are more than an isolated
activity (Wolf, 2007). The format of written messages and their symbols define how we read. How we read and interpret messages not only
provides basic knowledge, but also determines how we think and interpret the world around us—and our ability to do so. Malcolm Gladwell
(2008), for instance, notes the differences in mathematical abilities
between Chinese students who have grown up using ideograms and

Western students who have grown up using numbers and the alphabet. Cultures that use traditional knowledge—which interweaves rich, complex, story-based messages for interpreting the world around them—have very different worldviews than cultures that depend on the scientific approach to interpret the world around them. The emerging globalized and normalized multimedia, staccato, sound-byte, efficient, immediate, multitasked interpretations of information provided by the Internet and other ICTs are quite distinct from those provided by our rich and varied cultural heritages. Like a single, normalized, self-aware growth engine, people are, through their use of ICTs, subtly being exposed to an array of processes and behaviors that are transforming the way we behave, think, and expect. The release of a new suite of search engines to respond to Internet queries the way an expert would, each with its thousands of processor cores and air conditioned bandwidth sufficient to host a ski resort in the Sahara Desert, should be the least of the environmental worries. The mind-bending informational shaping of human thought processes—fundamentally reorganizing how we think, search for, and use information; and reference and validate data—is now transforming the informational resources made accessible by previous versions of search engines and making computable those informational resources, shifting farther away from human imagination and creativity the process to achieve a result and yielding instead a singular end result these computable knowledge tools decide is relevant. The implications for shaping the trajectory of globalization is virtually—pardon the pun—mind blowing!

Carr even goes so far as to suggest that it is in the economic interest of Google to drive the Internet experience to distraction. In that manner, users are more likely to access a greater number of websites—complete with advertising and commercial messages—and companies are better able to capture and analyze our behavior for profitable gain.

The decision, if not the premise, to apply ICTs hinges on their ability to generate an income or profit—to somehow be manipulated to fuel the growth engine. "The European experience with telecenters suggests that for such projects to be sustained over the long term, local people must be able to make money by running them as a business" (O'Meara, 2000, 140). Can the romantic beliefs or ideological determinism of ICTs be cultivated to nurture more sustainable consumption?

"The notion that technologies can prescribe their own course of action is mythical: the responsibility for technological outcomes lies in the social order—individuals, groups and institutions—through which lives are organised" (Davison et al., 2000, 5). In other words, we can choose how ICTs bring about the shaping of society—the implementation of essential guardrails and establishment of new and effective global institutions and frameworks to change behavior and lifestyles and entire decision-making architectures—that will lead to more sustainable consumption. That choice remains highly influenced by social factors that affect those decision-making architectures, which remain largely beyond the ability of individual action. Powerful social interests wield substantial control—incredibly and profoundly enhanced through ICTs—over those social factors, and are largely uninterested in altering existing prevailing structures they currently derive substantial benefits from.

SUMMARY AND DISCUSSION

During the August 2003 blackout, information and knowledge about "the big picture" were in short supply. It is the "big picture" that has become increasingly lost in a world that fixates on ever smaller details as it is flooded by data and information. There was simply no mechanism to assess the enormous amounts of data flowing across the computer screens and telephone conversations of literally hundreds of utility operators, supervisors, and managers responsible for maintaining the electrical grid supply. Compound these challenges with the data and calls from customers and other actors, and the operators at utilities and institutions responsible for the electrical grid never had a chance once the cascade began. In the immediate crisis, no single individual or agency was aware of the overall situation, and conjectures, as demonstrated by separate and almost simultaneous comments from First Energy employees, were not cross-fertilized. Despite the unimaginable amount of data and information flashing across computer terminals, warning messages, and complex process innovations afforded by ICTs, these features at best only contributed to the rapidly cascading deterioration of electrical energy trickling through the North American power grid.

This is one of the paradoxes of the information age as it is currently structured and spliced into the prevailing social framework: that in a time of voluminous amounts of data and information, its effective use, or, more accurately, knowledge of how to effectively use it, and its appropriate application—certainly for a more sustainable world—can sometimes be lacking. In particular, the lack of regular snapshots and trends in the big picture's unfolding social events are failing to impart the necessary wisdom we need for effective and sustainable decision making. This is also true in the environmental sector, where data from geopositional satellite systems, millions of documents on the Internet, instantaneous communications, and armies of armchair environmentalists have failed to slow many of our most pressing environmental challenges, especially global challenges. Despite the remarkable quantity of data and information, the quality of change necessary remains blissfully deficient.

In the late nineteenth century, when the telephone ushered in new communications potential, global competition rose dramatically for a few decades. The result was lower costs, increased affordability, and a sudden growth in telephone use. State-owned monopolies capitalized on this opportunity. Nearly a century later, the WTO brokered a deal permitting 90 percent of the world's telecommunications revenue markets to be opened to foreign competition (O'Meara, 2000). A frenzied series of mergers and acquisitions followed, leading to a dramatic rise in transnational ownership and convergence of these formerly national media.

Back in the early twentieth century, the telephone permitted a spectacular increase in the global movement of goods and services. Borders were opened and powerful empires spread globally, inspiring visions of the free market. Europe was one massive transnational trading block. During those exuberant years of trade and economic growth, people believed these opportunities were universal, unshakable truths.

Many pundits of modern globalization or ICTs insist that technology is far more advanced today—complex, uniting, and sustaining—justifying and solidifying those universal, unshakable truths. Yes, of course technology has advanced. It is the social framework out of which technology advances that has not sufficiently progressed to realize the quantum gains possible from these new discoveries and their application. We continue to transplant, splice, and graft the new technologies into—and interpret their meanings and uses out of—the global, market-based, growth-obsessed social framework. We need instead an evolution, transformation, and maturation of the social framework: society 2.0, rather than web 5.0! This might now be within reach, thanks to the incredible ability of ICTs to self-organize complex information flows.

Saul comments that those in power "believe that their job is to understand power and management and perhaps make minor corrections to what they accept to be the torque of events. But they take for granted the reigning truths of the day and so are fundamentally passive" (2005, 11). Is it perhaps too naïve to expect that ICTs could help transform those prevailing beliefs? Might we, in time to save our species, recognize and appreciate the critical role of ICTs in supporting what appears to be a fundamentally unsustainable social structure and therefore transform the reigning truths and the current trajectory of globalization?

9

Redefining Reality, Transforming Values

> If efforts to protect the planet and its peoples from environmental harm are to be effective, they will have to follow that shift in power . . . downstream to the ideologies, symbols, relationships and practices that drive consumption. (Conca, 2001, 55)

Heilbroner (1985) describes capitalism as a form of social structure intending, through its structure and institutions, to shape behavior. The fact that even the most impassioned supporters of sustainable consumption have sunk to the level of materialism and continued economic expansionism to promote their messages and enhance their "effectiveness" suggests a deeply pervading, incredibly flawed value structure.

Fundamentally, if we are to achieve progressively more sustainable consumption in our increasingly constrained globalized world, we will need a transformation of value structures and practices, the institutions that service them, and the mechanisms that enable these changes. *Daunting, idealistic, unrealistic,* and a host of similar adjectives might be employed to describe this goal.

Yet ICTs might just offer the model and opportunity to realize this goal. Here's the opportunity: if ICTs can be used as a tool to shape unsustainable behavior, why could they not be used just as effectively as a tool to shape more sustainable behavior? A hammer, after all, if designed properly, can be used just as effectively to remove nails as to install them. If ICTs can serve as a conduit for global cultural hegemony, is there any reason they could not serve ethical purposes? Certainly this has been one prominent stated objective or expectation driving their advance. If ICTs are to serve a more sustainable purpose and take advantage of this incredible opportunity, they will need a model. Historically, this has proven to be an enormous barrier—calls for value changes fall on deaf ears without a solid, realistic plan. Now, emerging out of the energy, environmental, and financial crises of the early part of the new millennium, we might just have such a model that would serve to develop a real, tangible plan.

The failure of the electrical grid in eastern North America in August 2003 demonstrated the incredible misalignment between our energy demands and supply. This serves as a metaphor for the increasing divergence of human energy demands and planetary processes and its physical properties. Just as evident is the increasing gulf between human aspirations, wants, and consumption with the biological and physical realities of the planet. A large reason for our increased energy and materials demand has been ICTs: they seem to have reorganized our lives, from the personal and local to the global, accelerating and magnifying the human economy in profoundly and deeply troubling ways. This challenge also holds the key to a solution: the distributive, self-organizing qualities of ICTs might be employed to sustainably restructure and spontaneously manage the energy grid, and by extension, human civilization. In the same manner that ICTs offer the potential to equitably redistribute information, they might also be applied to equitably redistribute energy, and simultaneously transform the social context within which energy and material artifacts come to be mediated. Using bottom-up or distributed forms of energy production, combined with the intelligent, self-organizing nature of ICTs, an organic transformation of energy, communications, and society might now be possible. Indeed, such a transformation might even be progressing beyond our peripheral of measurement.

FORGING AHEAD

When the lights finally flickered back on following the August 14, 2003, North American blackout, it took many months to decipher the causes. The large centrally controlled and managed energy and electrical grids of the world have been known to contain flaws. One of these has certainly been their vulnerability to just such events as the August blackout. Distributed electrical networks would help solve this problem. Forging such a network, however, has been an incredibly difficult task—until now.

The "Final Report on the August 14, 2003, Blackout in the United States and Canada: Causes and Recommendations" tended to focus on conventional solutions. Despite the horribly conservative nature of the final report's causes and recommendations, it does fortunately contain a number of enlightening opportunities and valuable insights.

One such insight was to ensure better situational analysis—understanding the big picture to guarantee adequate regional-scale interpretation of the bulk power system. Translation: the report calls for additional top-down command-and-control management and technologies. Wouldn't the addition of more energy and resource intensive technology simply compound the management and organizational complexity of the energy grid? Wouldn't the increasingly unwieldy, expensive, and complex task of managing a growing electrical grid only posit a more fragile, unsustainable, insecure, and inequitable system—an efficiently operating, consumer-oriented, management and regulatory nightmare obsessed with anachronistic economic growth? The recommendation for improved top-down command-and-control management of the energy grid, and current conceptualizations of the smart grid endeavor, reveal the insight that our decision makers have yet to grasp and appreciate: the importance of a distributed structure and the role ICTs can perform in such a structure for providing a more sustainable future.

A distributed democratic organic structure, just like natural systems—and just like ICTs are purported to offer (and perhaps create, albeit unsustainably!)—would nurture superior resiliency, flexibility, security, equality, and long-term sustainability, balancing demand and supply right down to the smallest device. Using ICTs, such a network could function autonomously, smoothing and lowering peaks across regions and throughout the day, shifting power, matching supply and demand, shutting off and turning on power where and when necessary, distributing production, constantly reevaluating and assessing system states and trends, and automatically reorienting the system as required. Since electrical energy must be used once it is produced, less any system storage capacity, loads must be shifted when and where required. This was one of the reasons for the August 2003 blackout: as transmission lines tripped, enormous amounts of power were rerouted through the network, causing a rapidly cascading series of events. An organic smart grid (unlike current conceptualizations that tend to use ICTs as a management tool) would be capable of maneuvering and manipulating smaller loads, with tremendously improved flexibility for rerouting power and shifting loads, and drawing on energy storage capacity as needed, as a single, self-aware, coherently functioning entity.

No single agency or individual was aware of the "big picture" unfolding on August 14, 2003. Initially, this might appear to be a problem. However, no single command-and-control top-down awareness need be construed. As an emergent self-aware organism, applying ICTs in a more sustainable manner can create that awareness as a natural inherent characteristic of the electrical network—or social framework. Einstein asserted that the problems we have today cannot be solved at the same level of thinking we were at when we created them. The August blackout was compounded by a top-down command-and-control structural shortcoming. In a bottom-up distributed framework, discourse, information, data, knowledge, and possibly even wisdom can be shared across global networks and cross-fertilized organically. There is no longer a need to top-down manage the voluminous data and information blinding the ICTs' ethernet. If we can unleash a self-aware global growth entity, perhaps we can nurture the emergence of a self-aware global sustainable consumption entity. We now have the opportunity to create a distributed democratic and sustainable social framework—ecologically astute, socially equitable, globally conscious—modeled upon and integral with a sustainable smart grid. Here's how.

A FORMULA

Jeremy Rifkin believes the confluence of new energy and communications frameworks have been accompanied by decisive transformations in human history (Rifkin, n.d.). For instance, across ancient societies—Mesopotamia, Egypt, China, and India—the harnessing of water and animals for energy combined with agriculture led to surpluses. These surpluses generated greater freedoms in terms of socially productive opportunities as fewer workers were needed to harvest crops. With these transitions came the need to manage the surpluses, and writing and bookkeeping were invented. The new communications tool of writing merging with the newly harnessed energies of water and animals gave rise to the agricultural revolution, utterly transforming society.

Similarly, key to the first industrial revolution, Rifkin argues, was the merging of steam power with printing, leading to increased literacy that propelled the steam-driven industrial revolution forward. The second industrial revolution, the result of merging oil and the telegraph, ignited the economic powers still very much apparent today that have generated incredible global wealth and distribution networks.

Rifkin next points to the current revolution in energy as putting power into the hands of everyone with the ability to install solar panels, geothermal heat pumps, wind turbines, and other forms of alternative energy in a distributive, democratic manner. Like the dinosaurs, "elite" or top-down energy structures—coal, nuclear, and oil and gas—are fading into oblivion. The structures that make massive blackouts possible and entire societies brittle and subject to terror-ism, social and political risks, class divisions, and ecological disasters are no longer feasible in the third Industrial Revolution. The huge investments required to make these mammoth projects possible are themselves responsible for massive loan guarantees, power struggles, and social and ecological disruptions on a global scale. This is one of the most important factors winking out these energy sources' future existence—like the land owners of the feudal era. Different from the top-down, large-capital intensive, centralized forms of energy produc-tion that powered the first two industrial revolutions, bottom-up en-ergy generation is distributed, fair, and accessible. Instead of grafting ICTs and alternative energy systems onto the existing technologies and management approaches of the current grid network, Rifkin and others argue the smart grid should integrate ICTs in a holistic manner to catapult global economies into the twenty-first century. These dis-tributed energies—a new energy framework and, thanks to the amaz-ing capabilities of ICTs, a new communications framework—will fuel the grid and global economic growth. It is, as Rifkin suggests, the third Industrial Revolution. Using the distributional democratic potential of the Internet as an analogy, Rifkin and others envision a distributed, democratic energy grid.

The manner in which this vision is constructed is pivotal. If, as we have seen with ICTs, the construction is not appropriately guided, amorphous growth might shape less sustainable behavior and devel-opment as much as it has the potential for more sustainable futures. That is why the Internet and ICTs only offer a *potential* to democrati-cally redistribute social wealth and restructure society; this potential has yet to be tapped.

Despite these uniquely visionary outlooks and all their promise, they remain grounded in a "spliced-onto" future. These visions insist that holistically integrating our new technologies—ICTs and alter-native distributed energy structures—to fabricate a completely new smart energy grid will result in new jobs, prosperity, and global eco-nomic growth. Such a framework would instead restrict, if not utterly impair, the incredible potential of this visionary new future with very likely catastrophic consequences.

The problem is that these present visionary futures are doing a lot of grafting themselves—grafting onto the second industrial economic foundation of growth, jobs, and implacable global market-based laws. Does this not impart the very same thing—a restricted future vision of untenable growth and distributive constraints, not to mention the collapse such a consumer society could and does engender?

Unlike these visions of a third Industrial Revolution, however, are the transformations to basic economic foundations and principles that are being catapulted forward by the merging of distributed alternative energy generation and ICTs. This—the Achilles' heel of the self-aware global growth entity—might instead be where the next global societal transformation occurs.

THE FOUNDATION

The shift to sustainability will come when the current conceptualizations of the smart grid allegiance shift from growth to degrowth—toward more sustainable consumption. Here's how this could transpire.

Frederick Soddy wrote during the 1929 depression years about the thermodynamic impossibilities of the current economy, and how, as we have seen, fiat currency creation can shift out of step with reality. As this happens, we have massive social and environmental crises.

Soddy suggested five important policy prescriptions. Eric Zencey, in the *New York Times*—as captured online thanks to the informational provisioning powers of the Internet—encapsulates Soddy's first four policy prescriptions (Zencey, 2009). While Zencey notes that each at the time was taken as virtually impossible—so unshakable were their truths—each has, in turn, tumbled like the economic turmoil that began in late 2008 to crumble the financial house of cards, or the winking out of power across the northeastern North American landscape in August 2003. These four prescriptions were to (1) abandon the gold standard, (2) let international exchange rates float, (3) use federal surpluses and deficits as macroeconomic policy tools that could counter cyclical trends, and (4) establish bureaus of economic statistics (including a consumer price index) in order to facilitate this effort. All of these are now the norm, despite their believed impossibility.

The fifth and most important policy prescription, which we discussed at length in the previous chapter, is that money cannot be created by private institutions at will in an exponential and continuously expanding manner. We have already seen the problems this practice creates, both socially and ecologically, from the standpoint of sustainable consumption. We have also explored the possibility that the Internet and ICTs within a global world have hatched a self-aware global growth entity to further fuel this process—our pathological prerequisite.

With the now emerging social framework of the twenty-first century, based on and integral to the smart-grid model, we no longer require private interests to create money—if we can nurture the emergence of this social framework. Since everyone can now create energy, or at least be given the opportunity to do so (as it is in both our ecological and social interests to do so), energy becomes the new currency. The shift will happen not as people trade energy with their local utilities in renewable energy standard offer programs or feed-in tariff programs for income or a credit on their energy bills as an economic incentive to propel growth. Rather, the shift will happen only after energy itself becomes the new global social currency, shifted where it is needed when it is needed—consistent with ecological and social realities—in a complex self-organizing system, all made possible by ICTs.

Our well-being and social framework will be linked with the real world—no longer guided by bits and bytes that represent mere numbers on a globally connected network of abstract money-creating systems. Our economy will be linked to the fundamental needs of the planet and the social structures that we nurture and create.

This transformation might already be underway around the world, as the smart grid begins to take shape. However, while the smart grid remains bound by a vision that courts economic growth, the current trajectory of market globalization continues to unfold, propelled further and fueled by short-sighted transplantation of new technologies and opportunities for growth into a framework of anachronistic global consumerism.

To overcome the limits of this trajectory and unleash the full global significance of ICTs, the organic smart grid model will need to be diffused throughout society, creating the synergies and rules, regulations and legislation, organizations and institutions and mechanisms to germinate, foster, nurture, and engender a flexible, resilient, organic, self-aware degrowth entity—an utterly transformed new social framework—focused on more sustainable consumption. The process will shift society from a large, top-down managed, command-and-control model to a bottom-up, distributed, cooperative, sharing model.

Throughout human history, power and wealth has gradually shifted away from the egalitarian, sharing, and cooperative structures seen in the small-group societies that survived sustainably for thousands of years within their immediate environments. Power and wealth has shifted instead toward increasingly rigid, unequal, individualistic, and competitive social structures—manifest through the enclosure movements and the gradual shift to capital ownership in a class-structured global village. But as that global village lost touch with reality, it quickly lost touch with the social and ecological needs of that reality. We now have the power—literally and figuratively—at our disposal to shift the global village back to the cooperative, sharing, sustainable egalitarianism not witnessed in ten thousand years of formal human social organization.

TRANSFORMATIONS

Our challenge: we have been attempting to splice a new emerging phenomenon, the significance of which nobody can yet fully appreciate or begin to understand its full implications onto an old, industrial-era set of instructions, structures, processes, expectations, lifestyles, and values.

At some point, those bits and bytes will represent a demand currency on tangible goods and services—goods and services that global actors have no intention, no ability, no substance, and no physical means of supplying. We're not a species about to run over a cliff. Our global oneness is on a collision course with an inviolable reality; the physical laws of thermodynamics and physics trump the assumptions, the values, and the belief structures that the present global society has been tenuously fabricated upon.

We have to stop thinking about ICTs and globalization as new tools to be applied in the old way, for global economic growth. We must now open up our minds and be the future we can be, the future that is sitting at our doorstep, the emergent global phenomenon that unites and connects humans everywhere with their environment and each other in a global currency compatible with ecological and social systems to propel our species toward sustainable consumption.

There are still a number of barriers. Obviously, the first is to recognize the choice we now confront. Connecting a social contract with the real world, or disconnecting it from fantasy, could benefit both social equalities and ecological realities. Once social structures and global institutions exist to permit that transformation, our values will become less contradictory.

This will be a critical step. For instance, were we to build up our stock of alternative energy and ICTs to match and continue to grow in lockstep with our current and growing—almost insatiable—global demand and aspirations for energy and materials, we might very well surpass planetary social and ecological tipping points. The pressure for the old economy to manufacture even our current demand—and continue to match the growing demand—would posit a continued physical expansion of the human economy. This is precisely why we must transform the social framework upon which society is constructed to one of degrowth from one of growth.

As buildings, hybrid cars, trucks, buses, cell phones, computers, and virtually all devices that contain energy storage capability are plugged into the smart emergent grid, they become power supplies or loads as the grid requires, organically, self-consciously. Since most vehicles are used very little over a twenty-four-hour period, they could offer considerable energy storage and supply this back to the grid at times of need. Rifkin estimates that if only 25 percent of the vehicles in the United States were employed in this manner, they would offset all the energy demands of all the power plants currently in the United States and the European Union (Rifkin, n.d.). Using ICTs, continental electrical grids could share electricity as simply as ICTs share information over the Internet today, with the powerful management and operational efficiencies ICTs furnish.

Vringer and Blok write that "dematerialisation of the consumption pattern does not seem to be an autonomous process" (2000, 713). The greatest hurdle this vision must overcome will be its creation—it will not emerge spontaneously. It will take work, planning, coordination, and the abandonment of materialist expectations, many firmly held beliefs and value structures, and even more firmly held power, wealth, and control structures. The risks that society will revert to global growth "can only be limited if appropriate social and ecological 'guardrails' are installed world-wide by politicians as part of the world's economic system" (Information Society Forum, 1998, 22). Those guardrails will be essential in the initial formative stages to shape a new world economic system, designed to establish an emergent form of social agreement and consciousness intended to nourish sustainable economic degrowth to match social and ecological realities. Specific policy tools and other actions will need to counter the consumer ethic, create information provisioning, achieve more sustainable social processes and lifestyles (for example, the denormalization of waste and excess consumption and the cultivation of immaterialism), create a culture of sufficiency (Reisch, 2001), maximize efficiency within this cultural sufficiency framework, establish regulations and legislation (such as the European Union's Restriction of the Use of Certain Hazardous Substances in Electrical and Electronic Equipment and the Directive on Waste Electrical and Electronic Equipment), and foster improved design and research.

Instead of using ICTs as a tool for productive expansionism, they will become the "neurons" of the emergent resilient, complex suprahuman social organism to redistribute and reduce in absolute terms the global consumption of energy and materials and the social impacts caused by expansionist values.

REALITY

Energy as the new currency!? A completely new social framework!? This sounds absurd. So too did Soddy's first four prescriptions. Until they come to be accepted socially, many new ideas are ignored or dismissed. Currency and money are purely social constructs. Despite the initial absurdity of energy as currency, many different forms of currency are already in existence today, from community dollars to various trading schemes, both within and outside formal economic structures. Fundamental differences between Islamic and Western banking structures exist. Despite what most people might believe, money is already virtually defined as bits and bytes. Electronic currency has become quite commonplace, used by transnational corporations to online users of debit and credit systems (for example, PayPal, digital cash and currency, e-wallets), and just about everyone in between. Electronic currency now sloshes into and out of real markets, shifting, altering, disrupting the ecologies that sustain us and the social networks that define who we are. Economic events of 2008/2009 demonstrate just how fragile a monetary system based on fractional reserve banking can be, and demonstrate the urgency to revamp the very structures and institutions splintering cyber- and real-space. Would it be more realistic to expect a self-aware, coherently functioning, synchronized growth entity—based on an artificial social construct for money (a bizarre, mystical, almost grotesque representation of social wealth) that is ultimately and literally loaned into existence—to continue indefinitely on a finite planet? Would it not be more realistic to theorize the cultivation of an economy based on tangible physical properties—social and ecological—linked through a new social construct based on available energy as a new currency? The system we currently have must continually expand—by design. Is it reasonable to expect this to continue indefinitely into the future? Of course not. Realistically, what we have now is a system that must disintegrate at some point in time, and that time seems to have arrived. We now need a new social contract to supersede the old, disintegrating past. ICTs are an available and critical tool that can now forge the foundation to enable, construct, and align values with ecological and social realities.

Clearly, it is essential to stop thinking of ICTs as an extension of the twentieth century industrial era to be grafted onto the old global growth economy. The power of ICTs in the anachronistic structures we have are rapidly catching up to us in surprising and unintended ways. The emerging supra-organism we have created through ICTs must be recognized for the culturally disruptive and marvelously empowering opportunity it is. We need to take those sparks and forge a new reality that accommodates the physical realities of our world and the ecosystems that enable life to exist on this planet.

ICTs will probably, and probably must, continue to be used to improve the efficiency of processes. Their strength, however, will not be in their application to applications. It will instead be realized in their application to transform values by restructuring the global world, our values, belief structures, and human behavior and decision making. When this power is unleashed, combined with a distributed, democratically structured smart grid, powerful synergies might just enable the self-organizing reorientation of global civilization so urgently needed.

The historical significance of this era will be the emergence of a culture possibly based on energy as currency, rather than a culture based on currency as power, where everyone should have the power to constructively engage in society. Our future currency can be linked with sharing and thermodynamics—social equality and environmental sustainability—in a global world that ensures through its self-organizing management more sustainable consumption. This is just one nonprescriptive, yet hopefully inspirational and motivational suggestion from the infinite number that we might envision, were we to let go of the bounds and social constructs that limit our imagination.

10

Global Transformations: Serious Considerations and Promising Opportunities

ICTs have infused every aspect of the lives of peoples around the world—reorganizing space and time across geographies and affecting lives at every level in every role. ICTs can and do interact in our lives in extraordinarily complex ways. Our values shape the institutions and social structures we construct. These in turn affect our decisions and help fuel and sustain our actions. These structures form complex decision-making architectures that we now know affect our health and well-being in critically important ways. Likewise, our global social institutions affect our consumption decisions in critically important ways. The trajectory of modern globalization is fueled by some remarkably contradictory values, which collide with sustainable consumption in amazingly questionable ways. Yet they remain largely unquestioned. The social structure out of which modern globalization has emerged and continues to project into the future is seriously flawed for achieving precisely that future in which it professes to believe. ICTs contribute to this future in profoundly complex and subtle ways to propel further, faster, and higher the growth of economies and consumption of planetary resources that are seriously compromising people and the health of local, state, and global cultures, as much as the ecological systems and processes upon which they depend.

ICTs are being applied across virtually every realm of social organization—globally—to solidify, anchor, instill, and install this incredibly flawed social structure. Whether it is the amazing power that specific applications or processes have to displace and substitute for energy and materially demanding activities, or the mystically mysterious efficiency promise others might offer, the fact that the human civilization remains just out of reach of that ephemeral promised future suggests that we have just to extend the reach of this or that application along its current locus of possibility just a little further.

The service orientation and dematerialization possibilities that ICTs offer have struggled to take root in a "political climate that does not favour policy intervention (such as heavy taxes on natural resource use), and a culture that does not favour curtailing consumption" (Heiskanen & Jalas, 2003, 196).

So why do such strong beliefs in the dematerializing properties, immaterializing properties, and social benefits of ICTs remain so firmly established despite the increasing evidence against their efficacy? Why are these beliefs increasingly ubiquitous, given the overwhelming evidence against them? Simply, we continue to project that locus of possibility downstream to possible future visions without following the locus of power upstream to where it emerges, and to where the values attributed to the forces that compel our current trajectory of globalization gestate. Like the salmon on their end-of-life run back up the river to lay their future offspring, their promises are swimming against an immense tide of powerful flows; this is a gestalt we fail to perceive, yet one that is critical to understand if we are to achieve more sustainable consumption. This can only be achieved if we follow the flow of power back upstream to its source, to where it originates.

We need to look up at the universe of possibilities rather than down into the world that created our problems if we are to find solutions. ICTs might best offer promise where they are applied to help us shape that turbulent flow.

A shift in these higher level structures will have a greater influence on lower level structures than the converse. That is, a shift in values and social processes will have a greater impact on behaviors than a behavioral shift will have on values and social processes. Brown and Cameron note that many unsustainable values are "moulded by the structure and constraints of the prevailing socio-economic system including the incentive structure reflected by the market and promotional messages" (2000, 33). Values and social processes serve as the organizing principles of how we view consumption.

More sustainable consumption will "require wide and deep social relearning of thinking, value structures, behavior patterns, and institutional arrangements" (Milbrath, 1995, 115). Brown and Cameron conclude that, in order to be successful, conventional tools and management techniques "require a fundamental shift in cultural value orientation away from self-interested consumer oriented motives and toward a prosocial pro-environmental value orientation that motivates limits" (2000, 31). These assertions, however important, have always abandoned the processes of achieving those objectives. ICTs might now provide insight into how that journey could be accomplished.

The blackout of August 2003 resulted from a complex set of events. A constantly increasing demand for energy (partly attributable to ICTs) combined with a series of human errors and technological mishaps in the immediate situation combined with the failure of existing systems and processes to suitably manage the network and inform network operators. This should not, however, be interpreted to suggest we need more top-down command-and-control management of the systems and processes that presently exist. Similarly, the social environment, which has an incredible influence on our behavior and choices, also exerts a profound influence on the tools we use and how they are defined and evolve. The fact that human social organization and behavior must become more sustainable does not necessarily imply greater attention to the specific products and processes we use to define and mediate our world. Nor does it imply that greater efficiency within the prevailing social framework would be a sufficient means test for either reducing demand or achieving a more sustainable and just global society. Little feedback exists on how these tools are shaping society, how society shapes its tools, and whether that global trajectory is even sustainable.

Deinstitutionalizing and denormalizing over-consumption, achieving more sustainable consumption, and improving population health is now both necessary and possible.

For decades, our governments have encouraged a consumption binge. We seem, sadly, to have lost our creativity and capacity to cultivate different ways in which to improve our well-being, so globally and pervasively ingrained in our institutions and social processes have growth-oriented market ideals become. Savings rates across Organisation for Economic Co-operation and Development countries are dismally low. We are simply compelled to spend all and more than we can get our hands on. We extend this, equally out of need and greed, to other cultures around the world. When caution compels people to reduce their spending, the global economy enters a tailspin, and all barriers are removed to renormalize society with growth, despite the clear inconsistencies with achieving more sustainable consumption. Despite our desire for greater well-being and global sustainability, when prodded, we are reluctant to consider stalling this trend. Every excuse is given, from the impact on economic growth and jobs creation, to the need to attract investment and increase productivity. Perhaps the most obtuse excuse is the wish to uphold free choice and not to interfere in individual choice or consumer sovereignty. Yet by encouraging and complacently accommodating growth, are we not explicitly and implicitly interfering in choice—limiting choice in this case to what global, growth-oriented market ideals can accommodate? How much freedom and choice does that permit?

In the era of virtually instantaneous transmission of information, there is no reason why that information cannot be used to benefit populations and ecosystems through social transformations that seek to achieve more sustainable consumption. Markets have demonstrated a powerful propensity to transmit information in the blink of an eye, causing tremendous market swings that can ripple globally in a matter of moments. They symbolize a compelling motivation to bend decision makers to their tightly focused, synchronized will. They manifest the persuasive capacity to influence the decisions and behavior of regions, nations, and international governments, often contrary to societal needs and environmental realities. There is no reason why this same phenomenon cannot be applied in a wider social context for more sustainable consumption. The inertial resistance of institutions and mechanisms, decision makers and governments, can be overcome if only the desire and self-awareness to do so exists.

Ronald Wright suggests that "[t]he rise in population and pollution, the acceleration of technology, the concentration of wealth and power—all are runaway trains, and most are linked together" (2004, 128). Modern market-based globalization hyper-charged by ICTs is taking us along a path typical of ancient societies that collapsed because of their folly—the path of greed and arrogance and resistance to change even though the evidence for the need to change was and, like today, is widespread. It is sadly ironic that, in the age of information and the knowledge economy, we have neglected the wisdom that human history can teach us, and lack the humility to embrace other ways of knowing and being.

As I conclude the writing of this book, the level of rhetoric in the ICT sector has reached new heights. With the awareness of global climate change becoming increasingly apparent, the ICT sector has peppered the media with reports expounding the benefits of rapid adoption of ICTs. Most fixate on the "efficiency" benefits of ICTs, as though climate change were the problem itself, rather than a symptom. As commented by Tom Kelly, Managing Director for Logicalis UK and posted on the Global Action Plan website upon the release of Global Action Plan's An Inefficient Truth Report, 2007, "efficient IT equals green IT" (Kelly, 2007, para. 13). Others recommend more efficient government policy interventions to enable the ICT sector to grow or more efficiently utilize existing technologies and processes.

Others consider reward, market, or tax mechanisms to boost growth in the presumably weightless ICT service sector, apparently unaware of the social and ecological dilemma these produce. The full potential benefits of ICTs to sustainable consumption in our increasingly globalized world have yet to be seriously pondered. While ICTs offer hope to contribute to a sustainable global transformation, widespread critiques and examinations of how to apply ICTs in a sustainable manner have been woefully scarce. Emerging reports and information in this realm leave little hope for success.

Emerging out of this dismal affliction are promising opportunities. The potential smart grid, and its diffusion across social structures, is one such opportunity. There are many developments that support this expectation. Application programming interfaces, open document formats, open source programming, social networking, and creative commons platforms all resonate with the self-organizing structural properties of ICTs for purposes other than simply amorphous capital and economic growth.

The strength of ICTs will not be in their ability to modify process efficiencies, product design, or other low-level applications. While existing tools can already achieve energy savings of an order of magnitude through various design features and technical specifications—reductions of 83.5 percent in electricity consumption for computing equipment can translate into a 94 percent reduction in other building system loads that support equipment loads (Eubank et al., 2004)—this will be insufficient without a transformation of the prevailing global social structures. Speaking only in these terms simply clouds their potential. A "blanket" approach to developing, promoting, and applying ICTs in every application where it is predicted, through some generalized assumptions and magical hand-waving, to achieve more sustainable consumption must be approached with caution, particularly where it can be brought to market. Indeed, if left to dominant social processes alone, such an approach may prove disastrous. Unless our increasingly unsustainable global consumption trends "are directly addressed by altering the underlying socio-economic processes, only limited progress is to be expected" (Spangenberg & Lorek, 2002, 134). Fuchs and Lorek argue that "globalization and global governance with their respective influences on the relevant actors strengthen rather than weaken the forces lined up in support of continued overconsumption" (2004, 3). It will be essential to shift global dialogue and progress on sustainable consumption "in order to re-articulate these concepts in ways not limited to the global management of contemporary capitalism in a green framework" (McManus, 1996, 70).

The strength of ICTs to reshape the current global trajectory will be in their ability to affect change at that social level, globally—to alter and transform our deepest beliefs and value structures and the institutional mechanisms that support and interact with these structures; to transcend conventional reductionistic, linear thought and behavior with complex, self-organizing actions, behavior, and decision making consistent with the natural ecosystems that we inhabit.

Bibliography

Aebischer, B., & Huser, A. (2000, November). *Networking in private house-holds: Impacts on electricity consumption.* Ittigen, Switzerland: Swiss Federal Office of Energy. Retrieved July 6, 2005, from www.electricity-research. ch/SB/haushaltsvernetzung-00-english.pdf

Aebischer, B., & Huser, A. (2002, December). *Energy analysis of the FutureLife House.* Ittigen, Switzerland: Swiss Federal Office of Energy.

Aebischer, B., & Huser, A. (2003). *Energy analysis of the FutureLife House.* Ittigen, Switzerland: Swiss Federal Office of Energy.

Aebischer, B., & Varone, F. C. (2001). The Internet: The most important driver of electricity demand in households. *European Council for an Energy Efficient Economy (ECEEE) 2001 Summer Study Proceedings,* 394–403. Retrieved November 25, 2005, from www.eceee.org/conference_proceedings/eceee/2001/Panel_2/p2_12/

Agility Forum. (1997). *Next generation manufacturing: A framework for action,* Agility Forum, Leaders for manufacturing, and technologies enabling agile manufacturing. Bethlehem, PA.

Alexander, C. J., & Stafford, A. P. (1998). The cutting edge? Gender, legal and ethical implications of high-tech health care. In L. Pal & C. J. Alexander (Eds.), *Digital democracy: Policy and politics in the wired world* (194–218). Toronto: Oxford University Press.

Amos, A., Gray, D., Currie, C., Elton, R. (1997, September). Healthy or druggy? Self-image, ideal image and smoking behaviour among young people. *Social Science & Medicine, 45*(6), 847–58.

Antipolis, S. (2001). *Free trade and the environment in the Euro-Mediterranean context. First synthesis report for the Mediterranean Commission on Sustainable Development.* Athens: United Nations Environment Programme—Mediterranean Action Plan for the Barcelona Convention.

Antonelli, C. (1991). *The diffusion of advanced telecommunications in developing countries.* Paris: Organisation for Economic Co-operation and Development.

Anzovin, S. (1997). The green PC revisited. Retrieved from www.computer-user.com/magazine/national/1519/covr1519.html

Arctic Monitoring and Assessment Programme (AMAP). (1997). *Arctic pollution issues: A state of the Arctic environment report.* Oslo: Author.

Arnfalk, P. (2002). *Virtual mobility and pollution prevention: The emerging role of ICT based communication in organisations and its impact on travel.* Unpublished doctoral dissertation. Lund University, Lund Sweden.

Arnfalk, P., & Kogg, B. (2002). Service transformation—Managing a shift from business travel to virtual meetings. *Journal of Cleaner Production, 11,* 859–72.

Arnott, R., de Palma, A., & Lindsey, R. (1991). Does providing information to drivers reduce traffic congestion? *Transportation Research, 25A,* 309–18.

ASSIST. (2002). Immaterialisation and lifestyle choice. *The European Journal of Tele-working, 8*(2), 8.

Aubrey, A. (2002, April). Activists push for safer e-recycling. National Public Radio.

Ayine, D., Blanco, H., Cotula, L., Djiré, M., Kotey, N. A., Reyes, B., et al. (2005, September). Lifting the lid on foreign investment contracts: The real deal for sustainable development. *Sustainable Markets Briefing Paper, International Institute for Environment and Development.* Retrieved from www.iied.org/pubs/pdfs/16007IIED.pdf

Ayres, R. U. (1995). Economic growth: Politically necessary but *not* environmentally friendly. *Ecological Economics 15,* 97–99.

Ayres, R. U. (1998). Towards a disequilibrium theory of economic growth. *Environmental and Resource Economics, 11*(3/4), 289–300.

Ayres, R. U. (2001). The minimum complexity of endogenous growth models: The role of physical resource flows. *Energy 26,* 817–38.

Ayres, R. U. (2002). Exergy flows in the economy: Efficiency and dematerialization. In R. U. Ayres & L. W. Ayres (Eds.), *A Handbook of Industrial Ecology* (185–201). Cheltenham, UK: Edward Elgar.

Ayres, R. U., Ayres, L. W., & Warr, B. (2003, March). Exergy, power and work in the US economy, 1900–1998. *Energy Journal, 28*(3), 219–73.

Balka, E. (2003). *From work practice to public policy: A case study of the Canadian health information infrastructure.* Unpublished research proposal.

Barber, B. (2007). *Consumed: How markets corrupt children, infantilize adults, and swallow citizens whole.* New York: W. W. Norton.

Barth, M. J. (1994). Evaluating the impact of IVHS technologies on vehicle emissions using a modal emission model. *National Proceedings of the Policy Conference on Intelligent Transportation Systems and the Environment,* Arlington, VA.

Baudrillard, J. (1988). The mirror of production. In Mark Poster (Trans.), *Selected writings* (98–118), Palo Alto, CA: Stanford University Press.

Beyers, W. B. (1998, March 21–23). Cyberspace or human space: Whither cities in the age of telecommunications? Paper presented at the *Telecommunications and the City Conference,* Athens, GA.

Binswanger, M. (2001). Technological progress and sustainable development: What about the rebound effect? *Ecological Economics, 36,* 119–32.

Binswanger, M. (2002). Time-saving innovations and their impact on energy use: Some lessons from a household-production-function approach. University of Applied Sciences of Northwestern Switzerland Discussion Paper No. 2002-W01.

Bodeen, C. (2002, May 31). Computer waste a threat to China's environment. *Associated Press.*

Brahic, C. (2007, December 3). Computer servers "as bad" for climate as SUVs. *New Scientist.*

British Broadcasting Corporation. (2005a, November 29). Climate change will dry Africa.

British Broadcasting Corporation. (2005b, December 8). Greenland glacier races to ocean.

British Telecom. (2001). Better world—Our commitment to society/e-business and the environment.

Brown, J. S., & Duguid, P. (2001). Knowledge and organization: A social-practice perspective. *Organization Science, 12,* 198–213.

Brown, P. M., & Cameron, L. D. (2000) What can be done to reduce overconsumption? *Ecological Economics, 32,* 27–41.

Bryden, H., Longworth, H. R., & Cunningham, S. A. (2005, December 1). Slowing of the Atlantic Meridional Overturning Circulation at 25° N. *Nature, 438,* 655–57.

Burch, M. (1995). *Simplicity: Notes, stories and exercises for developing unimaginable wealth.* Gabriola Island, BC: New Society Publishers.

Canadian Broadcasting Corporation. (2000, November 13). B.C. infestation rages out of control. Retrieved January 3, 2007, from archives.cbc.ca/IDC-1-75-1254-6967/science_technology/tree_pests/clip8

Canadian Broadcasting Corporation. (2002, October 22). Marketplace: Hi-tech trash.

Canadian Broadcasting Corporation. (2003, October 10). Canada's least wanted. Retrieved January 3, 2007, from archives.cbc.ca/IDC-1-75-1254-6969/science_technology/tree_pests/clip10

Canadian Broadcasting Corporation. (2006a). Arctic ice shelf collapse poses risk: Expert. Retrieved January 2, 2007, from www.cbc.ca/technology/story/2006/12/28/tech-ellesmereiceshelfcollapse-20061228.html?ref=rss

Canadian Broadcasting Corporation. (2006b, December 28). Development boom may hurt northern communities: Researcher. Retrieved January 2, 2007, from www.cbc.ca/canada/ottawa/story/2006/12/28/development.html

Canadian Broadcasting Corporation. (2006c, December 29). Global warming could transform Amazon into savanna in 100 years: Researchers.

Canadian Broadcasting Corporation. (2006d, December 26). In many villages, Alaskans face physical and cultural erosion.

Canadian Broadcasting Corporation. (2009). Profs say students lack maturity, feel entitled. Retrieved August 11, 2009, from www.cbc.ca/sunday/2009/04/041209_6.html

Canadian Public Health Association. (1997, March). *Health impacts of social and economic conditions: Implications for public policy*. Ottawa, ON: Author.

Carr, N. (2008, July/August). Is Google making us stupid? *The Atlantic*. Retrieved April 15, 2009, from www.theatlantic.com/doc/200807/google

Cas, J. (2005, Spring). Privacy in pervasive computing environments—A contradiction in terms? *IEEE Technology and Society Magazine*, 24–33.

Castells, M. (1996). *The rise of the network society*. Cambridge, MA: Basil Blackwell.

Castells, M. (2000). Information technology and global capitalism. In W. Hutton & A. Giddens (Eds.), *Global Capitalism* (52–74). London: Jonathan Cape.

Cerf, V. (2000). *Engineering tomorrow*. Los Alamitos, CA: IEEE Press.

Choi, W. S., Ahluwalia, J. S., Harris, K. J., & Okuyemi, K. (2002). Progression to established smoking: The influence of tobacco marketing. *American Journal of Preventive Medicine, 22*(4), 228–33.

Ciais, P., Reichstein, M., Viovy, N., Granier, A., Ogée, J., Allard, V., et al. (2005, September). Europe-wide reduction in primary productivity caused by the heat and drought in 2003. *Nature, 437*(7058), 529.

Clark, M. E. (1989). *Ariadne's thread: The search for new modes of thinking*. New York: St. Martin's Press.

Clark, M. E. (1995). Changes in Euro-American values needed for sustainability. *Journal of Social Issues, 51*(4), 63–82.

Cleveland, C. J., Kaufmann, R. K., & Stern, D. I. (2000, February). Aggregation and the role of energy in the economy. *Ecological Economics 32(2)*, 301–18.

Cogoy, M. (1999, March). The consumer as a social and environmental actor. *Ecological Economics, 28*(3), 385–98.

Cohen, N. (1999, October). Greening the Internet: Ten ways e-commerce could affect the environment and what we can do. *Information Impacts Magazine*.

Cohen, S. S., & Zysman, J. (1987). *Manufacturing matters: The myth of the post-industrial economy*. New York: Basic Books.

Coleman, R. (2004, April). Less may be more. *Reality Check: The Canadian Review of Well-Being, 4*(1), 1.

Commissioner of the Environment and Sustainable Development. (2001). Report of the Commissioner of the Environment and Sustainable Development to the House of Commons (Chapter 5—Integrating the Social Dimensions: A Critical Milestone). Ottawa, ON: Author.

Conca, K. (2001). Consumption and environment in a global economy. *Global Environmental Politics, 1*(3), 53–71.

Cook, D. (1999, December). *No Purchase Necessary: Newsletter of the Consumers, Commodities and Consumption Special Interest Group of the American Sociological Association, 1*(1).

Costanza, R., d'Arge, R., de Groot, R., Farber, S., Grasso, M., Hannon, B., et al. (1997, May 15). The value of the world's ecosystem services and natural capital. *Nature, 387*, 253–60.

CTV globemedia Inc. (2009, April 6). "Profs say students lack maturity, feel entitled." Retrieved from www.ctv.ca/servlet/ArticleNews/story/CTV News/20090406/student_study_090406/20090406?hub=Canada

Czech, B. (2001). A potential catch-22 for a sustainable American ideology. *Ecological Economics, 39*, 3–12.

Dalton, M. A., Tickle, J. J., Sargent, J. D., Beach, M. L., Ahrens, M. B. (2002, May). The incidence and context of tobacco use in popular movies from 1988 to 1997. *Preventive Medicine, 34*(5), 516–23.

Daly, H. E. (1996). *Beyond growth: The economics of sustainable development.* Boston: Beacon Press.

Daly, H. E., & Cobb, J. B. Jr. (1994). *For the common good: Redirecting the economy toward community, the environment, and a sustainable future.* Boston: Beacon Press.

Davison, R., Vogel, D., Harris, R., & Jones, N. (2000). Technology leapfrogging in developing countries: An inevitable luxury? *The Electronic Journal on Information Systems in Developing Countries, 1*(5), 1–10.

Department of Energy. (2008, June 23). Annual energy review 2007, Report No. DOE/EIA-0384(2007). Retrieved from November 15, 2008, www.eia.doe.gov/emeu/aer/contents.html

Diamond, J. (2003, June). The last Americans: Environmental collapse and the end of civilization. *Harper's Magazine*, 43–51.

Dominguez, J., & Robin, V. (1992). *Your money or your life: Transforming your relationship with money and achieving financial independence.* New York: Penguin Books.

Douce, G. K., Moorhead, D. J., & Bargeron, C. T. (2006). *Center for Invasive Species and Ecosystem Health website.* Project Coordinators, University of Georgia. Retrieved January 3, 2007, from www.invasive.org

Durning, A. (1992). *How much is enough? The consumer society and the future of the earth.* New York: W. W. Norton.

Durning, A. (2006, June 9). The currency of parenting #8.Weblog for the year of living car-lessly experiment. Retrieved January 4, 2007, from www.sightline.org/research/sprawl/res_pubs/durning-carless

Dürrenberger, G., Patzel, N., & Hartmann, C. (2001). Household energy consumption in Switzerland, *International Journal of Environment and Pollution, 15*(2), 159–70.

Dworschak, M. (2008, March 31). Server farms as polluting as air traffic: Computer centers and even individual PCs are responsible for massive amounts of carbon dioxide, and the problem is growing. *BusinessWeek*. Retrieved July 9, 2008, www.businessweek.com/globalbiz/content/mar2008/gb20080331_274500.htm

Easter, W. (2005, July). *Empowering Canadian farmers in the marketplace: Report to the Minister of Agriculture and Agri-Food.* Canada: Agriculture and Agri-Food Canada. Retrieved from www.agr.gc.ca/cb/min/pdf/rpt0705_e.pdf

Ehrlich, P. R., Wolff, G., Daily, G. C., Hughes, J. B., Daily, S., & Dalton, M. (1999). Knowledge and the environment. *Ecological Economics, 30*(2), 267–84.

Eisler, R., (1987). *The chalice and the blade*. San Francisco: Harper Collins.

Ekins, P. (1996). "Limits to growth" and "sustainable development": Grappling with ecological realities. In K. P. Jameson & C. K. Wilber (Eds.), *The political economy of development and underdevelopment* (53–69), New York: McGraw-Hill.

Elgin, D. (1993). Voluntary simplicity: Toward a way of life that is outwardly simple, inwardly rich. New York: William Morrow and Company.

Ellger C., & Scheiner J. (1997). After industrial society: Service society as clean society? Environmental consequences of increasing service interaction. *The Service Industry Journal, 17*(4), 564–79.

Ensley, L. (2005). Information and communications technological leapfrogging in developing countries. Retrieved January 2, 2006, from www.ischool. utexas.edu/~i385q/archive/ensley_l-Technological%20Leapfrogging.doc

EnvirosRIS. (2000, October). *Information technology (IT) and telecommunications (telecom) waste in Canada*. Gatineau, Quebec, Canada: Environment Canada.

Epstein, S. S. (1998). *The politics of cancer revisited*. Freemont Center, NY: East Ridge Press.

Erdal, D., & Whiten, A. (1996). Egalitarianism and Machiavellian intelligence in human evolution. In P. Mellars & K. Gibson (Eds.), *Modelling the early human mind* (139–50). Cambridge: McDonald Institute Monographs.

Erdmann, L., Hilty, L., Goodman, J., & Arnfalk, P. (2004). The future impact of ICTs on environmental sustainability. *European Commission Directorate General Joint Research Centre Technical Report EUR 21384 EN.*

Eubank, H., Aebischer, B., Lewis, M., Koomey, J., Tschudi, W., Rumsey, P., et al. (2004). High performance data centers. Building Performance Congress: Report from the Data Center Design Charrette, February 2–5, 2003, Snowmass, CO.

European Environment Agency. (2002). *Update on the environmental dimension of the EU sustainable development strategy from environmental signals* (Working Paper). Copenhagen: European Environment Agency.

Fawcett, T., Lane, K., & Boardman, B. (2000). *Lower carbon futures DECADE project*. Oxford: Environmental Change Institute, Oxford University.

Federal, Provincial, Territorial Advisory Committee on Population Health (1994, September 14–15). Strategies for population health: Investing in the health of Canadians. Paper presented at the Meeting of the Ministers of Health, Minister of Supply and Services Canada, Halifax, Nova Scotia.

Federico, A., Hinterberger, F., & Musmeci, F. (2002). Application of the MIPS concept in Italy: Two case studies. Paper presented at the Ecological Economics Conference, Sousse, Tunisia.

Fellenius, E., & Andersson, I. (2001, May). Bridging the gap: Sustainability research and sectoral integration. Chairman's conclusions presented at the International Conference, Sweden, May 9–11.

Fichter, K. (2001). Sustainable business strategies in the internet economy. Sustainability and the information society. In *15th International Sympo-*

sium Informatics for Environmental Protection, Zurich (109–18). Marburg: Metropolis Verlag.

Fichter, K. (2003). E-commerce: Sorting out the environmental consequences. *Journal of Industrial Ecology, 6*(2), 25–41.

Fischer-Kowalski, M., & Amann, C. (2001, September). Beyond IPAT and Kuznets Curves: Globalization as a vital factor in analysing the environmental impact of socio-economic metabolism. *Population and Environment, 22*(1), 7–47.

Fishbein, B. K. (2002). *Waste in the wireless world: The challenge of cell phones.* New York: INFORM, Inc.

Fodor, E. (1999). *Better, not bigger: How to take control of urban growth and improve your community.* Gabriola Island, BC: New Society Publishers.

Folke, C., Pritchard, L. Jr., Berkes, F., Colding, J., & Svedin, U. (1998). The problem of fit between ecosystems and institutions (Working Paper No. 2). Bonn, Germany: International Human Dimensions Programme on Global Environmental Change.

Frank, L. (2007, March). *The role of the built environment in promoting public health and sustainable ecosystems.* Health Canada Policy Research Presentation.

Frank, L., Kavage, S., & Litman, T. (2006). *Promoting public health through smart growth: Building healthier communities through transportation and land use policies and practices.* Vancouver, BC: SmartGrowth BC Report.

Frank, L. D., Sallis, J. F., Conway, T. L., Chapman, J. E., Saelens, B. E., & Bachman, W., et al. (2006). Many pathways from land use to health. *Journal of the American Planning Association, 72*(1), 75–87.

Frey, S. D., & Harrison D. J. (2000). Environmental assessment of electronic products using LCA and ecological footprint. *Joint International Congress and Exhibition: Electronics Goes Green,* Berlin, Germany.

Fuchs, D. A., & Lorek, S. (2001). *An enquiry into the impact of globalization on the potential for 'sustainable consumption' in households, program for research and documentation for a sustainable society.* Oslo, Norway: ProSus.

Fuchs, D. A., & Lorek, S. (2004, March). *Sustainable consumption: Political debate and actual impact* (SERI Background Paper, No. 4). Vienna: Sustainable Europe Research Institute.

Gard, D. L., & Keoleian, G. A. (2003). Digital versus print: Energy performance in the selection and use of scholarly journals. *Journal of Industrial Ecology, 6*(2), 115–32.

Gardner, P. M. (1972). *The Paliyans.* In M. G. Bicchieri (Ed.), *Hunters and gatherers today: A socioeconomic study of eleven such cultures in the twentieth century* (404–47). New York: Holt, Rinehart and Winston.

Garrison, W. (2000, February 21–22). Sustainable information societies in the U.S. In *Conference Proceedings Report.* Towards a sustainable information society.

Gaspar, J. & Glaeser, E. L. (1996). *Information technology and the future of cities.* Cambridge, MA: Harvard Institute of Economic Research, Harvard University.

Geels, F. W., & Smit, W. A. (2000, November). Failed technology futures: Pitfalls and lessons from a historical survey. *Futures* 32(9–10), 867–85.

Giampietro, M., & Mayumi, K. (1998). Another view of development, ecological degradation, and north-south trade. *Review of Social Economy, 56*(1), 20–36.

Gillespie, A., Richardson, R., & Comford, J. (1995). *Review of telework in Britain: Implications for public policy*. Newcastle, England: University of Newcastle upon Tyne, Centre for Urban and Regional Development Studies.

Gladwell, M. (2008). *Outliers: The story of success*. New York: Little, Brown and Co.

Global Action Plan. (2007). *An inefficient truth*. London: Author.

Global eSustainability Initiative. (2008). *SMART 2020: Enabling the low carbon economy in the information age*. Brussels, Belgium: The Climate Group.

Global Social Policy Forum. (2001). A north-south dialogue on the prospects for a socially progressive globalization. *Global Social Policy 1*(2), 147–62.

Goehring, B. (1993). Indigenous peoples of the world: An introduction to the past, present and future. Saskatoon: Purich Publishing.

Goldberg, C. (1998). Where do computers go when they die? Technology Circuits. *New York Times.* Retrieved from www.ce.cmu.edu/greendesign/comprec/nytimes98/12die.html

Gough, I. (2001). Globalization and regional welfare regimes: The East Asian case. *Global Social Policy 1*(2), 163–90.

Gowdy, J. M. (1994). *Coevolutionary economics: The economy, society and the environment*. Boston: Kluwer Academic Publishers.

Grahame, T. J., & Kathan, D. (2001, May). Internet data centers and electricity growth. *Broadband Wireless Online, 2*(5).

Green, K. (1992). Creating demand for biotechnology: Shaping technologies and markets. In R. Coombs, P. Saviotti, V. Walsh (Eds.), *Technological change and company strategies: Economic and sociological perspectives* (164–84). San Diego: Academic Press Limited.

Greening, L. A., Greene, D. L., & Difiglio, C. (2000). Energy efficiency and consumption: The rebound effect—A survey. *Energy Policy 28*(6/7), 389–401.

Greiner, C., Radermacher, F., & Rose, T. (1996). Contributions of the information society to sustainable society. Ulm, Germany: FAW.

Hachman, M. (2009, January 26). Internet users top one billion, most of them Asian. *PCMagazine.* Retrieved February 26, 2009, from www.pcmag.com/article2/0,2817,2339592,00.asp

Hamilton, C. (2007, May–June). Building on Kyoto. *New Left Review 45.* Retrieved from www.newleftreview.org/?view=2671

Hamm, S. (2008, March). It's too darn hot: The huge cost of powering—and cooling—data centers has the tech industry scrambling for energy efficiency. *Business Week.* Retrieved July 9, 2008, from www.businessweek.com/magazine/content/08_13/b4077060400752.htm

Hawkes, K., O'Connell, J. F., & Blurton-Jones, N. G. (1991). Hunting income patterns among the Hadza; Big game, common goods, foraging goals and the evolution of the human diet. In A. Whiten & E. Widdowson (Eds.), *Foraging strategies and natural diet of monkeys, apes and humans*. Oxford, UK: Clarendon Press.

Haynes, K., Lall, S., Stough, R., & Yilmaz, S. (2000). *Network usage patterns and the substitution and complementarity effects between telecommunications and transportation: A demand side approach*. Washington, DC: The Institute of Public Policy, George Mason University. Draft.

Health Canada. (2001). *Report from the first annual National Health and Climate Change Science and Policy Research Consensus Conference—How will climate change affect priorities for your health science and policy research?* Ottawa, Ontario: Climate Change and Health Office, Health Canada. Retrieved December 10, 2005, from www.hc-sc.gc.ca/ewh-semt/pubs/climat/research-agenda-recherche/index_e.html

Health Canada. (2003). *e-Health solutions—First Nations health care in transition: The Alberta story*. Ottawa: Author.

Heaton, L., Kishchuk, N., & Picot, J. (2004). Conflicting accounts: Operating assumptions and the evaluation of telemedicine. In *Proceedings of the Communication, Technologies and Health Working Group*. International Association for Media and Communications Research (15–24).

Hedges, C. (2009). *Empire of illusion: The death of literacy and the rise of spectacle*. Toronto: Knopf Canada.

Heilbroner, R. L. (1985). *The nature and logic of capitalism*. Toronto, Ontario: Penguin Books Canada.

Heinonen, S., Jokinen, P., & Kaivo-oja, J. (2001, May). The ecological transparency of the information society, *Futures* 33(3–4), 319–37.

Heiskanen, E., & Jalas, M. (2000). *Dematerialization through services—A review and evaluation of the debate*. Finland: Ministry of the Environment.

Heiskanen, E., & Jalas, M. (2003). Can services lead to radical eco-efficiency improvements? A review of the debate and evidence. *Corporate Social Responsibility and Environmental Management, 10*, 186–98.

Held, D., Mcgrew, A., Goldblatt, D., & Perraton, J. (2003). Rethinking globalization. In D. Held & A. McGrew (Eds.), *The global transformations reader* (67–74). Oxford, UK: Blackwell Publishers.

Herring, H. (1999). Does energy efficiency save energy? The debate and its consequences. *Applied Energy, 63*, 209–26.

Herring, H., & Roy, R. (2002). Sustainable Services, electronic education and the rebound effect. *Environmental Impact Assessment Review, 22*(5), 525–42.

Hesse, M. (2002). Shipping news: The implications of electronic commerce for logistics and freight transport. *Resources, Conservation and Recycling, 36*(3), 211–40.

Hilty, L., Behrendt, S., Binswanger, M., Bruinink, A., Erdmann, L., Fröhlich, J., et al. (2005, February). *The precautionary principle in the information society: Effects of pervasive computing on health and environment*. Report of the Centre for Technology Assessment, TA46e/2005.

Hilty, L. M., & Ruddy, T. F. (2000). Towards a sustainable information society. *Informatik*, No. 4, 2–9.

Hirsch, F. (1976). *Social limits to growth*. New York: Twentieth Century Fund.

Hochschild, A. R. (1997). *The time bind: When work becomes home and home becomes work*. New York: Metropolitan Books.

Hoogendijk, W. (1993). *The economic revolution: Towards a sustainable future by freeing the economy from money-making*. Utrecht, Netherlands: Jan van Arkel.

Hopkinson, P., & James, P. (2002). *Teleworking at BT—The economic, environmental and social impacts of its workabout scheme. Report on survey results.* Prepared for Sustainable Telework, Project of the European Community "Information, Society, Technology" Programme.

Huber, P. W., & Mills, M. P. (2005). *The bottomless well: The twilight of fuel, the virtue of waste, and why we will never run out of energy*. New York: Basic Books.

Information Society Forum. (1998). *Forum info 2000: Challenges 2025—On the way to a sustainable world-wide information society*. Ulm, Germany: FAW.

Intergovernmental Panel on Climate Change. (1990). *Potential impacts of climate change. Report of Working Group 2, Intergovernmental Panel on Climate Change, 1-1 to 2*. Geneva: World Meteorological Organization/United Nations Environment Programme. Retrieved from www.ciesin.org/docs/001-011/001-011.html

Intergovernmental Panel on Climate Change. (1998). *IPCC special report on the regional impacts of climate change: An assessment of vulnerability intergovernmental panel on climate change*. Retrieved February 2, 2006, from www.grida.no/climate/ipcc/regional/index.htm

International Society for Ecological Economics. (1998). Special issue: The environmental kuznets curve. *Ecological Economics, 25*(2), 143–232.

Internet World Stats. (2009). *World internet users and population stats*. Retrieved April 15, 2009, from www.internetworldstats.com/

Jackson, T. (2005). Live better by consuming less: Is there a "double dividend" in sustainable consumption? *Journal of Industrial Ecology, 9*(1–2), 19–36.

Jackson, T. (2009). *Prosperity without growth? A transition to a sustainable economy*. London: Sustainable Development Commission.

Jackson, T., & Marks, N. (1999). Consumption, sustainable welfare, and human needs—With reference to UK expenditure patterns, 1954–1994. *Ecological Economics, 28*(3), 421–41.

Jalas, M. (2000). *A time-use approach on the materials intensity of consumption* (p 29). Helsinki: Helsinki School of Economics and Business Administration, Department of Management.

Jalas, M. (2002). A time-use perspective on the materials intensity of consumption. *Ecological Economics, 41*, 109–23.

James, P., & Hopkinson, P. (2002). *Science innovation for sustainability: A new option for UK environmental policy?* London: Green Alliance.

Jespersen, J. (1999). Reconciling environment and employment by switching from goods to services? A review of Danish experience. *European Environment, 9*, 17–23.

Jevons, W. S. (1866). *The coal question—An inquiry concerning the progress of the nation and the probable exhaustion of our coal mines* (2nd ed.). London: Macmillan.

Jokinen, P., Malaska, P., & Kaivo-oja, J. (1998, August). The environment in an "information society": A transition stage towards more sustainable development? *Futures 30*(6), 485–98.

Jones, R., Rogers, R., Roberts, J., Callaghan, L., Lindsey, L., Campbell, J., et al. (2005). What is eHealth (5): A research agenda for eHealth through stakeholder consultation and policy context review. *Journal of Medical Internet Research, 7*(5). doi:10.2196/jmir.7.5/e54/; PMID:16403718. Retrieved from www.jmir.org/2005/5/e54/

Kaivo-oja, J., Luukkanen, J., & Malaska, P. (2001, November). Sustainability evaluation frameworks and alternative analytical scenarios of national economies. *Population and Environment, 23*(2), 193–215.

Kanninen, B. J. (1996). Intelligent transportation systems: An economic and environmental policy assessment. *Transportation Research A, 30*(1), 1–10.

Kaplan, H., & Hill, K. (1985). Food sharing among ache foragers: Tests of explanatory hypotheses. *Current Anthropology, 26,* 223–45.

Kawamoto, K., Koomey, J. G., Nordman, B., Brown, R. E., Piette, M. A., Ting, M., et al. (2001, February). *Electricity used by office equipment and network equipment in the U.S.: Detailed report and appendices.* Washington, DC: U.S. Department of Energy.

Kelly, H. (1999, October). Information technology and the environment: Choices and opportunities released. *Impact Magazine.*

Kelly, T. (2007). *Inefficient ICT sector's carbon emissions set to surpass aviation industry.* Global Action Plan website. Retrieved October 15, 2008, from www.globalactionplan.org.uk/news_detail.aspx?nid=62992fb1-c745-4738-bf96-f4acfd08088a

Kilbourne, W. E., Beckmann, S. C., Lewis, A., & Van Dam, Y. (2001). A multinational examination of the role of the dominant social paradigm in environmental attitudes of university students. *Environment and Behavior, 33*(2), 209–28.

King, B. (2002, March 4). Kazaa: A copyright conundrum. *Wired News.* Retrieved from www.wired.com/techbiz/media/news/2002/03/50788

Kirkpatrick, C., & Lee, N. (1999). *WTO new round: Sustainability impact assessment study, phase two report—Executive summary.* Manchester, UK: Institute for Development Policy and Management and Environmental Impact Assessment Centre, University of Manchester. Retrieved January 22, 2002, from www.europa.eu.int/comm/trade/pdf/repwto.pdf

Klein, N. (2000). *No logo: Taking aim at the brand bullies.* Toronto, ON: Vintage Canada.

Knauft, B. M. (1991). Violence and sociality in human evolution. *Current Anthropology, 32,* 391–428.

Knorr-Cetina, K. (1999). *Epistemic cultures: How the sciences make knowledge.* Cambridge, MA: Harvard University Press.

Koestler, A. (1975). *The ghost in the machine.* London: Pan Books.

Kohn, A. (1992). *No contest: The case against competition.* Boston: Houghton Mifflin Company.

Koomey, J. G. (2000, August). *Rebuttal to testimony on "Kyoto and the Internet: The Energy Implications of the Digital Economy"* (LBNL-4659). Berkeley, CA: Lawrence Berkeley National Laboratory.

Koomey, J. G. (2007, February). *Estimating total power consumption by servers in the U.S. and the world.* Oakland, CA: Analytics Press.

Kovacs, E. (2001, Winter). Increase community protection from extreme weather events, ISUMA. *Canadian Journal of Policy Research, 2*(4), 57–61.

KPMG. (1997). *The influence of the information society on traffic and transportation: Final report.* Den Haag, Netherlands: Dutch Ministry of Transport, Transport Research Centre.

Krenz, J. H. (1984). *Energy conversion and utilization.* Toronto: Allyn and Bacon.

Labonte, R. (2002, November). *Globalization, trade and health: Unpacking the linkages, defining the healthy public policy options.* Saskatoon: Saskatchewan Public Health and Evaluation Research Unit Report.

Labonte, R. (2004). Globalization, health, and the free trade regime: Assessing the links. *Perspectives on Global Development and Technology, 3*(1–2), 47–72.

Labonte, R., Schrecker, T., Sanders, D., & Meuss, W. (2004). *Fatal indifference: The G8, Africa and global health.* Cape Town: University of Cape Town Press and International Development Research Centre. Retrieved from www.idrc.ca/en/ev-45682-201-1-DO_TOPIC.html

LaFraniere, S. (2005, August 25). Cellphones catapult rural Africa to 21st century. *New York Times.* Retrieved December 28, 2008, from www.nytimes.com/2005/08/25/international/africa/25africa.html

Lalonde, M. (1974). *A new perspective on the health of Canadians: A working document.* Ottawa, ON: Minister of National Health and Welfare, Minister of Supply and Services Canada.

Langhelle, O. (2000, October/December). Why ecological modernization and sustainable development should not be conflated. *Journal of Environmental Policy and Planning, 2*(4), 303–22.

Lazaroff, C. (2002, April 13). High-tech U.S. trash floods Asia. *Albion Monitor.* Retrieved July 9, 2009, from www.albionmonitor.com/0204a/hightechtrash.html.

Lee, R. B. (1979). *The !Kung San: Men, women and work in a foraging society.* Cambridge: Cambridge University Press, 1979.

Lenski, G. E., & Lenski, J. (1978). *Human societies: An introduction to macrosociology.* New York: McGraw-Hill.

Lewontin, R. C. (1991). *Biology as ideology.* Concord: House of Anansi Press.

Linder, S. B. (1970). *The harried leisure class.* New York: Columbia University Press.

Lintott, J. (1998). Beyond the economics of more: The place of consumption in ecological economics. *Ecological Economics, 25*(3), 239–48.

Livingston, J. (1994). *Rogue primate.* Toronto: Key Porter Books.

Lowe, M. D. (1990, October). *Alternatives to the automobile: Transport for livable cities.* Washington, DC: Worldwatch Institute.

Lynch, B. S., & Bonnie, R. J. (Eds.). (1994). *Growing up tobacco free: Preventing nicotine addiction in children and youths* (p 71). Washington, DC: Committee on Preventing Nicotine Addiction in Children and Youths, Institute of Medicine, National Academy Press.

MacFadyen, L., Amos, A., Hastings, G., Parkes, E. (2003, February). "They look like my kind of people": Perceptions of smoking images in youth magazines. *Social Science and Medicine 56*(3), 491–99.

MacNeill, J., Winsemius, P., & Yakushiji, T. (1991). *Beyond interdependence: The meshing of the world's economy and the earth's ecology.* New York: Oxford University Press.

Malaska, P. (1997). *Sustainable development as post-modern culture* (FUTU publication no. 1). Turku: Turku School of Economics, Finland Futures Research Centre.

Manno, J. (2000). Commodity potential: An approach to understanding and ecological consequences of markets. In D. Pimentel, L. Westra, & R. Noss (Eds.), *Integrating environment, conservation and health.* Washington, DC: Island Press.

Marmot, M. G., Davey Smith, G, Stansfeld, S. A., Patel, C., North, F., & Head, J. (1991). Health inequalities among British civil servants: The Whitehall II study. *Lancet, 337,* 1387–93.

Marmot, M. G., & Mustard, J. F. (1994). Coronary heart disease from a population perspective. In R. G. Evans, M. L. Barer, & T. R. Marmor (Eds.), *Why are some people healthy and others not? The determinants of health of populations.* New York: A. de Gruyter.

Marvin, S. (1997). Environmental flows. Telecommunications and the dematerialisation of cities? *Futures, 29*(1), 47–65.

Marx, K. (1867/1965). *Capital: A critical analysis of capitalist production* (vol. 1). Moscow: Progress Publishers.

Matthews, H. S., & Hendrickson C. (2001). *Economic and environmental implications of online retailing in the United States* (65–72). Sustainability and the Information Society, 15th International Symposium Informatics for Environmental Protection, Zurich. Marburg: Metropolis Verlag.

Matthews, H. S., Williams, E., Tagamic, T., & Hendrickson, C. T. (2002, October). Energy implications of online book retailing in the United States and Japan. *Environmental Impact Assessment Review 22*(5), 493–507.

Max-Neef, M. (1995). Economic growth and quality of life: A threshold hypothesis. *Ecological Economics, 15,* 115–18.

Maybury-Lewis, D. (1992). *Millennium: Tribal wisdom and the modern world.* New York: Viking Penguin.

Mayer, D. (1998). Institutionalizing overconsumption. In L. Westra & P. Hogue Werhane (Eds.), *The business of consumption: Environmental ethics and the global economy.* Lanham, MD: Rowman & Littlefield.

McCool, J. P., Cameron, L. D., & Petrie, K. J. (2001, May). Adolescent perceptions of smoking imagery in film. *Social Science and Medicine 52*(10), 1577–87.

McCool, J. P., Cameron, L. D., & Petrie, K. J. (2003, March). Interpretations of smoking in film by older teenagers. *Social Science and Medicine 56*(5), 1023–32.

McGregor, D. (2004). Traditional ecological knowledge and sustainable development: Towards coexistence. In M. Blaser, H. A. Feit, & G. McRae (Eds.), *In the way of development: Indigenous peoples, life projects and globalization* (72–91). New York: Zed Books in association with the International Development Research Centre. Retrieved from www.idrc.ca/en/ev-64525-201-1-DO_TOPIC.html.

McManus, P. (1996). Contested terrains: Politics, stories and the discourses of sustainability. *Environmental Politics 5*(1), 48–73.

McMichael, A. J., Butler, C. D., & Douglas, R. M. (2002). Globalisation and environmental change: Implications for health and health inequalities. In R. Eckersley, J. Dixon, & R. Douglas (Eds.), *The social origins of health and well-being.* Cambridge: Cambridge University Press.

McMurtry, J. (1998). *Unequal freedoms: The global market as an ethical system.* Toronto: Garamond Press.

Mead, M. (1963). *Sex and temperament in three primitive societies.* New York: William Morrow.

Menzies, H. (1996). *Whose brave new world? The information highway and the new economy.* Toronto: Between the Lines.

Michaelis, L., & Lorek, S. (2004). *Consumption and the environment in Europe: Trends and futures* (Environmental Project Number 904). Danish Environmental Protection Agency, Danish Ministry of the Environment.

Milbrath, L. W. (1989). *Envisioning a sustainable society.* Albany: State University of New York Press.

Milbrath, L. W. (1995). Psychological, cultural, and informational barriers to sustainability. *Journal of Social Issues, 51*(4), 101–20.

Miller, R. (2008, May 22). Down on the server farm: The real-world implications of the rise of internet computing. *The Economist* (83–84).

Mills, M. P. (2000, February 2). *Kyoto and the Internet: The energy implications of the digital economy.* Testimony of Mark P. Mills, before the Subcommittee on National Economic Growth, Natural Resources, and Regulatory Affairs, U.S. House of Representatives. Retrieved August 14, 2009, from www.tech-pundit.com/page.html?pageid=42

Mills, M. P., & Huber, P. W. (1999, May 31). Dig more coal—The PCs are coming. *Forbes,* 70–72.

Mitchell-Jackson, J., Koomey, J. G., Blazekc, M., & Nordman, B. (2002, October). National and regional implications of Internet data center growth in the US. *Resources, Conservation and Recycling, 36*(3), 175–85.

Mokhtarian, P. L., & Meenakshisundaram, R. (1998). *Beyond tele-substitution: A broader empirical look at communication impacts* (California PATH Working Paper UCB-ITS-PWP-98-33). Davis: University of California, Davis.

Monbiot, G. (2005, December 6). The most destructive crop on earth is no solution to the energy crisis. *The Guardian.*

Monbiot, G. (2006). *Heat: How to stop the planet burning.* London: Allen Lane.

Morris, B. (1982). *Forest traders: A socio-economic study of the hill pandaram.* London: Athlone Press.

Moss, M., & Townsend, A. (1997, November). *The role of the real city in cyberspace: Understanding regional variation in Internet accessibility and utilization.* Paper prepared for the Project Varenius meeting at Pacific Grove, CA.

Moss, M., & Townsend, A. (1998a, April 23–25). *Spatial analysis of the Internet in U.S. cities and states.* Paper prepared for "Technological Futures—Urban Futures" Conference at Durham, England.

Moss, M., & Townsend, A. (1998b). Technology and cities. *Cityscape: A Journal of Policy Development and Research* 3(3), 107–27.

Moynihan, R., & Cassels, A. (2005). *Selling sickness: How the world's biggest pharmaceutical companies are turning us all into patients.* Vancouver: Greystone Books.

Murphy, T. (2000, January 23). Developers rush to meet demands of e-commerce. *New York Times.*

Myers, N. (1995). Economics of the environment: A seismic shift in thinking. *Ecological Economics, 15,* 125–28.

Naiman, J. (1997). *How societies work: Class, power and change in a Canadian context.* Scarborough, ON: Irwin Publishing.

National Research Programme. (2000). *National Research Programme on transport and the environment: Overview of Projects, Telecommunications do not reduce traffic volume.* Bern: Swiss National Science Foundation.

Nokia. (2005, September 21). Press release: Major milestone reached—One billionth Nokia mobile phone sold this summer. Retrieved September 22, 2005, from press.nokia.com/PR/200509/1012651_5.html

Norwegian Ministry of the Environment. (1995). *Elements for an international work programme on sustainable production and consumption: Oslo ministerial roundtable on sustainable production and consumption.* Oslo, Norway: United Nations Commission on Sustainable Development.

Novek, J., & Kampen, K. (1992). Sustainable or unsustainable development? An analysis of an environmental controversy. *Canadian Journal of Sociology, 17*(3), 249–73.

Nuij, R. (2002). Eco-innovation: Helped or hindered by integrated product policy. *The Journal of Sustainable Product Design 1,* 49–51.

O'Meara, M. (2000). Harnessing information technologies for the environment. In L. Stark (Ed.), *State of the world 2000: A Worldwatch Institute report on progress toward a sustainable society.* New York: W. W. Norton & Company.

Ory, D. T., & Mokhtarian, P. L. (2005). *When is getting there half the fun? Modeling the liking for travel* (University of California Postprints, Paper 549, Transportation Research 39A[2–3], 97–124). Davis: University of California.

Ontario Trade and Investment Mission to China. (2005). *Directory of participants.* Ontario: Ontario Trade and Investment Mission to China.

Ottawa, City of. (2000, August 16). *Growth in Ottawa-Carleton, 1996–1999 and infrastructure plans*. Region of Ottawa-Carleton Report from the Commissioner of Planning and Development Approvals Department to the Coordinator Planning and Environment Committee.

Ottawa Macdonald-Cartier International Airport. (1998a, December). *Ottawa Macdonald-Cartier International Airport Master Plan*. Ottawa Macdonald-Cartier International Airport Authority.

Ottawa Macdonald-Cartier International Airport. (1998b). Press Release. Retrieved April 15, 2009, from www.ottawa-airport.ca/Newsroom/press ReleasesZoom-e.php?prID=7

Ontario Tobacco Research Unit. (2003, June). *The economic impact of a smoke-free bylaw on restaurant and bar sales in Ottawa, Canada*. Ontario: Author.

Pamlin, D., & Szomolányi, K. (2008). *Saving the climate @ the speed of light: First roadmap for reduced CO_2) emissions in the EU and beyond*. Brussels, Belgium: World Wildlife Fund & European Telecommunications Network Operators Association.

Pan American Health Organization. (2002). *Profits over people: Tobacco industry activities to market cigarettes and undermine public health in Latin America and the Caribbean*. Washington, DC: Author, Division of Health Promotion and Protection.

Patel, R. C. (2007). *Stuffed and starved: Markets, power and the hidden battle for the world food system*. New York: Harper Collins.

Pearce, F. (2005, November 22). Forests paying the price for biofuels. *New Scientist Magazine*, No. 2526, 19.

Peddle, K. (2004). *Telehealth in context: Socio-technical barriers to telehealth use in Labrador, Canada—Proceedings communication*. Porto Alegre: Technologies and Health Working Group, International Association for Media and Communications Research.

Peet, J. (1992). *Energy and the ecological economics of sustainability*. Washington, DC: Island Press.

Penaloza, L. (2001, November). An institutional perspective on the study of consumption. *Newsletter of the Consumers, Commodities and Consumption Special Interest Group of the American Sociological Association*, 3(1), 4–5.

Phillips, P. (1998). Self-censorship and the homogeneity of the media elite. In *Censored 1998: The news that didn't make the news*. New York: Seven Stories Press.

Physicians for a Smoke-Free Canada (2001, February). *Summary of research on economic impact of smoking restrictions*. Ottawa, ON: Author. www.work safebc.com/news_room/campaigns/ets/assets/pdf/ecoimpact.pdf

Plepys, A. (2002, October). The grey side of ICT. *Environmental Impact Assessment Review*, 22(5), 509–23.

Pout, C. H., Moss, S. A., & Davidson, P. J. (1998). *The non-domestic building energy fact file*. London: Construction Research Publications.

Power, M. (1991). *The egalitarians: Human and chimpanzee*. Cambridge: Cambridge University Press.

Princen, T. (1997). The shading and distancing of commerce: When institutionalization is not enough. *Ecological Economics 20*, 235–53.

Princen, T. (1999). Consumption and environment: Some conceptual issues. *Ecological Economics, 31*(3), 347–63.

Pucci, L. G., & Siegel, M. (1999, November). Exposure to brand-specific cigarette advertising in magazines and its impact on youth smoking. *Preventive Medicine, 29*(5), 313–20.

Radermacher, F. J., (1996). Die Informationsgesellschaft: Langfristige Potentiale für eine nachhaltige Entwicklung und die Zukunft der Arbeit. In *Oracle Welt—Die globale Informationsgesellschaft als Chance 3*, S. 36–39.

Raphael, D. (2002). *Social justice is good for our hearts: Why societal factors—not lifestyles—are major causes of heart disease in canada and elsewhere.* Toronto: Center for Social Justice Foundation for Research and Education.

Raphael, D. (2004). *Social determinants of health: Canadian perspectives.* Toronto: Canadian Scholars Press.

Raphael, D. (2007). *Poverty and policy in Canada: Implications for health and quality of life.* Toronto: Canadian Scholars' Press Incorporated.

Rattle, R. (2005, March). *Northern sustainable development. Diamond mining: An investigation of socio-economic factors affecting Aboriginal community well-being.* Report Prepared for Indian and Northern Affairs Canada, Gatineau, QC.

Rattle, R. (Forthcoming). Aboriginal health and well-being: The paradox of globalization. In J. White and J. Peters (Eds.), *Aboriginal policy research: Gender and health.* Toronto: Thompson Educational Publishers.

Rattle, R., & Kwiatkowski, R. (2003). Defining boundaries: Health impact assessment and social impact assessment. In H. A. Becker & F. Vanclay (Eds.), *The international handbook of social impact assessment: Conceptual and methodological advances.* Cheltanham, UK: Edward Elgar.

Rechtschaffen, S. (1996). *Timeshifting: Creating more time to enjoy your life.* New York: Doubleday Books.

Rees, W. E. (1995, October/November). More jobs, less damage: A framework for sustainability, growth and employment, *Alternatives, 21*(4), 24–30.

Rees, W. E. (1998). How should a parasite value its host? Special section: Forum on valuation of ecosystem services. *Ecological Economics, 25*, 49–52.

Rees, W. E. (1999). Consuming the earth: The biophysics of sustainability. *Ecological Economics, 29*(1), 23–28.

Reichart, I., & Hischier, R. (2001). Environmental impact of electronic and print media: Television, internet newspaper and printed daily newspaper. In *Sustainability and the Information Society, 15th International Symposium Informatics for Environmental Protection, Zurich* (91–98). Marburg: Metropolis Verlag.

Reijnders, L. & Hoogeveen, M. J. (2001, July). Energy effects associated with e-commerce: A case study concerning on-line sales of personal computers in the Netherlands. *Journal of Environmental Management, 62*(3), 271–82.

Reisch, L. A. (2001). The Internet and sustainable consumption: Perspectives on Janus Face. *Journal of Consumer Policy, 24*(3/4), 251–86.

Rejeski, D. (2003). E-Commerce, the Internet, and the environment. *Journal of Industrial Ecology, 6*(2), 1–3.

Richardson, A. J., & Schoeman, D. S. (2004). Climate impacts on plankton ecosystems in the northeast Atlantic. *Science 305*, 1609–12.

Rifkin, J. (n.d.). *Leading the way to the third Industrial Revolution and a new distributed social vision for the world in the 21st century: White paper.* Bethesda, MD: Foundation on Economic Trends.

Rifkin, J. (1995). *The end of work: The decline of the global labour force and the dawn of the post-market era.* New York: G.P. Putnam's Sons.

Rip, A. (1995). Introduction of new technology: Making use of recent insights from sociology and economics of technology. *Technology Analysis and Strategic Management 7*, 417–31.

Roberts, L. G., & Crump, C. (2001). *US Internet IP traffic growth.* San Jose, CA: Caspian Networks, Inc.

Rodrik, D. (2001, October). *The global governance of trade: As if development really mattered.* (UNDP Background Paper). New York: United Nations Development Programme.

Romanow, R. (2002, November). *Building on values: The future of health care in Canada—Final report.* Ottawa: Commission on the Future of Health Care in Canada.

Romm, J. (2002). *The Internet and the new energy economy.* E-Vision 2000 Conference Proceedings—Supplementary Materials: Papers and Analyses. Santa Monica, CA: RAND Science and Technology Policy Institute.

Ropke, I. (1999, March). The dynamics of willingness to consume. *Ecological Economics, 28*(3), 399–420.

Ropke, I. (2001, September). New technology in everyday life—Social processes and environmental impact. *Ecological Economics, 38(3)*, 403–22.

Rosa, E. A., & Dietz, T. (1998). Climate change and society: Speculation, construction and scientific investigation. *International Sociology, 13*, 421–25.

Roseland, M. (1992). *Toward sustainable communities: A resource book for municipal and local governments.* Ottawa: National Round Table Series on Sustainable Development, National Round Table on the Environment and the Economy.

Rowbotham, M. (1999). *The drive behind globalisation: The debt-based financial system and the growth of wasteful trade.* Unpublished paper.

Royal Commission on Aboriginal Peoples. (1996). *Report of the Royal Commission on Aboriginal Peoples.* Gatineau, QC: Author.

Saffer, H., & Chaloupka, F. (2000, November). The effect of tobacco advertising bans on tobacco consumption. *Journal of Health Economics, 19*(6), 1117–37.

Sahlins, M. (1972). *Stone age economics.* Chicago: Aldine-Atherton.

Salomon, D. (1996). Telecommunications, cities, and technological opportunism. *The Annals of Regional Science 30*, 75–90.

Sanne, C. (2002, August). Willing consumers—or locked-in? Policies for a sustainable consumption. *Ecological Economics 42*(1/2), 273–87.

Sarkar, M. B., Butler, B., & Steinfield, C. (1995). Intermediaries and cybermediaries: A continuing role for mediating players in the electronic marketplace. *Journal of Computer Mediated Communication* (Special Issue on Electronic Commerce). Retrieved August 16, 2009, from jcmc.indiana.edu/vol1/issue3/sarkar.html

Saul, J. R. (2005). *The collapse of globalism and the reinvention of the world.* Toronto: Viking.

Saunders, H. (1992). The Khazzoom-Brookes postulate and neoclassical growth. *Energy Journal, 13*(4), 131–48.

Schandl, H., & Schulz, N. B. (2002). Industrial ecology: United Kingdom. In R. U. Ayres et al., *Handbook for Industrial Ecology.* Cheltenham, UK: Edward Elgar.

Schauer, T. (2000, February 21–22). *What are the conditions for a sustainable information society?* Proceedings: Towards a Sustainable Information Society. Retrieved from www.jrc.es/pages/projects/AsisProceedingsFinal.pdf

Schnaiberg, A. (1980). *The environment: From surplus to scarcity.* Oxford: Oxford University Press.

Scholte, J. A. (1997, July). Global capitalism and the state. *International Affairs, 77*(3), 427–52.

Scholte, J. A. (2000). What is "global" about globalization. In *Globalization: A critical introduction* (41–61). New York: Palgrave.

Schor, J. (1991). *The overworked American: The unexpected decline of leisure.* New York: Basic Books.

Schor, J. (1998). The overspent American: Upscaling, downshifting, and the new consumer. New York: Basic Books.

Schumpeter, J. (1954). *History of economic analysis.* New York: Oxford University Press.

Science Daily. (2003). Major Greenland glacier, once stable, now shrinking dramatically. *Science Daily.* Retrieved December 8, 2003, from www.sciencedaily.com/releases/2003/12/031208140730.htm

Scott, C. (2004). Conflicting discourses of property, governance and development in the indigenous north. In M. Blaser, H. A. Feit, & G. McRae (Eds.), *In the way of development: Indigenous peoples, life projects and globalization.* New York: Zed Books in association with the International Development Research Centre.

Shadman, F., & McManus, T. J. (2004). Comment on "The 1.7 kilogram microchip: Energy and material use in the production of semiconductor devices." *Environmental Science and Technology, 38*(6), 1915.

Silicon Valley Toxics Coalition. (2000). *Water use and other materials and wastes associated with semiconductor production.* San Jose, CA: Silicon Valley Toxics Coalition.

Simmons, S. (2000, August). Telework for sustainability. *Informatik: Journal of the Swiss Computer Society, 4,* 27–29.

Simmons, S. (2001). *Immaterialisation—The new reality.* Venice, Italy: E-work and E-commerce Proceedings.

Simmons, S., & Leevers, D. (2001). *The case for immaterialisation.* Venice, Italy: E-work and E-commerce Conference.

Sindhav, B., & Balazs, A. L. (1999, December). A model of factors affecting the growth of retailing on the internet. *Journal of Market-Focused Management, 4*(4), 319–39.

Singh, P. M., Wright, C. A., Wilson, D. C., Boytsov, A., & Raizada, M. N. (2007). Language preferences on websites and in Google searches for human health and food information. *Journal of Medical Internet Research, 9*(2), e18. Retrieved August 16, 2009, from www.pubmedcentral.nih.gov/articlerender.fcgi?artid=1913940

Smyth, D. (1990). *From technological fix to appropriate technology, planet under stress: the challenge of global change.* Oxford: Oxford University Press, Don Mills.

Sonntag, V. (2000, July). Sustainability—In light of competitiveness. *Ecological Economics 34*(1), 101–13.

Soskolne, C. L., & Bertollini, R. (1999, December 3–4). *Global ecological integrity and 'sustainable development': Cornerstones of public health. A World Health Organization discussion document based on an international workshop at the World Health Organization European Centre for Environment and Health, Rome Division.* Rome, Italy: World Health Organization.

Spangenberg, J. H., & Lorek, S. (2002, December). Environmentally sustainable household consumption: From aggregate environmental pressures to priority fields of action. *Ecological Economics 43*(2/3), 127–40.

Statistics Canada. (2006a). *Human activity and the environment* (Catalogue no. 16-201-XIE). Ottawa: Statistics Canada Environment Accounts and Statistics Division, System of National Accounts.

Statistics Canada. (2006b, November). *Our lives in digital times: Connectedness series* (Research Paper, Catalogue no. 56F0004MIE–no. 014). Ottawa: Statistics Canada Science, Innovation and Electronic Information Division.

Steinmueller, E. (2001). ICTs and the possibilities for leapfrogging by developing countries. *International Labour Review, 140*(2), 193–210.

Stern, D. I. (1997). Limits to substitution and irreversibility in production and consumption: A neoclassical interpretation of ecological economics. *Ecological Economics 21*(3), 197–215.

Stern, P. C. (2000). Toward a coherent theory of environmentally significant behavior. *Journal of Social Issues, 56*(3), 407–24.

Stern, P. C., Dietz, T., Ruttan, V. W., Socolow, R. H., & Sweeney, J. L. (1997). *Environmentally significant consumption: Research directions.* Washington, DC: National Academy Press.

Sui, D. Z., & Rejeski, D. W. (2002, February). Environmental impacts of the emerging digital economy: The e-for-environment e-commerce? *Environmental Management, 29*(2), 155–63.

Symons, D. (1979). *The evolution of human sexuality.* Oxford: Oxford University Press.

Taylor, S., Button, K., & Stough, R. (2000). Telecommunications and transportation effects—A review of interaction tendencies and travel. *Journal of Public Affairs 1*(1), 140–74.

Terrachoice. (2009, April). *The seven sins of greenwashing: Environmental claims in consumer markets. Summary report*. Ontario: Author.

Tew, J. (2002, July 24). Computer waste: With electronics, it's not easy to be green. *Courier News* (Elgin, IL).

Thrift, N. (1996). *Spatial formations*. London: Sage, 1996.

Tisdell, C. (2003, July). Socioeconomic causes of loss of animal genetic diversity: Analysis and assessment. *Ecological Economics, 45*(3), 365–76.

Tobacco Documents Online. (1989, November 10). tobaccodocuments.org/landman/2021593776-3779.html

Tobin, J. (1965, October). Money and economic growth. *Econometrica, 33*(4), 671–84.

Tooby, J., & DeVore, I. (1987). *The reconstruction of hominid behavioral evolution through strategic modelling, the evolution of human behavior: Primate models* (W. G. Kinzey [Ed.]). Albany: State University of New York Press.

Traxler, J., & Luger, M. I. (2000, December). Businesses and the Internet: Implications for firm location and clustering. *Journal of Comparative Policy Analysis, 2*(3), 279–300.

Tulbure, I. (2002). The information society and the environment: A case study concerning two Internet applications. In B. Standford Smith, E. Chiozza, & M. Edin (Eds.), *Challenges and achievements in e-business and e-work* (125–32). Amsterdam: IOS Press. Retrieved from www.terra-2000.org/htdocs/Documents/Prague/Papers/THe%20IS%20and%20the%20Environment.pdf

Turnbull, C. (1965). *Wayward servants*. London: Eyre and Spottiswoode.

United Kingdom Department for Transport. (1999, March). *Sustainable distribution: A strategy*. Retrieved August 16, 2009, from www.dft.gov.uk/pgr/freight/sustainable/sustainabledistributionastrategy

United Nations, Department of Economic and Social Affairs, Population Division. (1998). *Measuring changes in consumption and productions patterns*. New York: Author.

United Nations, Department of Economic and Social Affairs. (2005). *The inequality predicament: Report on the world social situation 2005*. New York: Author.

United Nations Development Programme. (1999). *Human development report 1999*. New York: Oxford University Press.

United Nations Environment Programme. (2005, December 6). *News release: Pacific Island villagers first climate change "refugees."* New York: Author.

Union of Concerned Scientists. (2007). *Smoke, mirrors and hot air: How ExxonMobil uses big tobacco's tactics to manufacture uncertainty on climate science*. Cambridge, MA: Author.

Vance, A. (2008, November 24). Sin City server farm keeping the world safe for data. *Wired Magazine*. Retrieved from www.wired.com/techbiz/people/magazine/16-12/st_robroy

Vayada, A. P. (1988). Actions and consequences as objects of explanation in human ecology. In R. J. Borden, J. Jacobs, & G. L. Young (Eds.), *Human ecology research and applications*. Bar Harbor, ME: Society for Human Ecology.

Victoria Transport Policy Institute. (2002). Freight transport management increasing commercial vehicle transport efficiency. In *Transportation Demand Encyclopedia.* Retrieved January 12, 2003, from www.vtpi.org/tdm/tdm16.htm

Vitousek, P., Ehrlich, P. R., Ehrlich, A. H., & Matson, P. A. (1986). Human appropriation of the products of photosynthesis. *Bioscience, 34*(6), 368–73.

Vringer, K., & Blok, K. (2000). Long-term trends in direct and indirect household energy intensities: A factor in dematerialisation? *Energy Policy, 28*(10), 713–27.

Wackernagel, M., & Rees, W. (1996). *Our ecological footprint: Reducing human impact on the earth.* Gabriola Island, BC: New Society Publishers.

Wagner, I. (1995). Hard times: The politics of women's work in computerized work environments. *The European Journal of Women's Studies 2*(3), 295–314.

Warde, A. E., Shove, E., & Southerton, D. (1998, March 27–29). *Convenience, schedules and sustainability.* Paper prepared for the ESF TREM Programme Workshop, Centre for the Study of Environmental Change, Lancaster University.

Warner, K. E., & Fulton, G. A. (1994). The implications of tobacco product sales in a nontobacco state. *Journal of the American Medical Association, 271*(10), 771–76.

Whitehead, A. N. (1925). *Science and the modern world.* New York: Macmillan.

Whiten, A. (1998). The evolution of deep social mind in humans. In M. Corballis & S. E. G. Lea (Eds.), *The evolution of the hominid mind.* Oxford: Oxford University Press.

Wilkinson, R., & Marmot, M. (2003). *Social determinants of health: The solid facts* (2nd ed.), R. Wilkinson & M. Marmot (Eds.). Copenhagen: World Health Organization.

Williams, E. D. (2000). *Global production chains and sustainability: The case of high-purity silicon and its applications in IT and renewable energy.* Yokohama, Japan: The United Nations University, Institute of Advanced Studies.

Williams, E. D. (2004a). Energy intensity of computer manufacturing: Hybrid assessment combining process and economic input-output methods. *Environmental Science and Technology, 38*(22), 6166–74.

Williams, E. D. (2004b). Environmental impacts of microchip manufacture. *Thin Solid Films, 461,* 2–6.

Williams, E. D., Ayres, R. U., & Heller, M. (2002, December 15). The 1.7 kilogram microchip: Energy and material use in the production of semiconductor devices. *Environmental Science & Technology, 36*(24), 5504–10.

Williams, E., Ayres, R. U., & Heller, M. (2004). Response to comment on the "1.7 kilogram microchip: Energy and material use in the production of semiconductor devices." *Environmental Science and Technology, 38*(6), 1916–17.

Wilska, T. A. (2003, August 15–17). *New technology and consumption styles among Finnish young people.* Paper presented at the Nordic Sociological Conference, Reykjavik.

Wilson, C., & Tisdell, C. (2001, December). Why farmers continue to use pesticides despite environmental, health and sustainability costs. *Ecological Economics, 39*(3), 449–62.

Wolf, M. (2007). *Proust and the squid: The story and science of the reading brain.* New York: HarperCollins.

Wood, E. M. (1995). *Democracy against capitalism: Renewing historical materialism.* Cambridge: Cambridge University Press.

World Health Organization. (1967). The constitution of the World Health Organization. *World Health Organization Chronicles, 1,* 29.

World Health Organization. (1984). Health promotion: A discussion paper on the concept and principles. Cophenhagen, Denmark: World Health Organization Regional Office for Europe.

World Health Organization. (2005, May 5). *Towards a conceptual framework for analysis and action on the social determinants of health: Discussion paper for the commission on social determinants of health (draft).* New York: World Health Organization.

World Information Technology and Services Alliance. (2004, October). *Digital planet: The global information economy.* Vienna, VA: Author.

World Wildlife Fund. (2004). *Living planet report 2004.* Retrieved November 12, 2005, from www.footprintnetwork.org/gfn_sub.php?content=lpr2004

Worm, B., Barbier, E. B., Beaumont, N., Duffy, J. E., Folke, C., Halpern, B. S., et al. (2006). Impacts of biodiversity loss on ocean ecosystem services. *Science, 314,* 787-790.

Wright, R. (2004). *A short history of progress. CBC Massey Lecture Series.* Toronto: House of Anansi Press.

Zencey, E. (2009, April 12). Mr. Soddy's ecological economy, Op-Ed Contribution. *New York Times.*

Zumkeller, D. (1996, September 9–11). Communication as an element of the overall transport context—An empirical study. In *Proceedings, International Conference on Survey Methods in Transport* (66–83). Oxford: Steeple Aston.

Index

About the Author

Robert Rattle is an independent researcher working with NGOs as well as business and governmental organizations. For the last two decades, Robert has conducted research and provided consulting services in the areas of sustainable development and sustainable consumption, eco-systems and human health, ecological economics, impact assessment, information and telecommunications policy, Aboriginal well-being, and globalization. Prior to that, Robert, a physicist by training, worked in the high tech sector in areas of artificial intelligence and telecommunications research. In his spare time, he writes a regular environment and health column; enjoys the outdoors; studies the art, philosophy, and sport of Taekwondo; and volunteers in his community.